T0326275

Kenneth Clarke

'Affable, invisible ... the man with a brilliant future behind him.' Thus *Varsity* magazine appraised Kenneth Clarke's term as President of the Cambridge Union in the summer of 1963. Dominated by his opposition to the admission of women students to the Union, Clarke's Presidency had been less than distinguished. But *Varsity*, like so many commentators throughout Clarke's political career, seriously underestimated a politician who, three decades later, has emerged as a strong man within a weak Conservative administration, often tipped as a possible successor to John Major should the bailiffs be summoned to Number Ten.

Clarke, as Andy McSmith explains in this fast-paced and highly readable biography, is above all a survivor who has been a government Minister since 1979. Despite his reputation as the 'thinking man's lager lout', Clarke is an old-fashioned 1960s One-Nation Tory who played the tough guy with considerable adroitness in order to survive under Thatcher's hard-line administration. Displaying the same joviality which had seen him sign up for both the Campaign for Social Democracy and the Conservative Club on arrival at Cambridge, Clarke frankly admitted in the 1970s that it was only the arithmetic of Britain's first-past-the-post election system which kept him in the same party as the British nationalists of the Tory right. His pragmatism served him well as he progressed from being the youngest high-flier in the Heath government to the Minister responsible for introducing the highly controversial 'internal market' in the NHS under Thatcher, and now to the happy position of Chancellor of the Exchequer with an economy recovering from recession.

Clarke's presence at the heart of the Tory government demonstrates that the mix of free-market liberalism and British nationalism to which Mrs Thatcher gave her name never really took root in the Conservative government. Right-wing Tory rebels who plead that the EC is destroying Britain as a nation-state, or free-market ideologues who want to privatize whatever remains of the welfare state, find Kenneth Clarke an obstacle to their ambitions. From Clarke's point of view, social instability and trade barriers are bad for business. The rise and rise of this most flexible of politicians, according to Andy McSmith's engaging account, may not be enough to stop the cracks in a Tory Party now beyond repair.

Andy McSmith is a political correspondent for the *Observer* who previously worked on the *Daily Mirror*. A long-standing Labour Party member, he is the author of the critically acclaimed *John Smith: Playing the Long Game*.

KENNETH CLARKE

A Political Biography

ANDY McSMITH

VERSO
London · New York

First published by Verso 1994
© Andy McSmith 1994
All rights reserved

Verso
UK: 6 Meard Street, London WIF OEG
USA: 20 Jay St, Suite 1010, Brooklyn, NY 11201

Verso is the imprint of New Left Books

British Library Cataloguing in Publication Data
A catalogue record for this book is available from the British Library

Library of Congress Cataloging-in-Publication Data
A catalogue record for this book is available from the Library of Congress

ISBN 978-1-78663-754-3

Typeset in Garamond by Lucy Morton, London SE12
Printed in the United States

CONTENTS

CHAPTER ONE

BOYHOOD

It was around the time of his elevation to the Cabinet in 1985 that the Right Honourable Kenneth Clarke QC MP came by a working-class boyhood. In addition to being a Gray's Inn barrister and a polished professional politician from Cambridge University, he became a "grammar school boy" and the son of a "former miner"[1] – a Nottinghamshire miner at that, in a year when the miners of Nottinghamshire were the height of fashion because of their part in breaking the NUM strike; they were not "scabs", they were "lions".[2] The days when more than half the Conservative Cabinet were Old Etonians had long gone. With a grocer's daughter in command, the party was indulging in a long bout of inverted snobbery – especially on the Tory right, where humble beginnings and a school-of-hard-knocks education are badges of honour. Although he was never on the right wing of the party, no Thatcherite could have had more politically correct beginnings than those attributed to Kenneth Clarke.

Clarke claims that this is not important to him. "Why are people on the left so obsessed with people's jobs and their fathers? ... I don't have any hang-ups," he says.[3] However, as a politician, he is continually in the business of talking about himself and projecting an image which suits his interests. More than once, using that "don't-take-me-seriously-if-you-don't-want-to" tone which he often adopts, he has likened himself to Britain's most celebrated working-class MP: "I always say my background was exactly the same as Dennis Skinner's: grammar school and Oxford in his case, grammar school and Cambridge in mine..."[4] "I had an accent of the kind Dennis Skinner is trying to keep."[5] If this were true, it could be the basis for an interesting psychological study, of the boy from the deprived background dominated by the smell of coal dust, shut out from the elite by the circumstances of his birth, who nonetheless fought his way in. Unfortunately, the comparison with

1

Skinner does not stand up to serious examination. Both men came from the East Midlands coalfields and won scholarships, but there the similarity ends. Skinner has genuine childhood memories of hunger and hardship; his father really was a miner, when he was in work at all; the son was expected to follow him, and did indeed spend more than twenty years down the pits, plus three months at Ruskin College, Oxford, paid for by the NUM.

Clarke, meanwhile, was neither a grammar-school boy nor the son of a coalface miner; nor had he inherited a place in the elite. He was from Middle England, a middle-class boy from the Midlands, blessed with a good brain and a capacity for enthusiasm. His father was a shopkeeper, like Alderman Alfred Roberts of Grantham, whose daughter Margaret has featured so prominently in Clarke's life. The younger Kenneth Clarke had the good fortune to be born at a time when the British ruling class was, figuratively speaking, opening its doors to bright boys from the provinces and inviting them to assume positions of responsibility above their native status. Kenneth, being very bright and fascinated by politics, seized his chance.

It is often assumed that in the lives of all successful people there lies a secret unhappiness or childhood trauma which has driven them to achieve great things. It appears that nothing of that sort has motivated Kenneth Clarke to become famous. He seems a happy character with a secure family background, doing a job he enjoys. The capitalist system and British parliamentary democracy have treated him well. He is grateful for that, and his life's work has been to preserve them both, as much as he can, from economic disaster, social dislocation, trade unions, and whatever else appears to threaten them. The most interesting person in his family tree seems to have been his maternal grandfather Harry Smith, a pattern maker employed by Raleigh Bicycles in Nottingham. He was, at first, an active member of the Labour Party, who helped sell the *Daily Herald*, but he broke with the party over the expulsion of George Lansbury. He then switched to the Communist Party, and took the *Daily Worker* for most of the rest of his life. "He was a pacifist, and became a communist on those grounds", says Clarke. "How far he was actually Marxist, I'm not sure. He was one of those communists who thought fondly of Uncle Joe Stalin, as a very nice guy. My grandfather was himself a nice man. He was certainly not totalitarian or anti-democratic. He was a naive idealist about the Soviet Union, like the Webbs. He thought the *Daily Worker* was the only newspaper that told the truth."[6]

The move up the social ladder began with the next generation, when Harry Smith's daughter Doris married Kenneth Clarke, who had been born in Sneinton, Nottinghamshire, in 1910, the son of a house decorator named Ernest Clarke. The house where he was born is still occupied by his two surviving brothers, uncles of the future Cabinet minister. Kenneth was a skilled man, good with his hands, who demonstrated in middle age that he was also good at book-keeping and at managing. The story that he was a miner originates in the fact that, as war was approaching, the demand for coal rapidly increased, and coal owners were hiring men in large numbers. Even Dennis Skinner's father, who had been blacklisted since the General Strike, was able to work underground again.

Moorgreen colliery was one of seven mines owned by a firm called Barber, Walker & Company Limited, which had its head office in Eastwood, Nottinghamshire. The Barbers were a local family with strong military ties. In fact, the firm was largely run by men with military titles: the chairman was Major Thomas Barber, and the directors included Major Hugh Campbell and Captain Andrew Bradford. In the mid thirties, Moorgreen had 499 pitmen working underground, and 183 other staff working above ground. Around 1938, the workforce expanded considerably. One of the men taken on was Kenneth Clarke, who was employed not as a miner but as a colliery electrician. (To a member of the Skinner family, an electrician was virtually a member of the boss class, working in relatively comfortable surroundings above ground, coming below only when he was needed, and socializing with the managers.)

One obvious advantage to the job was that, as it was in an industry vital to the war effort, Kenneth Clarke was able to stay there throughout the war. Given that he was recently married and about to become a father, the front line would not have held many attractions for him. Doubtless his pacifist father-in-law approved of him staying where he was. The war was also causing a labour shortage, enabling him to earn extra money in the evenings as part-time manager–electrician at Eastwood cinema. He may have voted Labour in 1945, but it is unlikely that he ever did so again. Certainly he did not stay to work for the nationalized Coal Board. The mines became publicly owned on 1 January 1947, but during the previous year Clarke had left the industry for good, and sunk his savings into a watch-repair shop in Mansfield Road, Eastwood. Eastwood is, of course, famous as the birthplace of D.H.

Lawrence, who was not then an honoured local son. The younger Kenneth Clarke says:

> My father knew a lot of people who had known the family, and Eastwood refused to acknowledge this man for years and years. They liked his father, who was regarded as a great character. They thought that his mother and D.H. Lawrence himself were a stuck-up pair who never really settled down there – and then he brought shame on the village by writing all those dirty books.[7]

By now, he and Doris had a growing family. Their first son, christened Kenneth Harry, was born on 2 July 1940. Two more children, a son and a daughter, followed. Michael Clarke, who is eight years younger than his famous brother, has settled for the life of a car salesman in the Lincolnshire village of Stickney, near Spilsby, where he is occasionally sought out by journalists in pursuit of a juicy quote. When Kenneth was appointed Chancellor of the Exchequer, his brother is reported to have said: "He is a swine. He has always risen to the top in everything he has ever done – from school, through university, and now in government. I am not at all surprised."[8]

Soon, the shop in Eastwood was prospering, and Kenneth Clarke was in a position to expand. He moved to better premises in Nottingham Road, and opened up a new and bigger jewellers' and watch-repair business at 25 Highbury Road, Bulwell, a suburb of Nottingham. Later he expanded again, opening a third shop in High Road, Beeston, which he kept for about ten years. At the time of his early death in 1974 he still had the two shops in Eastwood and Bulwell. The latter is still open for business, run by Ivan Deacon, former apprentice of Kenneth Clarke senior. The Chancellor of the Exchequer called in there in February 1994 to have his watch mended.

Generally, the impression one gets of the older Kenneth Clarke is that his life was a happy and successful one, until he was struck prematurely by an illness which killed him at the age of only sixty-four. (He was taken into Rushcliffe Hospital for an operation in August 1974, and died there in September. Within three years, Clarke's mother had also died.) Here was a man who achieved security and prosperity through his own efforts, and commanded respect in the little community in which he spent his life. Having to close the third of his three shops in the mid 1960s was perhaps a small setback, but it hardly compares, say, with the financial disaster that forced Abraham Thomas Ball, aka Tom Major, to sell his Surrey home and move to

Brixton, where his son John left school early, with no O-levels. As a business-man, Kenneth Clarke senior was as successful as Alderman Roberts of Grantham; but he had the sense to stick to what he did well, so avoiding having his social pretensions shattered by the socialists who ousted Alfred Roberts from the aldermanic bench, an act which his daughter Margaret never forgave. The younger Clarke's childhood went by without trauma or hardship. "I've never claimed to have been poverty stricken", he says. "Father always had a little car. We weren't well off, but we weren't poor."[9]

The big event in the younger Kenneth Clarke's boyhood was the move to Bulwell. It made such an impression on him that he can reel off the precise date from memory: it was on 1 June 1950, just before his tenth birthday. Until then, the family had lived at 73 Upper Dunstead Road, Langley Mill, a pit village in Derbyshire, close to the Nottinghamshire border. He started his education there, first at Aldercar infants school, then at Langley Mill primary school. This school, housed in a building dating from the reign of Queen Victoria, evidently looms large in Clarke's memory. In one of his first speeches in the House of Commons, he deplored the fact that buildings of that age were still being used to educate Nottinghamshire children. "The worst ones are in the north of the county, in the mining towns and villages", he said, adding: "The most important decision which this government have taken was to give such high priority to improving the facilities and eradicating the disgraceful conditions in these schools."[10] Later, as Secretary of State for Education, he berated the conditions "in the places I used to go to", blaming the abolition of the eleven-plus and changes in teaching methods for their deterioration. He told *Teacher* magazine in May 1991: "The losers have been working class children with genuine ability." Remarks like this have not pro-duced a wholly favourable reaction from those who teach in such schools. Lyn Winsor, who was head teacher of Langley Mill primary school when Clarke became Education Secretary, told a journalist: "We are always extremely surprised at Mr Clarke's interest in the state education system, because he has no real experience of it."[11] Certainly, given his low opinion of Langley Mill primary school, Clarke was lucky to be moved out of it, and into Highbury primary school in Bulwell, at the age of ten. Previously, he was destined to go to Heanor Grammar school in Derbyshire, assuming that he had passed his eleven-plus. In his *Teacher* interview, he implied that he might then have become a miner, rather than a barrister and politician. Now he was at a school which often acted as a feed for the far more prestigious and academically successful Nottingham High School for Boys.

Its name may make it sound like a grammar school run by the local education authority, which doubtless explains the number of times that Clarke has been called a "grammar school boy". Sometimes even Clarke seems to be caught in the confusion.[12] Actually, it is one of the oldest independent schools in the country, founded in 1513 by Agnes Mellers, widow of Richard Mellers, a former Mayor of Nottingham, and granted its first charter by King Henry VIII. It was moved to its present site at Waverley Mount in Nottingham in 1868. The institution benefits from an oddity in British law which permits private schools to register themselves as charities, and is, in fact, administered by the Charity Commissioners. Its charitable work consists in taking in a number of bright young children from Nottingham every year and educating them free of charge, alongside pupils whose parents are paying fees. Its academic record has long been outstanding, and it has produced a succession of prominent old boys. The most famous, once again, is D.H. Lawrence, but in Clarke's day the school neither acknowledged him nor encouraged its pupils to read his work. Others, who did not embarrass the old school, included Sir Douglas Wass, permanent secretary to the Treasury 1974–83, and Baron Richardson of Duntisbourne, governor of the Bank of England 1973–83 – neither of whom was much in favour with the Thatcher regime because they were suspected of clinging to Keynesian economics – and at least two Tory MPs, Jim Lester and Piers Merchant, who were not Thatcherite either. After Clarke, as Secretary of State for Education, had inaugurated league tables comparing exam results achieved by individual schools, it turned out that, of the old schools attended by Cabinet ministers, Nottingham High School was second only to Eton.

This does not mean that, as a scholarship boy, Clarke endured the same sort of miseries that blighted George Orwell's days at Eton. First, in the unlikely event that he had failed to win a scholarship, his father could probably have afforded to pay the fees anyway, although "whether he would have done is a different matter."[13] Anyway, about half the school was made up of scholarship boys. It was also streamed, with the inevitable result that the top streams were made up almost exclusively of scholarship boys, who were the only ones to stay on into the sixth form. Clarke was consequently receiving an elite education without sharing the same classroom as the children of the elite. When he emerged he was well educated, down to earth, and very sure of himself. One thing he lost at Nottingham High School was the Derbyshire accent he had picked up in Langley Mill. He now describes himself as having a "strangulated accent", but it could just as accurately be described as the sort of functional accent which can see him comfortably through glittering social occasions without marking him out as effetely upper class.

What made Kenneth Clarke an unusual schoolboy is the passion with which he pursued his hobbies. He has a magpie-like curiosity. Something stimulates his interest and he is off, and in no time he can talk about his latest craze with a dilettante's expertise. This is a useful quality for politicians, who are required to move from one job to another, mastering one topic and speaking to the nation with an expert knowledge about it before moving on to the next.

One of Clark's first and lasting enthusiasms was for football. His father did not like the game, which is after all associated with the class he had left behind. But grandad Harry Smith loved it. So did great-grandfather Ronald Smith, who, remarkably, was still alive in the early 1950s. In 1947 – "the year that QPR won the third division" – the two older men started calling round at the house on Saturday mornings to take seven-year-old Kenneth out to watch Notts County play at home. Great-grandfather was strict in his devotions: he refused to go to the rival Notts Forest ground. Kenneth Clarke has sensibly refused to risk alienating part of his electorate by being an exclusive fan of either of the Nottingham teams, or of any other. When the occasion arises, he slips away to the nearest convenient ground to watch whoever is playing. One night in the early 1980s, for example, he bought a ticket from a tout outside Tottenham's White Hart Lane ground, and found himself standing behind the goal amid a crush of West Ham supporters.

> I was there wearing a grey pinstriped suit, striped shirt, smart tie... and we were so jampacked that when they jumped in the air, I jumped in the air. When they stood still, I stood still. And when they surged forward, I surged forward. I was surrounded by those guys who were shrieking hatred at the Spurs supporters – most of the time trying to clamber over barriers to get at the Spurs supporters and otherwise singing *I'm Forever Blowing Bubbles*.
>
> Policemen were peering at me curiously. There were cameras trained on us... I rapidly decided I was a West Ham supporter. I learnt all the words of the songs and anything I didn't know before I picked up very rapidly... West Ham

won 4–0. So these guys surrounding me, who I do think could have got rather savage, were in the best of humour... [14]

Clarke's other sporting interest is cricket. He has boyhood memories of watching Reg Simpson, a Nottinghamshire and England batsman and fielder from the late 1940s and early 1950s, and other names from the same era, like Joe Hardstaff and Bruce Doolidge. One of his social contacts is an Indian businessman who has a box at Lords, which allows him to enjoy the good life when a Test is on. Once he visited his friend in Bombay and they decided, after dinner, to take a look at the Test ground.

> We went to the ground, got in without too much trouble and walked out to the middle. We walked round and round and up and down the pitch. It was midnight and there was a huge, bright moon in the sky. Then some officials came and made us go... [15]

A slightly more risky pastime for a government minister was watching prize fights. Once when Barry McGuigan was fighting in the open air, Clarke was spotted at the back of the crowd, "seated happily among a contingent of Irishmen from West Belfast, totally camouflaged by his shabby raincoat and 'catholic' shoes... "[16] Another time, when he was Minister for Health, he was seen at the ringside at the Albert Hall.

His attention to sport is unmatched by any ability as a player. As he reached maturity, Clarke became notoriously averse to physical exercise in any form. In his teens he had played football for the Midland Amateur Alliance, but by his own account he only just scraped his way into a team, and "wasn't any great shakes". He gave up the game when he reached university and "became unfit".[17] As a departmental minister, in 1986, he travelled to a Cotswold village for a cricket match against industrial correspondents, during which he bowled, and even took a catch in the slips, because "the ball was coming straight at me and I couldn't get out of the way fast enough". In the return match, a year later, he succeeded in hitting one of the balls bowled at him, set off to make a run, and pulled a calf muscle. Several national newspapers reported at the time that he returned to Westminster limping painfully. His humiliation was compounded by the umpire following him off the pitch to ensure that the scorer understood that he had not made a run. The scorer was Clarke's wife, Gillian. "Retired hurt for 0. I hung up my bat."[18]

Clarke's interest in sports-car racing, remarkably, has been as a driver rather than as a spectator. Since the 1970s, he has been a participant in the annual race at Brands Hatch between the Commons and the Lords, driving his own red Ford Escort XR3. In the 1970s he always teamed up with Jim Lester, and often won. In June 1993 he came last. And there are other hobbies which do not demand physical fitness. Clarke was, surprisingly, an avid train spotter. In recent years, this particular hobby has become inextricably linked in the public mind with odd-looking young men in shabby anoraks and cheap glasses. However, in the late fifties it was a common craze. The ABC guides, which listed twenty thousand locomotives, sold about a million copies a year. On bank holidays the police would have to come out to deal with the crowds of enthusiasts who poured into stations like Tamworth, on the west-coast main line to Birmingham. As a teenager, Clarke says, "I spent much of my life looking at steam locomotives in various parts of the British Isles and abroad." He was a paid-up member of the Railway Correspondents and Travel Society and the Birmingham Locomotion Society. Even as a transport minister in the early 1980s he could boast of being a shareholder in the Great Central Preservation Society at Loughborough, and say that "the sight of the Great Western 'Castle' still excites me more than most other locomotives."[19]

His absorbing interest in professional jazz is another surprising foible for a right-wing politician, given the anti-authoritarian attitudes and wild lifestyles of the players, and the subversive nature of the medium itself. It appears to have began tamely with the likes of Chris Barber, but then drifted into the risky music of black Americans. "I bought a very early Louis Armstrong record and found it didn't remotely sound like Chris Barber, though Chris Barber might fondly imagine that it did. So I went through the big bands – Basie, Ellington, and then on to Charlie Parker, which was thought dangerous discordant stuff."[20] Apparently, it was the very rebelliousness of jazz music that appealed to him in the first place; like so much else, the interest dates back to Nottingham High School:

> I can well remember the moment when, in the sixth-form common room, one of my masters came in and told me he had discovered a guy called Gerry Mulligan and put a new record on the turntable. We all sat round in a little row and listened to *Walking Shoes*...
>
> Initially, I was seduced by parts of the lifestyle that went with jazz music. I am naturally rebellious... Jazz rather went with a slightly rebellious lifestyle. I'm glad to say I wasn't completely taken by it, because the lifestyle of Charlie Parker

was a rather sad disaster. But the kind of disorganised lifestyle of jazz people, the late nights, the strange views, the approach to life which is fairly laid back of jazz people, yes, I enjoy it... It is the sort of thing that is bound to intrigue a young man, but it never wore off because I enjoyed the music as well...

For a politician, feeling a bit beleaguered with the world, worn down by the cares of the world, it does put a bit of fire back in your belly.[21]

Having once discovered Charlie Parker, Clarke became expert on any jazz saxophonist. When he was invited onto *Desert Island Discs* in 1994, he toyed with the idea of selecting nothing but records by alto sax players, but was persuaded to throw in recordings by Little Richard and Bessie Smith for variety. Even a devoted friend like Jim Lester, who was first lured to Ronnie Scott's jazz club by Clarke, sees something slightly odd in an enthusiasm so narrowly focused on one instrument. "Ken has got this fantastic knowledge of such a narrow field of music", he says.[22] Clarke has admitted several times to having a private fantasy that, if life had worked out differently, he might have been a tenor sax player.

Occasionally it has been a problem for Kenneth Clarke, as a Conservative Cabinet minister, to be spotted in London's jazz clubs where the audiences, like the performers, are generally left wing and anti-establishment. In the early eighties, Clarke was in the audience at the Bass Clef during a live recording of the British performer Stan Tracey, whose visiting American saxophonist, Sal Nistico, happened to be one of his favourites. He had the recording played on *Desert Island Discs*, whereupon the club revealed that it was facing bankruptcy owing to a raid by officers from Customs and Excise, whose employer, ultimately, was Kenneth Clarke as Chancellor of the Exchequer. This at once promoted a reader's letter to the *Guardian* saying that "If the VAT men have allowed the club to re-open on the understanding that Kenneth Clarke never again darkens its doors, I and many other jazz lovers will breathe a sigh of relief."[23] Clarke also complains that middle age and ministerial responsibilities make it impossible for him to stay on until 2 or 3 a.m. listening to the music. Nonetheless, when the pressure of Commons business is light, he will still slip off to imbibe the atmosphere of London's jazz scene. According to Lord Hayhoe, a former Tory MP who succeeded Clarke as Minister for Health in 1985, "Given a choice between meeting someone who was uncongenial but might help his career, and going off to Ronnie Scott's Club, Ken wouldn't think twice – he'd be in Soho straight away."[24] It is a world that will still be open to him if or when his political career comes to an end.

There are other hobbies. Like Michael Heseltine and Norman Lamont, Clarke is an inveterate bird-watcher, an interest that apparently dates from an occasion when he was out walking with his wife, Gillian, on holiday in Cornwall. He said: "What's that beautiful bird?" Said she: "It's a blue tit, and we have lots in the garden at home."[25] In addition, he devours political biographies whenever the opportunity arises, and professes an interest in Romanesque architecture.

Something which has undoubtedly helped him keep an undamaged mind is that he was wise enough not to destroy his private life in pursuit of his ambitions. While other high-flying politicians seem to use their families as a political asset, to be put on display at critical moments, Clarke sensibly kept his home life separate. For most of his political career, his family home was in Birmingham, a safe distance away both from Westminster and from his constituency. One of his knickknacks safely hidden away there was a toby jug designed by Fluck and Law, creators of *Spitting Image*, featuring a hideous, long-nosed caricature of Margaret Thatcher.[26]

One schoolboy enthusiasm Clarke developed – very odd indeed for a child from a normal family – was for politics. To some extent this was inspired by his communist grandfather, but largely it seems to have been an interest he developed on his own and remarkably early.

> I was interested in politics from about the age of six or seven, because I read the paper – the *Daily Mail*. My father was addicted to the *Daily Mail*. Our family were pretty non-political.[27]

It was, nonetheless, an absorbing interest which his parents did not discourage. Bright boy that he was, he evidently worked out that if he lacked the exceptional talents to make a career in jazz, he could handle himself in politics. And that is Kenneth Clarke: not a visionary driven by some trauma to change the world, but a happy-go-lucky character who was fascinated by politics in the same way that he was fascinated by football or train spotting, and who has been one of those rare individuals fortunate enough to be able to turn a hobby into a successful career.

CHAPTER TWO

THE ORIGIN OF THE CAMBRIDGE MAFIA

By the time Kenneth Clarke arrived at Cambridge University in autumn 1959, he had a career in politics in mind but no ideology to guide him through it. He was not at all like Margaret Roberts, who already knew she was a Conservative before she arrived at university. On the contrary, Clarke was quite promiscuous in his approach to student political circles. He joined the Bow Group, which was then identified with the left wing of the Tory Party; the Campaign for Social Democracy, which was loyal to the Labour leader Hugh Gaitskell; a Liberal club; and "practically everything that was in sight".[1] By about the end of his first year he had decided which of these three mistresses was to be his bride, and during 1961 he emerged as one of a circle of ambitious young Conservatives who made quite an impact on student politics in their day and on national politics later. Incredibly, no fewer than five of Clarke's Cambridge contemporaries later sat with him in Mrs Thatcher's Cabinet at different times. They were Leon Brittan, Norman Fowler, John Gummer, Norman Lamont and Michael Howard. The six of them became known as the "Cambridge mafia".

And therein lies the most likely explanation of what made Clarke decide to be a Conservative. Cambridge in the early sixties was feeling the stirrings of social change, which erupted nationally in 1963. From being a haven for wealthy public-school boys who, if they were considering a career in politics, expected it to be arranged for them when they went down, Cambridge had become more middle class; its students more socially conscious and quicker to question the wisdom of their elders. During Clarke's first year in Gonville and Caius College, one of its older undergraduates, David Frost, was a well-known figure around the college. Peter Cook, a recent graduate, was working on his review, *Beyond the Fringe*. In November 1960, the student newspaper *Varsity* ran a large feature entitled "What is Sociology?", which revealed that there were no less than five sociologists lecturing at the university. Interest in sex was also spreading, with particular reference to Eastwood's bad boy, D.H. Lawrence, whose novel *Lady Chatterley's Lover* was the subject of a famous trial in 1960.

In that year, the Cambridge Union earnestly debated the question of whether censorship should be abolished. Two of the students sticking up for censors were Ken Clarke and his best friend, John Gummer, who was known at the time as "Gum-gum". *Varsity* gave them a good write-up: "Ken Clarke was cogent and to the point and John Gummer yet again displayed his gem-like talents." Unfortunately, none of Clarke's "cogent" points was recorded for posterity; but Gummer argued that "the censor does not hope to raise moral standards but to prevent their falling; he is concerned with the protection of the citizen from exploitation."[2] The reviewer may not have been wholly unbiased; although he did not sign his name, the comments appear to have been written by their friend, Norman Fowler.

· The general election of 1959, just a few weeks after Clarke's arrival at university, was the worst defeat for the Labour Party since the war, with the Conservatives coming back into power with an overall majority of more than 102. For the next three years, the Labour Party was riven by a split between the right, who supported NATO and wanted to remove the reference to nationalization from the party programme, and the pro-CND left. This split was replicated in the university, with the difference that the Labour Club was dominated by the left, and the smaller Campaign for Social Democracy broke from it in 1960–61. The left attracted a number of talented students who later made their mark in their chosen fields, but not in parliament. The CND club was run by the future historian Angus Calder, and the leading figure in the Labour club was John Dunn, now Professor of Political Theory at Cambridge. The leading Gaitskellites seem to have been worthy, plodding individuals who disappeared into normal life after university.

The biggest political club, the Cambridge University Conservative Association (CUCA), was also affected by social change. One survey early in 1962 suggested that no more than 42 per cent of the student body supported the Conservatives. The public-school element was losing its hegemony. The proportion of former public-school pupils dropped during Clarke's time there from something like two-thirds of the total student body to about half. In 1960, the Union daringly staged a debate on the motion "The Public Schools do more Harm than Good", in which, according to the commentary by an anonymous reviewer who was himself probably ex-public school, "Norman Fowler, proposing, was first of all funny, and then purely destructive...", whilst "Nick Budgen, opposing, was labelled as a blimp before he got to his feet. The audience ridiculed him, but he managed to describe some of the advantages inherent in a Public School system." The public schools won the day by 349 votes to 188.[3]

These changes, curiously, seem to have done CUCA the world of good. In summer 1961, the newspaper carried a perceptive piece on the student political societies by an undergraduate named David Saunders, then the university's leading Gaitskellite. He complained that the Labour Club had been taken over by a "rather rigid form of socialist orthodoxy", an "obsession with CND", a "mad love affair with neutralism" and "the concomitant neurosis about public ownership"; but meanwhile:

> During the past four years, the Tories have altered out of all recognition.... Smooth young men of good family have gone ... from solidly right wing and upper class, CUCA has become radical and middle class.
>
> The tragedy for the Labour Club is that radicals who ought on any examination of their views to be active Labour Club members are finding their way and a welcome in the Tories.
>
> They admit that they are not Conservatives ... but claim that in the Tories and in the Bow Group they can find expression for radical ideas, which are swamped in the Labour Party.[4]

During Clarke's time, the Liberal and Labour Clubs turned out no career politicians of note; David Owen, who was there studying medicine in the late 1950s, went to one Cambridge Union debate, but was so put off that he never returned.[5] But the list of undergraduates who went through CUCA between 1959 and 1963 on their way to becoming Conservative MPs is amazingly long. In addition to the six who made up the so-called "mafia", there were David Howell and John Nott, who were both members of the 1979 Cabinet, Peter Temple-Morris, Peter Viggers, Peter Lloyd, Nick Budgen, Hugh Dykes, Christopher Tugendhat, Michael Latham, and Michael Spicer. Peter Lilley was also at Cambridge, but was too shy to be involved in politics. Lloyd, Fowler, Viggers, Temple-Morris, Gummer, Clarke, Dykes and Lamont were all chairmen of CUCA at various times between 1959 and 1963. The Association also attracted a number of bright students who went on to be successful academics, including Colin Renfrew, now Professor of Archaeology at Cambridge, Norman Stone, now Professor of History at Oxford, and John Barnes, an LSE lecturer and lifelong friend of Clarke's. At the time, Colin Renfrew and Leon Brittan were regarded as the brightest of the bunch.

Mostly, these were not boys from famous Conservative families or from major public schools. Leon Brittan was the son of an immigrant doctor from Lithuania, and had been through a direct-grant school. Fowler, who was to be more important to Clarke's career than any of the others, had been through King Edward VI Grammar School in Chelmsford. John Gummer, the son of a Welsh Anglican vicar, had been a scholar at Rochester, and was well known even then for combining politics with devout Christianity. Lamont, who came from the Shetland Islands, had been a scholar at Loretto, and was known as the "fish finger connoisseur from Grimsby". Howard was a shopkeeper's son, from Llanelli Grammar School. Even Nick Budgen, the "blimp" who had defended the public schools, had been through one of the less expensive ones. He now says:

> We were part of the general mood that a new middle class had arrived, with wider aspirations. I suspect that in an earlier age, the Brittans and the Renfrews would have made it anyway, but whether the Fowlers and the Budgens would is another matter. I suspect that Budgen would have been a discontented provincial lawyer, Fowler would have been a discontented provincial journalist, and Clarke would have been a circuit judge.[6]

It is not difficult, therefore, to see why Clarke threw in his lot with the Conservative Club. It was full of people just like himself: earnest young men from the provinces intent on successful careers in politics. He could ease his way in via the Bow Group, whose self-proclaimed purpose was to stimulate "constructive thought" within the Conservative Party. At that time, there was nothing "establishment" about the Bow Group; none of its members had even been elected to parliament, let alone served in government. It had been founded in 1952, in Bow in London's East End, by young Conservatives who had recently graduated from university, primarily from Cambridge, with which it kept in continuous contact. Bright students like Leon Brittan used to travel to London to speak at Bow Group meetings.

In his student days, Clarke had already formed some of the opinions that would shape his political outlook. He was self-consciously a One Nation Tory. His political hero was Iain Macleod, whom he met while he was a student. He also described Harold Macmillan, just before his death in 1986, as the man "who once converted me to Conservatism". This was not as trite a statement as it might sound, because at the time it was uttered the elderly ex-Premier was berating the Thatcher government for rejecting the good old Conservative virtue of "paternalism".[7] At the age of twenty-one, Clarke was already firmly committed to the Common Market, after hearing Macmillan speak to the party conference at Llandudno. In one student debate, he proclaimed: "The Commonwealth is founded on history and sentiment and it has no future in an association with an independent Britain, while Britain's entry into Europe would open wide new fields."[8] A year later he claimed that "admission is still only a matter of time. I still feel myself a European."[9]

CUCA's other attraction was its formidable election machine, known as the "crocodile", which placed its nominees into prized positions in the Cambridge Union. Tugendhat, Nott, Brittan, Renfrew, Gummer, Howard, Clarke and Lamont were all presidents of the Union at various times between 1959 and 1963. Of those, Howard was the only one not put there by CUCA. Its own internal elections, however, were dull affairs. The general perception was that there were no real elections inside CUCA at all, but an informal and highly efficient selection process by which it was worked out three terms in advance who would hold which of the Society's main offices. Similarly, CUCA's candidates for office in the student union waited in a queue for a year or more. This is where Clarke and his contemporaries learned how to plan a political career.

They were not, perhaps, a brilliant social set, like the celebrated Cambridge communists of the 1930s. Other students would not have looked upon them enviously, wishing they could be included in their circle. John Dunn says:

> It didn't strike me that I was in the presence of people that would run the country. They were all tremendously unformidable. The most impressive, in an out-of-date sort of way, was Leon Brittan, who was clearly very bright and a fluent orator. But most of them seemed to be in a stage of prolonged adolescence. It was inconceivable that they would be running the country, even scary.[10]

This flavour of retarded adolescence is captured in a contemporary account of a social occasion held by the Disraeli Society, an offshoot of CUCA, organized by an undergraduate named Rodney Stewart-Smith:

> When the dinner-jacketed luminaries slipped into the Caius Parlour and passed the security check at the door they began with prawn cocktail and Forster Attenburg 59. Then the dignitaries, including Gummer, Renfrew, Clarke and Dykes, munched Chicken Maryland, drank Troplong Mondot 55 from crystal glasses, went on to Bombe Glacée Vanilla, and struggled through to gland teasing soufflé.

The Society exists, according to Stewart-Smith, "to encourage gastronomic well-being. We believe in the good life."[11]

There were other times, though, when the "luminaries" took themselves and their student politics very seriously indeed. An annual event in the Union was to debate a vote of no confidence in the government of the day, which was almost always won by the Conservatives. It was, after all, a conservative institution. However, in 1960, when Norman Fowler was chairman of CUCA and the main student speaker against the motion, he and his guest, a government minister named Hugh Fraser, were trounced in debate by the Labour team, and heavily outvoted as a result. Fowler takes up the story in his memoirs:

> I was working in my rooms at Trinity Hall... There was a knock at the door. Two young undergraduates a year behind me entered and explained the purpose of their visit. They were worried at the damage the Union debate had done to the Conservative cause and they wanted urgent action to correct the position. The first of the undergraduates was ... Kenneth Clarke and the second another law student from Peterhouse named Michael Howard...[12]

Clarke was twenty years old, and Howard was nineteen, when they took it upon themselves to reverse the damage "done to the Conservative cause". In no time, the little band of friends had found another important issue, which brought the three of them together on the same side as Leon Brittan. They were all scandalized by the fact that some of the wealthier young Tories who did not have to worry about finding a job after university were staying on for an extra year, apparently for no other reason than to hold some sort of office, such as the chairmanship of CUCA or the presidency of the Union, which might stand them in good stead should they opt for a career in politics later. This was thought to be terribly unfair on students like Clarke and Howard, who would have to earn their living as soon as they had taken their finals. Brittan and Fowler consequently ran a campaign to change CUCA's rules to bar fourth-year students from holding office, with the overt intention of knocking two right-wing students out of the queue and making room for Clarke and Howard. Otherwise they feared the pair were fated to be "the two best ex-future chairmen we have".[13] Given that Howard emerged many years later as one of the right-wing "bastards" infesting John Major's Cabinet, it is worth emphasizing that then he was on the party's far left. He had staked out his ground by leading a call for South Africa to be expelled from the Commonwealth. Nevertheless, the issue of whether fourth-year students should hold office seems to have been as ill-chosen as it was inconsequential. John Gummer, for example, was already planning ahead to become Union president in his fourth year, and Clarke would soon be following his example; but in the short term, it worked. One of the offending students was knocked out of the way, and the path to success as a student politician was open again for Kenneth Clarke.

He took over from John Gummer as chairman of the Conservative Association for the autumn term of 1961, obviously intending to make an impact. In this he succeeded, by means of a reckless piece of exhibitionism which dogged him for the rest of his time at university. To make sure that at least one of CUCA's meetings secured a big turnout, he invited the notorious old fascist Sir Oswald Mosley to come and speak. It was at a time when race relations were tense, and there was a serious argument about whether the growing ultra-right groups should be given opportunities to spread racist ideas. The invitation to Mosley set off an immediate reaction in student political circles. Under attack from all sides, Clarke exhibited the qualities that would stay with him during his political career: he refused to give an inch and answered criticism with bluster. Only members of the Conservative Association had a right to decide who spoke at CUCA meetings, he claimed. Moreover, he added: "Mosley's views are so intrinsically ridiculous that no one will agree with him."[14] That being the case, there seemed little point in inviting Mosley in the first place. His comment provoked a stiff letter from Mosley to Hugh Dykes, who was then secretary of CUCA, objecting to being dismissed out of hand without a hearing, and challenging Clarke to a debate in which they each had half an hour to state their positions. It was a challenge that Clarke could hardly refuse; Dykes, in fact, announced that "if Kenneth Clarke doesn't do it, someone else will."[15] On the other hand, he would be up against someone who, for forty years, had had the reputation of being one of the most powerful speakers in the land. Clarke experienced what he now calls "a rather surprising loss of confidence",[16] and insisted that there must be two students, himself and John Gummer, pitted against Mosley.

Meanwhile, his explanations were not accepted outside the Conservative Association. He had to defend himself in front of the student union, where he insisted that CUCA's policy was to invite speakers from right across the political spectrum, and that Mosley was a "serious political figure" who had "got to be faced". *Varsity* reported scathingly that "Ken 'it's only a novelty' Clarke made CUCA sound like a sort of multi-racial Fabian Society",[17] but acknowledged that he had fought his corner "vigorously". He was, of course, heavily defeated in the vote, but stuck to his line that it was nobody's business who they invited but the Conservatives'.

When the meeting occurred, before a crowd of some 1,500 in the university's Examination School, Mosley easily outwitted his young opponents. He devoted the first part of his speech to the Common Market, which he supported, before rattling through an explanation of why he thought a third of Africa should be cordoned off as "white territory" and why his views were not "racist". And, when he took questions from the audience, he answered at great length if they were on Europe, and evaded them if they strayed on to more uncomfortable subjects. Soon, the 10.30 deadline was approaching and the proctors were at the door to ensure that the future world leaders ended their meeting and went back to their colleges on time. "During the final minutes, the shouts of 'irrelevant' and 'answer the questions' grew apace with the realization that Mosley had sidestepped almost every important question put to him..."[18]

Afterwards, Clarke invited his guest back to his room in Caius College for coffee, but Mosley insisted he had to get back to London and got in his car to hurry away to what turned out later to be a secret rendezvous with four students who were his only active supporters in the university. The event had made Clarke a minor celebrity in the university, but it almost ruined his plans to take his career as a student politician any further. He had himself said that the only opinions which mattered to him were those of his fellow members of CUCA. Unfortunately, there was one who was furious about the invitation to Mosley, and resigned from CUCA's committee in protest. This was Michael Howard. A student photographer caught Clarke and Howard sitting side by side, staring in opposite directions. The caption read: "We used to be friends..."[19] Clarke insists now that they remained "extremely good friends" throughout.[20]

Soon afterwards, there was an election in the Cambridge Union which developed into a political scandal all of its own, attracting the attention of national newspapers. It centred around a highly gifted student named Brian Pollitt, son of Harry Pollitt, who was every bit as hardline a communist as his father. His idea of a summer vacation was to drive a tractor on a collective farm in Kazakhstan. There were fewer than twenty pro-Soviet communists in the entire university, but Pollitt was such an outstanding speaker that even Conservatives would vote for him. He featured in one debate on the merits of a planned economy, speaking against Enoch Powell, with Douglas Jay as his seconder, whilst Clarke seconded Powell. Even Clarke's friend and mentor, Norman Fowler, who disapproved of Conservatives throwing their votes away on a communist, was compelled to admit that "Pollitt and Powell outshone Jay and Clarke."[21] In the summer of 1961, Pollitt caused a sensation when he beat John Gummer to the post of vice-president, "despite considerable pressure to get Conservatives to the polls".[22] This put him in with a serious chance of becoming the first communist president of the Union since the onset of the Cold War. He had increased his chances by running the campaign to discredit Kenneth Clarke. To stop him, CUCA's "crocodile" went into overdrive, and secured a narrow victory for a very right-wing American student by methods which, it turned out afterwards, were flagrantly illegal even by the loose standards applied to student elections. At the same time, it was reported that John "now thank we all our God" Gummer had slipped quietly into the vice-presidency. The ballot for the presidency had to be rerun when the students returned from their Christmas break, bringing victory to what *Varsity* described as "the quiet, career men who have slid into political seats of power in the shadow of the Union's greatest hullabaloo – and nobody has ever heard of them. At the top is unassuming John Selwyn Gummer, the Union's third choice for the Presidency ... CUCA's new chairman is efficient and unspectacular Hugh Dykes."[23]

With all this going on, the struggle for the other prized Union posts attracted very little interest. Clarke, who had the "crocodile" working for him, was counting on winning, so that he could move on from there to be Union vice-president, and then president; but afterwards, *Varsity* announced: "The most disappointed man in the union must be CUCA chairman Ken Clarke, who was being confidently tipped for secretary. Instead he came third."[24] He had been beaten by Michael Howard, who had split the Conservative vote and persuaded the left to support him in recognition of his principled stand against fascism. Even if Howard appears a little wobbly on his ideology, we can see that even then he was icily clear about his main objective, to get on in politics. While he was Union secretary, he insisted on maintaining a balance by putting in an appearance at an equal number of meetings of the Conservative Association and the Labour Club whilst showing "at all times a keen interest in Liberal affairs; and all this whilst retaining the goodwill of CND and worse..."[25] In March 1962, he was triumphantly elected Union president, without letting on which party he now supported. Later, he reputedly went up to Kenneth Clarke at a party, slapped him on the back, and told him: "Politics is easy when you've got principles."[26] Clarke suspects to this day that he had, in fact, joined the Labour Party.[27] His success certainly mystified the anonymous commentator in *Varsity*, who appealed to him:

> Step forward Michael Howard and take a bow. Show us all exactly how it should be done. First of all you run with CUCA until Ken Clarke beats you. Then Mosley gives you a few cheap votes. A loud approach to the Labour club, a public promise to speak on their platform, is followed by an agonising reappraisal...[28]

A year later, Michael Howard was still taking part in the activities of the Labour Club, and his name appeared on an "investigation" into why Cambridge Conservatives appeared to be intellectually moribund, despite having the university's most effective political machine and the backing of two-fifths of the student population. The article concluded acidly: "The CUCA bandwagon is for those who are hoping for the offer of a safe seat when they go down... There are, in fact, no thinking Conservatives in Cambridge."[29] When his friends read this extraordinary piece, they were sure that Michael had burned his boats with the Conservative Party for good. Not at all: the very next week, a furious letter from Michael Howard appeared in the same newspaper, disowning the entire article and claiming that his name had been appended to it without his knowledge. In March 1963 it was reported that:

> Michael Howard has almost finished his monumental ideological rethink. However, one nagging fear still prevents him fully embracing the philosophy of democratic socialism. Will he, as a Labour MP, be able to wear a clean shirt and own an E-type Jaguar?[30]

Later that year, Howard was chosen as one of the two student speakers for a biennial debating tour of the USA. When he returned, he threw his energies back into the Bow Group.

Meanwhile, Clarke had to pick up the pieces of his disappointed political ambitions, which he did in a manner that was to become a mark of his character: he went straight back and tried again. In January he ran for the post of vice-president, only to be beaten 99–86 by the "extreme left winger" John Dunn, who won over a few waverers by speaking "eloquently" on why homosexuality should be decriminalized.[31] In March he ran again for the secretaryship. In November he was elected vice-president of the Union. The following March he finally won the prize he wanted: with CUCA's crocodile working for him, he cruised to victory. For the summer term of 1963, his last at the university, he was to be president of the Cambridge Union.

It was an undistinguished term which did not do much for Clarke's reputation in the university. For a number of reasons, the Union seems to have been in a trough during the year Clarke was president, from which it recovered after he had left. During the summer of 1963 the student body had suddenly become more interested in listening to Beatles records than earnestly discussing the future of the world. Only 385 students had bothered to vote in the contest for the presidency. Drastic steps were taken to draw them back, ranging from the practical – a self-service cafeteria was installed – to the absurd. Clarke and his fellow officers dug out and polished up a ceremonial sword which had been donated to the Union some years earlier by Lord Mountbatten, and initiated a practice of carrying it in solemn procession into the debating hall. Despite these efforts, a group of undergraduates launched a serious attempt to abolish outright the offices of president, vice-president and secretary. Just forty-nine students turned out to debate the matter, the lowest turn-out at any Union debate for three years. Norman Lamont addressed them from behind the ceremonial sword on the importance of retaining these ancient offices, and the motion was defeated. *Varsity* commented: "When little more than one per cent of the membership resident in Cambridge turns up to vote for or against a motion as radical as that involving the abolition of the president and other offices, there is little to be done to stop the rot."[32] The last mention of the Union president in the university newspaper described him as "affable, invisible Ken Clarke, the man with the brilliant future behind him."[33]

The rot had something to do with the Union's image as a self-satisfied club where self-important young men dressed up in dinner-jackets and black ties to listen to each other speaking. The word "men" is chosen advisedly. Women students were barred from joining. This had been a lively source of contention for the whole of the time that Clarke had been at university. During the course of the long arguments, three of the "Cambridge mafia" – Norman Fowler, Michael Howard and Norman Lamont – came across as enlightened and sympathetic to the feminists. Others said things that they would probably prefer to forget. In March 1961, there was an energetic campaign to change the rules, centred on a petition sent out to every member of the Union. Most of its supporters were from the left, just as the opposition to women seems to have come almost exclusively from Conservative students. However, the Conservative Association was not monolithic. Norman Fowler, who had recently taken over as political editor of *Varsity*, was leading the pro-feminist campaign, with energetic support from Michael Howard. In his memoirs, Fowler tactfully glosses over the part played by other students who went on to be famous Tories,[34] but the contemporary record survives. When seventy students gathered for a private Union meeting to discuss the issue, the university's two most respected Conservative students, Leon Brittan and Colin Renfrew, insisted that women must be kept out. "People would not listen to them as speakers. They would look at them as women", Brittan explained. John Gummer warned that if women were admitted as members they would lose more than they gained because "they would no longer be able to come to debates as guests of men". According to the report that Fowler wrote at the time, "this argument failed to convince anyone",[35] and very soon Gummer was himself convinced that he had been wrong and changed sides. The campaign failed nonetheless, because it had an impossible hurdle to cross: any rule change required a majority of at least three to one in favour. A quarter of the all-male membership was sufficient to keep women out.

In October 1961, exasperated women students pushed their way into the first debate of the term, demanding their right to take part. They were "howled down", with shouts of "keep these bloody women out!" and "this is a gentleman's forum!" One woman fainted and had to be taken into hospital overnight for observation.[36] As a gesture, two of their leaders were allowed in as a one-off the following month, to speak on the motion that "this Union would welcome women". The opposition was led by Hugh Dykes, who claimed that "the admission of women would have a disastrous effect on the Union and that most women do not want to join."[37] The pro-feminist majority was 225 to 125, nowhere near the requisite 75 per cent. After the direct approach had failed, sympathetic males decided on a change of tactics. In the term when Michael Howard was Union president, two sympathetic young Conservatives, John Barnes and Norman Lamont, ran a campaign to bring the majority required for a rule change down from three-quarters to two-thirds, and succeeded. But when the vote was taken on whether to admit women, it was 371 for and 220 against, just short of the necessary majority. "The result must come as a great disappointment to the president, Michael Howard", *Varsity* commented. "A victory for the feminists would have been a memorable ending to his term in office."[38]

The next time a female voice was heard in the Union was in the autumn of 1962, when the communist Brian Pollitt had succeeded in becoming Union president, and used his position to extend a special invitation to selected "ladies of distinction" to speak in an emergency debate called to gauge student reaction to an extraordinary development in one of the men's colleges: an undergraduate had been caught with a nurse from a nearby hospital in his bed and sent down. "In spite of the boos which greeted his announcement that he would admit female members of the University to future debates, the House was restrained as it listened to what speakers from Girton and New Hall had to say."[39]

As to Kenneth Clarke, he is surprised now to be reminded, first, that women were still barred from the Union when he was its president and, second, that he supported the ban.[40] However, the contemporary record is clear. At the same time that Clarke was elected president, the Union voted, once again, to retain the ban, despite the news that the Oxford Union had decided to admit women students. The incoming president's thoughts on the matter were also recorded, both in the university newspaper and in *The Times*:

he had "always" opposed the admission of women – Cambridge should wait at least another year; and "the fact that Oxford has admitted them does not impress me at all. They will soon realise what a mess they are in."[41] *Varsity* also posed the question "How much do women care anyway?" However, it was while Clarke was president that the Union finally voted to admit women, starting from the winter term of 1963. The first woman president, Ann Mallalieu, was elected in 1967.

Whilst he was president, Clarke also had his final examinations to think about. Back in 1959 he had begun as a history student, but had switched to reading law on the sound premiss that lawyers found it easier than most other professionals to enter politics. He also imagined that his ability to absorb a lot of detail quickly would allow him to come away with a first. In fact, "it wasn't quite the doddle I expected it to be. I never quite got the first which I thought I would get. It was the first time I began to realize that you could not just assume that all these things were just going to happen."[42] However, given the amount of time he was devoting to politics, and to other student pursuits like playing bridge late into the night with Norman Stone and others, it says something for his stamina that he passed his examinations at all. He could not rely on wealthy parents to see him through long vacations either, and had to take whatever jobs he could find. Between school and university he worked for a time in a solicitor's office in Nottingham and took a night job in a bakery for "a couple of months... I opted deliberately for permanent night work and sought the maximum amount of overtime... I did all sorts of unpleasant jobs, such as greasing tins in the middle of the night."[43]

Of all the people he had met at university, the one who was most valuable had not taken any part in the shenanigans at the Cambridge Union. This was Gillian Edwards, a teacher's daughter from Sidcup, who was reading medieval history at Newnham College. Her final degree was better than Clarke's, good enough for her to have taken up an academic career; but by the time she had completed her M.Litt., they were married with a baby son, and her husband was about to enter parliament, so she settled down to keep house. She never aspired to be a national figure, but has for years been an active Conservative at constituency level, as well as giving time to Oxfam and other causes. The marriage has lasted when so many others in politics have failed.

The closest male friendship Clarke formed at university was with John Gummer, of whom it was said at the time, "When Gummer comes can God be far behind?" One thing they shared was their undergraduate sense of humour. For about a year both of their names crop up in every issue of *Varsity* with comments attached which are dressed up as insults, as if they were the most talked-about students in the university. Frequently they were writing jokes about one another. Later, Gummer acted as best man at Clarke's wedding. Of his other political contacts, Norman Fowler turned out to be vital to Kenneth Clarke's survival as a junior minister in the Thatcher government. The link to Geoffrey Howe, through the Bow Group, also served him well. But generally the expression "Cambridge mafia" can mislead, because it gives the impression of a group who were all for one and one for all, whereas even as students, Clarke and Howard were competing intensely with each other, and Norman Lamont would find out just what his "mafia" links were worth when his position as Chancellor of the Exchequer was hanging in the balance in 1993. Nonetheless, the competitive atmosphere in the Cambridge Conservative Association certainly spurred its members on. Peter Lloyd now recalls how, as a moderately successful businessman in the mid 1970s, he became acutely aware of how many of his university contemporaries had entered parliament ahead of him, which motivated him to find a safe seat in time for the 1979 election. Nearly all of Clarke's contemporaries who became Conservative politicians were in parliament by 1974 at the latest. The glaring exception was Michael Howard, who left it as late as 1983 to get in.

Having been "called to the Bar" at Grays Inn in November 1963, Clarke set himself up as a practising barrister on the West Midlands Circuit, in chambers headed by Michael Davies – now the Honourable Sir Michael Davies, a retired judge – specializing in industrial and criminal law. The reason he moved to Birmingham is simply that he could not afford the cost of living in London. He had a bedsit in Castle Bromwich for a year, then he and Gillian moved into a flat when they were married, but it was several years before they could afford a stable home. Their first child, christened Kenneth Bruce, was born in 1965. Their daughter Esther Susan, usually known as Sue, followed in November 1968. Clarke's trouble was that he was spending too much time on politics to earn a comfortable living in law. In 1963–64 he followed in Gummer's footsteps by being chairman of the National Federation of Conservative Students, which took him to meetings at universities around the country. Between 1964 and 1966 he was research secretary for the Birmingham Bow Group. In addition, he kept up his membership of the

North Nottingham Conservative Association. Simultaneously, he was a member of the Young Conservatives National Advisory Committee, the general-purposes committee of the National Union of Conservative Associations, the British National Committee of the World Assembly of Youth, and the Joint Action Group for Understanding Among Races.

The Bow Group link brought him back into contact with one of his former university contemporaries, Nick Budgen, who was also practising as a barrister on the Midlands Circuit. He and Clarke co-wrote a pamphlet called *Immigration, Race and Politics* which was intended to be a detailed and generally liberal commentary on race relations and immigration law. They called for legislation to outlaw racial discrimination along the lines of the recently defeated Race Discrimination Bill, government funds for more Community Centres on the lines of the one which was then operating in Sparkbrook in Birmingham, aid for New Commonwealth immigrants to help them buy their own homes. On the other hand, they wanted a five-year ban on New Commonwealth immigrants, except for holders of special vouchers, which the government would issue at a rate of sixty thousand a year, and only to those who were in good health and fluent in English.[44] Clarke put his name to other Bow Group publications, including an interesting one on local government reform. He and his co-authors proposed to abolish county councils and divide England into seven regions, each with its regional council, with assemblies for Scotland and Wales.[45] That was very similar to the proposals which Labour and the Liberal Democrats put forward during the 1992 general election against determined opposition from the Conservatives.

In March 1964, at the age of only twenty-three, Clarke was adopted as prospective Conservative candidate for Mansfield, in south Nottinghamshire. On the day the association held its selection meeting he was at an inquest at Shifnal, Shropshire. He had to drive to Mansfield as soon as the hearing was finished. The following morning, he reassured his pupil master, truthfully, that he had "not a hope" of winning the seat.[46] It was, as Clarke later described it, "very traditional, old fashioned mining country with an immovable Labour base."[47] It has been Labour without interruption since 1945, despite the bitter rift caused by the 1984–85 miners' strike, during which most of the miners in the area kept working. Contesting it was simply a way of establishing himself as parliamentary material, in the hope that a better prospect would come his way at the next election. The previous prospective candidate, Richard

Whiteley, had pulled out only months away from a general election because of ill health. The local association soon learnt that his young replacement was not only healthy, but keen. Little more than twelve hours after being adopted, Clarke turned up at a coffee morning in the constituency, bringing his 23-year-old fiancée, Gillian Edwards.[48]

He fought Mansfield twice, in 1964 and 1966. The second time, he was up against Don Concannon, a miner and town councillor who went on to hold the seat for twenty-one years. Clarke fought him on a six-point formula for economic revival, which he set out at his formal adoption meeting in March 1966 – low taxes, better management, education, more power to the Monopolies Commission, reform of Britain's "archaic" industrial-relations law, and membership of the Common Market – but lost by a margin of almost twenty thousand.

After the 1966 election, more interesting prospects than Mansfield came on offer. Clarke was shortlisted for Wellingborough, a marginal Labour seat where a by-election was held in 1969, but during the selection conference he had "a long harangue"[49] with one member of the audience who supported Ian Smith and the white supremacists in Rhodesia, which may have cost him the nomination. He also entered the running for South Bedfordshire, but lost. Meanwhile Sir Martin Redmayne, former Tory Chief Whip and MP for Rushcliffe, in south Nottinghamshire, had been narrowly defeated by Labour's Anthony Gardner, and granted a life peerage. The seat was a curious patchwork, as Clarke explained later in the House of Commons:

> It is necessary to go over a one inch ordnance survey map with a microscope to find the word "Rushcliffe" and one needs to have been born, educated and resident in Nottingham to know that it is part of Nottinghamshire. Even fewer people know that the name "Rushcliffe" comes from that of a wapentake, which was an old local government area at the time of Danish settlement of Notts...
>
> There are mining towns at one end and rolling farm acres at the other over which the Quorn has been known to hunt. In between, Beeston and Stapleford are satellite towns of the city of Nottingham. Rushcliffe contains a great deal of industry, mostly light industry, but including mining and textile industries in which there has been difficult change and reform.[50]

Here the Labour majority was only 380, so there was a clear chance of the seat reverting to the Conservatives in four or five years' time. About sixty hopefuls put their names forward for the seat. The association's General

Council whittled that down to fourteen, all of whom were interviewed in November 1966. The committee sent two names forward for the final run-off: Kenneth Clarke and David Penfold, who had fought Nottingham West in the previous election. Both went in front of a full meeting of the association's Central Council at the beginning of December, where there were some rumblings about the fact that both were rather young, and that the respected Tory MP Tom Boardman had not been shortlisted, as expected. There was a "record attendance" of ninety.[51] Clarke emerged as the winner, and his status as prospective candidate was confirmed at a formal adoption meeting at the Roundhill School, Beeston, on 31 January 1967, before an audience of three hundred. Gillian Clarke had to turn out for the second meeting, but was asked only one question about whether she would put time into the constituency, which she undertook to do.

At twenty-six, Clarke was ahead even of the galaxy of young politicians he had known at Cambridge. In 1968, Leon Brittan and Norman Fowler fought one another for the nomination in the neighbouring Labour marginal of Nottingham South. Fowler won, and it took Brittan until after the 1970 election to find a seat. John Gummer also won a nomination, in the Labour marginal of West Lewisham. Michael Howard slogged it out in Liverpool, Edge Hill, without a real hope of success. Lamont settled for Hull East, another hopeless prospect. Clarke nursed his new constituency by constant hard work, and by being a master of the colourful phrase which could be picked up by local journalists. Here, for instance, he is describing a 1969 Vietnam peace march:

> The same people seem to march for endless different causes, or the marchers tend to look and dress very much alike. Whatever the issue, they all sing the same old songs which are usually cribbed from the American civil rights movement and which have a terrible dirge-like quality...[52]

Harold Wilson called the general election suddenly, on the strength of an opinion poll which predicted a decisive Labour win, the result that most observers expected up until the count. On the night, Clarke not only took the seat off Labour, he achieved a majority of 6,168 – the largest since the last boundary revision fifteen years earlier. At school he had told his history master that he would be an MP by the time he was thirty. He fulfilled that boast with just a fortnight to spare. In the morning, he learnt that his party was back in government.

CHAPTER THREE

"HE COULD HARDLY HAVE MORE APPEAL TO THE PRIME MINISTER IF MR HEATH HAD INVENTED HIM"

The parliament that Kenneth Clarke entered at the age of only twenty-nine was disconcerted by the unexpected change of government. It took Harold Wilson a couple of days to admit defeat and vacate Downing Street. The Conservative Party took even longer to discover what manner of political leader they had in the little-known Edward Heath. Both his enemies on the left and some of his supporters on the right anticipated that he might be the sort of prime minister which Margaret Thatcher later became: courageous and unflinchingly strong in his principles, or hard-nosed, right wing and ideologically driven – according to taste. Their expectations had been built up by a declaration issued after a weekend Conservative Shadow Cabinet at the Selsdon Park Hotel. To Norman Tebbit, another of the new intake of Tory MPs, the Selsdon declaration was "the Tory party's first repudiation of the post-war Butskellite consensus."[1] Here was a prime minister hardened by the experience of having fought his way to the top from genuinely humble beginnings, who would surely dispose of the upper-class paternalism of the Macmillan years that had made the likes of Tebbit almost ashamed to be Conservative.

In reality, it did not take Heath long to discard the Selsdon declaration, which seems only to have been a device to motivate the party when its fortunes were low. Before the election, the bane of Heath's life was Enoch Powell, who was much more famous than the party leader and had a far more dedicated base of support among party activists and among lower-middle-class and working-class voters in the country. The prospect of Powell becoming prime minister was spoken of in the pubs and clubs. After the election, the balance of power within the Conservative Party was dramatically transformed. Having won an election against the odds, Heath acquired an unchallengeable personal authority within the party and could concentrate on governing, for which he needed the assistance of forces rather larger than the far right of the Tory Party. He tried to construct an economic policy around British membership of the Common Market and collaboration between industry, trade unions and a Conservative government. Sadly for him, the trade unions had also taken the Selsdon rhetoric seriously – with much encouragement from Harold Wilson, who coined the phrase "Selsdon Man". The Heath government, like the Labour government that succeeded it, was driven out of office when its attempts to win union support for a pay policy ended in disaster. Mrs Thatcher, who was a member of the Heath Cabinet throughout, now claims that:

> After a reforming start, Ted Heath's government … proposed and almost imple-mented the most radical form of socialism ever contemplated by an elected British government. It offered state control of prices and dividends, and the joint oversight of economic policy by a tripartite body representing the Trades Union Congress, the Confederation of British Industry and the Government, in return for trade union acquiescence in an incomes policy. We were saved from this abomination by the conservatism and suspicion of the TUC…[2]

This is where Kenneth Clarke's career as a professional politician began: not as an observer, like Norman Tebbit, but as a young and ambitious participant in the Heathite project. He joined the government as its youngest member at the age of thirty-one. Before that, he had taken part in the draft-ing of the 1971 Industrial Relations Act. Unlike Thatcher, he has never since shriven from his association with Heath, and still says that he is an "admirer" of the man, although the record of his government amounted to "a glorious failure":

> He is a tragic figure really, except in one respect: the big historical thing that he did was to get us into Europe. Otherwise, that government had no lasting achievement to its name. He was a great man. He still is. He's a statesman of quality, a class act: he's got star quality. Ever since he fell from power he's been a completely wasted talent. He should have been on the world stage.[3]

At the outset of his career, Clarke had to cope with the dilemma that faces any backbencher who wants to establish his reputation and be devotedly loyal to the government of the day. He obviously wanted to distinguish himself from the grey mass of lobby fodder who fall over one another in their desperation to excel in sycophancy, and yet he did not want to criticize the prime minister. It was a difficult act, but Clarke proved remarkably good at it. Instead of relying on dumb loyalty to receive its reward, he chose a quicker and riskier means to get on, by wading into all of the most delicate and divisive issues of the day – Europe, immigration, industrial relations and comprehensive education, and in all of them he was a little bit more anti-Powellite than the prime minister, more "Heathite" than Edward Heath. This was some achievement, because until 1972 there was general confusion about what being "Heathite" meant, other than a commitment to the Common Market. The Selsdon declaration was abandoned in practice in 1972, when the government became alarmed by the unemployment figures and embarked on a policy of subsidies for loss-making industries and pay restraint. Clarke says that, like most Conservatives, he disapproved of the U-turn at first, but he obviously adapted to it very quickly.

Before the new government had set out its programme in the Queen's Speech, on 2 July 1970, there had been two highly contentious announcements by Cabinet ministers, both of which strengthened the impression that the postwar consensus was about to end. The first was from the Foreign Secretary, Alec Douglas-Home, who wasted no time in announcing the resumption of arms sales to South Africa. The government's law officers, Peter Rawlinson and Geoffrey Howe, claimed that the Wilson government, which had ended the arms trade reluctantly under the threat of a backbench rebellion, had broken the Simonstown Agreement. Home's view was that he was doing no more than carry out a treaty obligation to protect the sea route round the Cape against the Soviet Navy. There were others, however, who were not as mindful of the danger that the Red Army might land in Cape Town. A group of twenty-nine Conservative MPs braved the anger of their own right wing by signing a Commons motion warning that the arms supplied to South Africa might be used to support apartheid. The signatories were not criticizing the decision. They were not saying that it should be reversed. Instead, they were rather lamely urging the government to ensure that the arms were not deployed against South Africa's blacks or the front-line states north of the Zambesi – as if the Pretoria government would want them for anything else – and they called upon ministers "to make clear that such supplies imply no approval of South Africa's policy of apartheid". Signing the motion, therefore, was not an overt act of disloyalty, but it did put a distance between the signatories and the party's white supremacists who supported apartheid. One of the signatures on the motion was that of Kenneth Clarke, who then had been in parliament barely a fortnight.[4]

Another decision that predated the Queen's Speech was the cancellation of a Labour government circular compelling local authorities to draw up plans to convert all their grammar and secondary-modern schools into comprehensive schools. All the shire Tories and agitated parents who had been fighting a rearguard battle to save the eleven-plus and selective education could take heart, because they obviously had the new Secretary of State for Education on their side. Kenneth Clarke could have been forgiven if he had put his finger to the wind and decided that this was the time to mount a staunch defence of the grammar-school system; or else that the issue was too hot to handle, because feelings were probably higher on this than almost anything else other than immigration. Instead, he chose to make his maiden speech on an afternoon when education was the chosen topic, only ten minutes after the Secretary of State had finished speaking. As is customary in a maiden speech, he spoke mainly about his own constituency. However, Rushcliffe was an interesting case, in that some of its schools were run by Nottinghamshire County Council, which was Conservative controlled, and others by Nottingham urban council, which was Labour. Both were in the process of converting to a comprehensive system. This allowed Clarke to take up a reasoned position in the centre. He disapproved of the way Nottingham was handling the reorganization, because a plan to reclassify three separate school buildings as a single school might mean that pupils would face a one-and-a-half-mile bus journey between classrooms. "I do not oppose such a system because I oppose any abolition of the 11 plus or because I believe in an elitist, selective form of education," he demurred, "but I should expect all honourable members on both side to oppose that sort of education nonsense."[5]

Meanwhile, Nottinghamshire was proceeding with an expensive plan for a purpose-built comprehensive school at Chilwell, which would not be affected by the new government circular. As the Education Secretary had pointed out just before Clarke began speaking, the circular specifically permitted developments to go ahead where "the local authority wishes it and it is appropriate for the area."[6] Clarke was at pains to praise such moderate and reasonable behaviour, in the stilted language required of MPs. "It will be quite clear to all honourable members who listened to what my Right Honourable Friend the Secretary of State said today that that projected development will go ahead ... without the slightest hindrance or obstruction."[7] Time proved that Clarke had guessed correctly what the government would do. There was a popular movement at the time behind comprehensive education, with only a few Conservative councils like Buckinghamshire and Manchester standing in its way. The circular simply relieved the government of the responsibility of forcing the small number of recalcitrant councils into line. Otherwise, it did nothing to hold up the spread of comprehensives. A year after his maiden speech, when Clarke was already bound by his position as an unpaid ministerial aide to support government policy, he said he was in favour of scrapping the eleven-plus and expanding comprehensive education "so far as possible", without making it "absolutely universal". He made a particular point that direct-grant schools should be saved,[8] That was basically the attitude of the government. Edward Heath's Education Secretary signed more orders permitting the creation of comprehensive schools than any Labour minister. Her name, of course, was Margaret Thatcher. There is a wonderful image to be savoured of Margaret Thatcher, only minutes after her first parliamentary speech as a Cabinet minister, having to listen in silence as she was praised by a bumptious new boy, just six days past his thirtieth birthday, for being so moderate. Perhaps it was then that she decided that Kenneth Clarke was very annoying.

By now, Clarke was well established as one of the brightest young MPs of the day. In October 1971 he was given the formal honour of "seconding the Loyal Address', which meant that he was the second MP to speak in the debate on the Queen's Speech which opened the new session of parliament, a prestige slot awarded annually to a promising newcomer. It meant that he was guaranteed a capacity audience, since the speech which followed his was Harold Wilson's, and then Edward Heath's. In line with tradition, Clarke did his best to be funny, with a rather daring joke about the French language which obliquely referred to the fact that, despite Heath's commitment to Europe, he was a notoriously poor linguist. Clarke jokingly claimed that the Nottinghamshire police were learning French in order to cope with continental motorists speeding up the M1, but spoke it so badly that they could only confuse French drivers. "However, if the prime minister is stopped on the M1 he may find he can get in useful practice with no risk of being misunderstood."[9] The story was promptly denied by the Nottinghamshire police.[10] He was also chosen to take part in a number of choice facility trips, including a visit to the USA for the mid-term elections of 1970. He spent election night, on 3 November, at the Maine headquarters of Senator Edmund Muskie, who had been the candidate for the vice-presidency two years earlier. In 1972 Clarke accepted office as a government whip, and was therefore prevented from making any public statements, but he hardly needed to: his reputation was so firmly established that the "Crossbencher" column in the *Sunday Express* commented: "Why, he could hardly have more appeal to the prime minister if Mr Heath had invented him."[11]

The first time Clarke made a formal parliamentary speech on anything other than a constituency matter, he picked the only topic that was more emotive than comprehensive education, which was immigration; and, as if he wanted to make the maximum number of enemies on the Powellite wing of the party in the shortest time possible, he chided the Home Secretary of the day, Reginald Maudling, for being too hard line. One of the measures in the government's new immigration bill created a distinction between black immigrants granted the right to settle in Britain, and voucher holders who would have temporary rights to stay, work and vote in Britain, but not to bring their families with them. It also proposed to compel voucher holders to register with the police. It was that proposal which Kenneth Clarke opposed as unenforceable, and pointedly compared with the South African pass laws. Immigrants from the Indian subcontinent or the West Indies who wanted to evade it could simply vanish into their own communities, he warned. "If the police are to chase them forcefully, looking in and among the immigrant community in the big cities for defaulting people who should be registered, that will give rise to tensions with the police", he warned. "I doubt whether such attempts to restrict their movements by any system of registration will be worth the troubles that will be involved."[12]

This was a bold stand for any Tory MP, especially one whose seat was on the edge of Nottingham, scene of the notorious 1958 race riot. However, Clarke was objecting to only one detail. The crux of the legislation was the so-called "grandfather" rule, which specified that any UK passport holder who had at least one parent or grandparent resident in the country was free from the restrictions proposed by immigration control. The bill's opponents claimed that, despite the neutral language in which it was written, this was implicitly racist, being deliberately formulated to ensure that English-speaking white settlers from the Old Commonwealth could enter Britain unchecked, whilst Indians, Pakistanis and West Indians were kept out. Clarke took this argument head-on. He admitted it was true, and accused liberal opinion of being "intellectually dishonest" by trying to pretend that immigration control was about anything else but race. He added:

> With the unfortunate racial tensions which have arisen here and which we all regret, it is desirable to restrict the number of coloured immigrants into this country.

And he asked rhetorically why the same restrictions should apply to Australians, New Zealanders or South Africans of British descent, who would then suffer

> a most undesirable hardship which ought not to be caused by this country simply in an effort to achieve a bogus uniformity in the way it treats would-be immigrants ... when, in fact, the problems which give rise to the necessity for restrictions are problems to which they make no contribution?[13]

Underneath Clarke's relatively liberal views on race can be seen the streak of hard-nosed pragmatism that argued that racial tension was a problem, "coloured" immigrants were its cause, and they must therefore be subjected to indignities which it would be wrong to inflict on the children of Britons returning to the homeland, even those who had been away seeking their fortunes in the land of apartheid, of which Clarke so stiffly disapproved.

In the year after the new immigration act was passed, white racism reached a new pitch in Britain, after Heath had courageously announced that thousands of Asians with UK passports, who had been expelled from Uganda by its new military dictator, General Idi Amin, would be permitted to enter the country. This would inevitably have repercussions in Clarke's constituency, among many others; but he firmly defended the Cabinet's position in the Rushcliffe Conservative Association newsletter, saying that the government had "no alternative at all, in terms of law and practical government, as well as for reasons of humanity and commonsense."[14] That alone would have destroyed any credit Clarke had with the Powellite wing of the party. The other great issue that divided Heath and Powell was at that time less emotive than immigration, but was to have greater long-term consequences.

The 1971 Industrial Relations Act was the flagship that led the Heath government to disaster. In outline, the Act laid down that strikes could, under specified circumstances, be banned and unions punished without trampling too blatantly on the individual rights of individual union members. The instrument for imposing the law was to be a new National Industrial Relations Court, chaired by a judge, which would have the power to order cooling-off periods and statutory ballots, and fine unions that failed to comply. The evidence is that Heath genuinely did not want confrontation with the trade unions. He wanted to legislate with their consent, if at all possible; and, if that failed, at least to get them to cooperate once the law was in place. His aim was not to eliminate the trade unions from British political life, but to tame them and coax them into becoming like the German unions, partners with management in the common pursuit of profit. He tried to achieve this in one great legislative leap. In retrospect, the legislation has few friends. As a barrister with some specialist knowledge of union law, Clarke played a part in drafting the legislation, but does not attempt to defend it now. "I think it was drafted in an unworkable fashion", he says. "It ground to a halt. It just never took off. The industrial court was never accepted."[15] The Tory right regard it as a shameful piece of corporatism, an unnecessary pandering to the self-importance of disruptive trade-union bosses. By contrast, it was controversial at the time because the left interpreted it as a provocative attack on the organized working class.

As they introduced the legislation, the Tories thought it necessary to give a show of authority by not consulting the unions. Unconsulted, the unions felt themselves honour bound to resist, especially since they had successfully resisted *In Place of Strife*, the Labour government's attempt to reduce strikes through legislation. In the early 1970s, British trade unionism was at the peak of its power, with a combined membership of 9,750,000. More work days were lost through strikes in 1970 than in any year since 1926. The head of the TGWU, Jack Jones, was thought to be the most powerful man in the land. There was even a song in the charts serenading the power of the union barons, with the refrain "You can't get me, I'm part of the union". Organized opposition, out in the streets, was what discredited the legislation and eventually brought down the government. By the time the NIRC opened for business, it had been effectively killed off by the union tactic of refusing to register with it, a prospect that the government had not foreseen and to which they had no answer. The ministers responsible "had expected the parliamentary process and the sheer reasonableness of the reforms to blunt opposition once the bill had gone through".[16] For the next year and a bit, the government did their desperate best to make sure that no trade-union members were jailed under the Act, knowing that it would only escalate industrial disruption. In the subsequent confrontation with the miners, the NIRC and the Industrial Relations Act were useless and unused.

The battle inside the House of Commons, which created the Act, was only an overture, but it was a long one. Unusually, the government decided that line-by-line scrutiny of the legislation would be conducted on the floor of the Commons rather than in a committee upstairs. The debate dragged on for six tedious weeks through January and February 1971, taking up more parliamentary time than any piece of legislation other than budgets since 1945, and ending with a record-breaking eleven-and-a-half-hour session during which MPs did nothing but vote in sixty-three separate divisions. Clarke had intended to take part as one of the loyal dissenters on the back benches, backing the government with a few minor reservations. For instance, he thought it was tactically inept for the Conservative Party to try to tar the entire trade-union movement with one brush. He made a point of praising Vic Feather, the TUC general secretary, and warned in December 1970 that there were "too many scare stories about communists in industry" – although, in the same sentence, he remarked that the Communist Party was "clearly and openly" organizing some of the agitation against the Industrial Relations Bill, which was undeniable.[17] He also put his name to a few proposed amendments, but pulled out in January when he was offered an unpaid job as parliamentary private secretary to the Solicitor General, Geoffrey Howe.

To be a PPS is to be on the lowest rung of government. It has the disadvantage of being required never to criticize or dissent from government policy, without the compensation of a minister's salary or status. A PPS's job is to be the eyes and ears of the minister within the Commons. To perform this task for the more junior of the government's two legal officers would usually be considered about as unrewarding as any political placement could ever be, but not in this case. First, Clarke had done very well to have been offered any promotion at all after only six months in parliament, three months of which had been taken out by the summer recess; second, his new boss was to be among the four or five most important figures in the history of the Conservative Party over the next two decades. To this day, Clarke considers Sir Geoffrey Howe to be one of the great prime ministers Britain never had. Such were the legal complications of the new legislation that Howe, rather than the Employment Secretary, Robert Carr, was the person most responsible for steering it through parliament. Throughout those long weeks, Clarke was at his side:

> I was a keen, attentive PPS and used to attend all the meetings at the old Department of Employment in St James's Square. Instead of being my usual taciturn, quiet, retiring self, I used to join in quite a bit and was very, very immersed in it. Geoffrey was the author of it and did all the work, and tried to get it drafted properly...[18]

Later in his career, Clarke established a reputation as a hammer of the public-sector unions and allied professional lobbies. In the early 1970s, he might deplore militancy on the fringes of a major dispute, but his general attitude was that industrial strife was best settled, and settled quickly, by compromise and negotiation. In the midst of the three-day week, when the British economy had been put on part-time working by the miners' strike, he acknowledged that the NUM leadership had the solid backing of its members, even in the traditionally moderate Nottinghamshire coalfield, and remarked of Employment Secretary Robert Carr's decision to reopen talks that "although I am an admirer of [his] nerve and sense of timing, I believe that this intervention has come not a moment too soon."[19]

He also rushed to Cannock on 8 February, intending to appear in court to defend two NUM pickets, who unfortunately had not been forewarned by their solicitor that their barrister was a Tory MP. They discovered his identity just before they were due in court, and objected, leaving an embarrassed solicitor with no choice but to ask the magistrates for an adjournment. To make matters worse, the prosecution objected to the delay, insisting that it was important that publicity be given to the laws on picketing. Then, in the press reporting of the incident, it was wrongly said that Clarke had refused to defend the men for political reasons, an accusation which could have landed him in serious trouble with the Bar and had to be quickly corrected.[20]

Trade-union militancy is self-evidently less of a problem for right-wing ministers who are not asking for cooperation from the unions than for those from the political centre who are. While Heath and Callaghan were brought down by union defiance, Thatcher thrived on it. So the fact that Clarke became more anti-union as the years went by does not signify, in itself, that he had capitulated intellectually to the right, who suspect him to this day of being a secret supporter of incomes policy. His old colleague Nick Budgen, for instance, says: "I thought perhaps he might have learnt something about pay policy, but he seems to have learnt nothing."[21] Clarke, on the other hand, says he has: that he finally abandoned the notion of pay policies around 1980, when he saw the Thatcher government getting by without one.[22]

There is another issue on which Clarke claims that his opinions have altered over the years, although if they have it is probably not by very much. As a student, he had been fired with enthusiasm for the Common Market. This issue now seemed perfectly suited to the new decade that was to follow the permissive sixties: dull but deeply important. A new breed of earnest young person was arising, to supersede the pot-smoking peaceniks of 1968. In June 1971, Trafalgar Square was once again filled with demonstrators: short-haired, smartly dressed and well-behaved, they were the young Conservatives showing their dedication to the European ideal. The platform speakers included Kenneth Clarke, John Gummer and Norman Lamont. By now, Clarke was helping to draft the legislation which took Britain into the EEC, a task so complicated that once again it been handed to his mentor, Geoffrey Howe. This was a cause Clarke believed in, and he was prepared to make enemies in the Conservative Party because of it.

In May 1971, months of tortuously complicated negotiations suddenly produced a French concession on sugar imports, in return for a British concession on farm prices. For old British Empire loyalists, this had emotive overtones: the French beet-sugar industry dated back to the Napoleonic Wars, when the English navy had prevented the French from importing cane sugar from the West Indies; now it was being proposed that centuries-old, British-owned plantations should, in effect, be abandoned by the motherland in the interests of the French. That argument, though, was ripped apart in a joint statement issued by two of the new intake of Tory MPs, who urged parliament to endorse the deal without delay, claiming that sugar production was "an outdated colonial labour system" whose importance to the Caribbean economies was declining in relation to tourism. They warned:

> The British people might not forgive those who would jeopardise our European future for the sake of perpetuating economies that should be encouraged to diversify, not ossify ... Caribbean workers prefer working in a modern hotel to sweating in a cane field.[23]

The statement was signed by Robert Adley, a former Powellite who was evidently trying to shed an embarrassing political connection, and by Kenneth Clarke, who seemed to want to establish himself as the young Mr Europe. On two occasions during 1971 he had the good fortune to be the first on the list of MPs called during the twice-weekly ritual of Prime Minister's Question Time. He used both opportunities to back Heath on Europe. He wanted the deal struck while there was an opening, and had no patience with those who said that there must be a long period during which the British public was educated in the consequences of membership. They were motivated, said Clarke, by nothing but "a desire to postpone the evil day".[24] As for the argument that Europe was not a democratic institution and that its parliament in Strasbourg was a sham, Clarke's solution was to hold elections to the Strasbourg parliament, despite the risk that this might threaten the sovereignty of the House of Commons. (He was consistent on this for the next decade: when the Callaghan government ran into opposition from the Labour left, Clarke urged the Conservative opposition, now led by Margaret Thatcher, to ignore the "little Englanders" on its own side and back the government.[25])

The crucial vote on Europe came in October 1971, when Edward Heath followed the advice of his Chief Whip, Francis Pym, and gave the Conservatives a free vote, enticing a large group of Labour pro-marketeers led by Roy Jenkins, and including the young John Smith, to break their whip and support the government. In the debate that immediately preceded the vote, Clarke kept quiet: the day belonged to the lead players like Heath himself and to Labour MPs like David Owen, who were risking their careers to secure British entry. He had already said his piece in July, when the Commons had spent almost a week debating the issue.

In the July debate, Clarke spoke immediately after the newest MP in the House, Neville Sandelson, a Labour pro-marketeer who had just made his maiden speech after winning a by-election in Hayes and Harlington. Normal parliamentary procedure demanded that Clarke congratulate him on his speech, even if it was the worst he had ever heard; and he was, in fact, quite sparing in his praise. However, what he did not need to do was enthuse about the by-election campaign, which had not been a happy one for the Conservatives, whose share of the poll had dropped drastically; but Clarke declared himself "delighted" that Hayes and Harlington should have sent such a man to parliament, since his "smashing victory" demonstrated that "my government's present unpopularity, which is undoubted, is not related to the Common Market issue to anything like the extent claimed and hoped for by the anti-marketeers."

His entire speech was admirably clear on detail and short on ambiguity. He did not confine himself to a few safe remarks on the benefits of being part of a free-trade area, although he did warn that the Common Market countries "are enjoying higher living standards than we are, and have a growing political influence in the world at a time when ours still seems to be declining", because they "took the right decision 12 years ago and we took the wrong one."[26] Even Margaret Thatcher and Norman Tebbit had accepted that Britain needed to remove the trade barriers that hindered access to European markets. The question that was agitating the Tory right was what would become of Britain as a self-governing nation-state, and of the "special relationship" with the USA, under a treaty which gave European law precedence over British law. Clarke's answer was that where the prosperity of British companies conflicted with the sovereignty of the British state, he was all for prosperity. He quoted the example of a new Ford plant in Bridgend, South Wales, which would never have opened if it had been "on the wrong side of tariff walls".[27]

Clarke did not quite say that Britain's long-term future was as a province in the European state in the way that Newfoundland is a province of Canada, but he did talk about the "new Europe" as a "very great and important power grouping in the world", with "common foreign policies" and with internal "political unity and common political aims". He plainly thought that it should have a single currency into which sterling would be subsumed. He managed to imply this in circumlocutory language without quite saying it: "I see a Europe committed to going on to the development of economic and monetary union."[28] In a later speech, he was more specific: "I have always regarded the development of a common monetary system as the natural corollary which would come in due course from the development of the common trading system." Outside Europe's monetary system, Britain was doomed to the role of a "second class, rather derided member".[29] As to the special relationship with the USA, he argued that it was on the wane anyway, and that domestic US pressures would eventually force Washington to withdraw a large part of the American garrison from Europe. To counter US isolationism, which "will happen regardless of what we do", he called for a joint Anglo-French nuclear programme and a common European policy for the procurement of aircraft and weaponry.[30]

If all this earned him credit with the prime minister, it did not necessarily do him any good in Rushcliffe. At that time, opinion in the country was probably more anti- than pro-Common Market, because of the traditional British xenophobia towards the French and Germans. Clarke himself admitted on a later occasion, "I cannot claim that all or even the majority of my constituents share my convictions."[31] While he was a government whip, he carried on fighting the European cause by conducting secret negotiations with the pro-European Labour rebels, whose informal whip was John Roper, later a founder of the SDP. Later still, he persisted in sticking his neck out over Europe when the Conservatives were in opposition and caution might have dictated that it was best to keep quiet.

By March 1974, there was a Labour government committed to "renegotiating" Britain's terms of entry and then submitting them for approval to a referendum. This, of course, was a device to evade the problem that the Labour Party was then more deeply divided over Europe than the Tories. As Clarke saw it, even with a second general election looming, it was not for the opposition to exploit the government's difficulties on this particular issue. Since the Cabinet was predominately pro-European, despite Michael Foot, Tony Benn and Peter Shore, it should be encouraged to face down its own rebels. Consequently, when the Foreign Secretary, Jim Callaghan, reported on the opening of the renegotiations, Clarke was soon up on his feet to congratulate him. Nothing he said could have "given much joy to anyone who still had any illusion that this country would leave the European Community"; through "renegotiation" the new government was "merely carrying on the process of the previous government, but paying lip service to one part of the Labour Party"; and consequently, Clarke said he hoped that "my party will respond in kind and will not obstruct reasonable discussions with the Europeans."[32]

In 1977–78, the House of Commons deliberated on the bill which introduced direct elections to the European parliament in Strasbourg. Because it was a constitutional measure, the detailed argument had to be dragged out on the floor of the House of Commons, rather than in a committee. Both the Conservatives and Labour were split, more or less along the same lines as they had been during the referendum campaign, with the opposition coming from the Labour left and Tory right. Their combined strength came to nearly one hundred and fifty MPs. There was an enormous opportunity here for the rebels to waste time by filibustering, clogging up the legislative programme of a government that had already lost its overall majority in the Commons and was living from day to day on the support of the Liberals and nationalists. The Leader of the Commons, Michael Foot, eventually had to resort to the guillotine to cut the debate short.

At this stage in Mrs Thatcher's leadership, the Conservative Party still prided itself on being more European than Labour. Mrs Thatcher herself, and her entire front bench, backed the government on the question of direct elections, even to the extent of supporting Foot's guillotine motion, although the rebels on the Tory back benches included a number of MPs who would later be among her most devoted allies – Norman Tebbit, Alan Clark and Ian Gow, to name three. Their argument was that an elected European assembly must necessarily become a competitor with the British parliament. For the first time, the powers of the House of Commons would be limited, and the foundation would have been laid for a supranational European state.

Kenneth Clarke was not obliged to involve himself in this argument. He had a position on the Tory bench as a spokesman on industry, to which the European Assembly Elections bill was wholly irrelevant. If caution had been his watchword, he would have done what most of the bill's Tory supporters did: stay out of the argument, and turn out to vote. Instead, he was constantly on his feet. The only criticism he had of the Labour ministers who were putting the bill through was that they underplayed its importance, by trying to dress it up as a purely technical measure. These were "dangerous short term tactics" which were bound to provoke allegations of ill faith later, said Clarke. In fact, elections would lead to "a much more powerful European

Parliament with more significant powers". He was prepared to accept the rebels' case that a parliament which commuted between Luxembourg and Strasbourg, and paid its members the same rates as deputies to the Bundestag, was a "ridiculous extravagance" that "enables anti-Europeans to batten on to the envy and malice which motivate too many of our people".[33] But, that aside, there was nothing "fearful" about increasing the powers of the European parliament; indeed, it was "an essential step towards a more unified Europe".[34] His remarks were so straightforward that one of the Labour anti-marketeers, Nigel Spearing, was moved to congratulate him on being "a new kind of Unionist, a European Unionist".[35]

To most people, the European Community is so remote, arcane and uninteresting that it must be bewildering that it could be an issue over which the Conservative Party, or the Labour Party, could tear itself apart. However, to those close to the centre of power, it goes to the heart of the question of what the Conservative Party is about. Nationalism is not usually recognized as a force in British politics, except on the Celtic fringes and in some of the more desperate parts of the inner cities. The Irish, the Scots, the Welsh and countries all around the world have nationalists, but not the English – except for flag-waving rowdies on the political fringe – or the British. Nonetheless, here is a country whose relative position in the world has been in decline for the whole of the twentieth century. From being the world's most powerful state, ruling an empire that encircled the globe, it has lost the power to rule over others and is relinquishing the right to rule itself. It would be a surprise indeed if this had no effect on the internal politics of the Conservative Party, which, more than any other mainstream party, likes to display the Union Jack and use nationalistic language and imagery. To the common-or-garden Tory Party activist, whose role is to organize social events and deliver leaflets at election time, the purpose of the organization is to protect the British way of life against all who threaten it: criminals, left-wing intellectuals, the organized working class, and foreigners. However, the Conservative Party is funded by large multinational companies and is closely linked to people who work in international money markets, who are not deeply sentimental about the sensitivities of small-time British patriots. The party is nationalist and Thatcherite at base, but at its head is more or less acclimatized to the idea that Britain's future is as part of a supranational European state.

From the moment he made his first political speech in the Cambridge

Union, Clarke has been part of the Conservative Party elite, his Hush Puppies and love of football notwithstanding. There is no evidence that his views on Europe have changed in any fundamental way during his long political career. In 1977, he rejected the description of himself as a "federalist", claiming it was a "misnomer". He said: "I do not approve of federal constitutions for the United Kingdom, the European Economic Community, or any other body".[36] However, his old friend Nick Budgen is convinced that he always has been and still is a "federalist",[37] and he is certainly no friend of those who want to halt Britain's integration into Europe.

When there is mutiny in government ranks, one course open to the prime minister is to hire and fire ministers and try to build a loyal team around himself like sandbags against the flood water. By April 1972, the Heath government was surrounded by trouble on all fronts. In foreign affairs, the European bill was grinding through the committee stage against determined and organized opposition from the Tory right. In Northern Ireland, the policy of internment had proved an unmitigated disaster and Heath had been compelled to abolish Stormont. When direct rule was introduced as a "temporary provision" Kenneth Clarke forecast that the government would return year after year to renew its powers and that "Stormont as we know it is dead", with much of the blame going to the Northern Ireland prime minister, Brian Faulkner.[38] This last comment provoked lively protests from Ulster Unionist MPs. And, on the industrial front, defeat by the NUM had been closely followed by the first U-turn on state intervention, when the government rescued an ailing shipyard in the Upper Clyde and then introduced an Industry Act that provided for systematic state aid to the regions.

It was time, obviously, for a change. The main casualties were the ministers at the Department of Trade and Industry, who could not be trusted to implement the new policy. Nicholas Ridley was called back from a visit to Portugal to be fired. The Secretary of State, John Davies, who was a rare example of someone brought into the Cabinet directly from the business world outside, stayed on for only a short period with a team that included Michael Heseltine. There was also a new Employment Secretary, Maurice Macmillan, son of the former prime minister. These changes created openings for members of the new intake to be brought into government for the first term, as assistant whips. The selection was left to the Chief Whip, Francis Pym, a member of the gentry whom Mrs Thatcher later axed from the Cabinet for being a "wet". Pym's view was that there was nothing more destructive of the inner cohesion of the Conservative Party than what he called "dogma", or what others might call political ideology. "Dogmatists cannot come to grips with the world because they cannot come to grips with themselves", he later observed, in what appeared to be a coded reference to Margaret Thatcher and her coterie. "Inflexible opinions defend against inner doubt, not outer adversaries."[39]

Unsurprisingly, the first of the new MPs picked out for promotion were a pair to whom inner doubt was as strange as a visitor from Mars. They were also carefully picked to give the appearance of regional and political balance. Marcus Fox was the sort of Yorkshireman who invites the adjective "blunt". His opinions were predictably right wing: he was against immigration, the EEC and comprehensive education, and for hanging and white South Africa. When Clarke was called into the whips' office, he assumed he was due for a dressing down for his speech on Ireland.[40] On the contrary, he was to be appointed government whip with special responsibility for employment and law, two of the more sensitive policy areas. Pym remembered him as a student who had come canvassing for him in a Cambridgeshire by-election back in 1961. He now recalls an efficient, keen young whip, not markedly different from all the other keen young men who have been through the whips' office on their way to greater things.[41] As a whip, he was forbidden to speak in the Commons on any subject for the next two years; but he was nonetheless required to spend a long time either sitting on the government benches in the debating chamber or being about the premises. In the year ending October 1973, there were 211 occasions when Tory MPs were required to vote for the government. Clarke was there for 206 of them. He was outdone only by Marcus Fox, who voted 207 times.[42]

Each whip, incidentally, is allocated a geographical area, and is responsible for making sure that MPs from his region are present at important votes. Clarke began as the West Midlands whip, which meant that nominally Enoch Powell was part of his flock. It would be interesting to record that his tasks included persuading Powell to keep in line with government policy, but untrue. In fact, Pym handled the Wolverhampton problem personally.

In November 1972, after the main industrial legislation had been through the House, Clarke was shifted to handling education and social security, to help pilot a 94-clause Social Security and Pensions bill through the Commons.

This was the attempt to bring the state pension system up to date, introduced by the Social Security Secretary Keith Joseph, who at the time appeared to be "the embodiment of the Liberal-Tory conscience".[43] Having scrapped Dick Crossman's proposed universal earnings-related pensions scheme, he legislated for a flat-rate basic state pension topped up either by a private earnings-related pension or a much less attractive state scheme. The measure was due to come into effect in April 1975. In 1973, Clarke acted as whip for another piece of legislation piloted by Keith Joseph, the National Health Service Reorganisation Act. This abolished the old hospital boards that had managed most of the health service since the previous century, and brought into existence a network of area and regional health authorities that ran Britain's health care for the next sixteen years, until Kenneth Clarke, by now Secretary of State for Health, undercut their powers by creating self-governing trust hospitals.

Each week, Clarke also went to meetings of the education ministers, presided over by their Secretary of State, Margaret Thatcher. "I thought she was quite good", he says. "I wasn't hostile to her, but never in a thousand years did I expect her to become leader of the party." He claims he had a minor role in persuading Pym to ask Heath not to sack her in 1972, when the decision to abolish free school milk had earned her the name "Thatcher the Milk Snatcher" and Heath was in the mood to strike out at the right.[44] Later in the year, Clarke's responsibilities were altered again. He now became the whip for the East Midlands, and was drafted into the team dealing with the EEC. His job was to keep the government informed on the extent of opposition or support for the EEC, to act as whip for Tory MPs sitting on Common Market committees, and to devote two or three days a month to meetings of one sort or another in Europe, including the Council of Europe, the West European Union and the North Atlantic Assembly. In January, he was promoted to the status of Lord Commissioner, one step up the pecking order in the whips' office, with a salary of £4,000 a year.

It was from the whips' office that Clarke witnessed the second and final humiliation of the government by the National Union of Mineworkers, and Edward Heath's ill-fated attempt to rescue his government, which had emerged from the February 1974 general election with more votes but fewer MPs than the Labour Party, by offering the Liberals the prospect of coalition. Although silenced in the Commons, he was still allowed to make speeches in his constituency; consequently it was to the Edwalton Ladies' Coffee Club that he confided his view that there was "nothing special" about the miners' case, and that "it cannot be right to give in to the claim on terms which show that blackmail had won".[45] But by now, even Clarke's loyalty to Edward Heath was being stretched. After the February defeat, without waiting for the next general election, which everyone knew must come soon, he resigned as a whip.

CHAPTER FOUR

IN OPPOSITION

For all his admiration for the "statesmanlike" side of Edward Heath's character, Clarke had been watching in exasperation from the whips' office as his leader seemed to withdraw into a bunker surrounded by civil servants and walled off from the Conservative Party. He could scarcely believe what he was seeing as he watched Heath make an undignified effort to evade electoral defeat by offering Jeremy Thorpe a place in his government. Clarke was not impressed by the Liberals. They had counted for nothing during his days as a student politician. He suspected that the Liberal candidate in his Rushcliffe seat had picked up the votes of Powellites who had refused to support Clarke because of his views on immigration and on Europe. He opposed the idea of coalition or its concomitant, reform of the parliamentary system to introduce voting by proportional representation, an idea beginning to interest some of the Tory intellectuals close to Heath. Moreover, he knew that the Conservative Party would not wear it, because one of his last tasks as a whip had been to telephone round to test opinion among Midlands MPs. One knight of the shires told him: "Just tell that man to stop messing about. We have lost an election, we cannot form a government, we have just been defeated, and we should leave with dignity." His views, says Clarke, were "remarkably close to my own".[1]

However, his motive for leaving the whips' office was more personal than political. He could not afford to be a full-time MP. He still did not have a home of his own. His family were in a flat near Birmingham and, while the Commons was sitting, he was spending the week in a house in Lambeth owned by John Gummer. Gummer was already an ex-MP, at the age of only thirty-four, having lost his London seat to Labour. He sold the house to a fellow member of the Bow Group named Robert Moreland, a management consultant and future member of the European parliament. Clarke stayed on as his lodger until the latter part of the 1980s. That solved the London end of his domestic arrangements, but not the more important Birmingham end. He consequently went back to practising law with the intention of making as much money as he could before there was a Conservative government again. In his legal career, he mostly handled jury trials in Birmingham, Coventry and Warwick. He also occasionally represented the union side, generally the GMWU, in claims for industrial accidents. One of his more unusual cases followed a stabbing in Leamington. The victim ran hundreds of yards from the Press Club, where he had been stabbed, down the street, before dropping dead. The trial consequently revolved around medical arguments over whether he had died from the stab wound, or from heart failure brought on by the exertion of running away. Clarke's client was acquitted of murder. Clarke also represented a litigant in what he claims was one of the last cases of "enticement" heard in a British court. His client was married to a shorthand typist, who was apparently not even a particularly good shorthand typist, but who was given an E-type Jaguar only three months after accepting a job. Clarke's client, suspecting that the employer's intentions were not honourable, took him to court. "It was a ridiculous action", says Clarke. "On the third day, nobody turned up, so the case was solemnly abandoned. The assumption was that the parties had settled it between themselves."[2]

His court work condemned Clarke to a frenetic life style. Friends remember him rushing to take the last train to Birmingham to be in court from 10 a.m. to 4 p.m., then back to London to appear in the Commons in the evening. He displayed the same energy later, as a junior minister, sometimes staying out at Ronnie Scott's until 2 a.m., then working on his ministerial papers before going to bed. But at least the Clarke family finances were back in reasonable order before 1979, and they could afford to buy a home at 8 Amesbury Road, in a middle-class enclave in Moseley, Birmingham, and pay to send their two children to independent schools – a fact that would return to haunt Clarke when he became Education Secretary. Meanwhile, he had built up a reputation as a hard-working constituency MP, which was as well for him because the boundaries of Rushcliffe constituency were redrawn in 1972, taking West Bridgford in from Nottingham South, which disappeared leaving its incumbent MP, Norman Fowler, seatless. Fowler chose to fight it out with Clarke over who would be MP for the revised Rushcliffe seat – evidence that the "Cambridge mafia" were not entirely all for one and one for all. They and two others went in front of 120 members of the constituency Executive Committee on 29 January 1972. Clarke won. Fowler then went on to find himself a safe seat in Sutton Coldfield, which, as events would prove, was fortunate for Kenneth Clarke.

As well as taking up local issues such as roads, an eternal obsession with constituents living near the M1, Clarke was outspoken in defence of the small number of Asian families among his constituents. For example, in July 1974 he wrote to the Foreign Secretary, James Callaghan, appealing to him to intercede with the Pakistani government over the treatment of the minority Ahnadiyya sect. In June 1975, he protested about the "disgraceful" case of a woman from Islamabad who had had to wait eighteen months for permission to join her husband in West Bridgford.[3]

One of the more unusual constituency cases he took up concerned a 21-year-old widow from Stapleford, whose husband, a corporal in the Royal Marines, vanished while diving off Gibraltar. Two life-insurance policies worth a total of £10,000 were outstanding on him, but because his body had not been found he was not officially considered dead, and after eighteen months his widow had still not been paid.[4] He was also involved in interminable debates and questions about the rights of people who owned caravans that they used as mobile homes. It was a popular practice in Nottinghamshire to take the summer break in a caravan on the Lincoln coast, but those who engaged in it were vulnerable to unscrupulous site owners. This was because their mobile homes were not very mobile in practice. Many had had their wheels removed, and a new pitch would be hard to find anyway, so if the owner fell out with the site owner, over an increase in rent for instance, the only way out was to sell the caravan on its site. That usually meant selling at a giveaway price to the site owner, who would then resell at a handsome profit to a new owner. Clarke was involved in endless exchanges with Labour's junior environment minister, Gerald Kaufman, to improve these people's rights.

In the months between the two 1974 general elections, most of the Conservative Party loyally said very little about their defeat or the record of the Heath government. The notable exception was Keith Joseph, who began a Pauline conversion to the views which soon became associated with his friend and ally Margaret Thatcher. "It was only in April 1974 that I was converted to Conservatism", he claimed the following year. "I had thought that I was a Conservative but now I see I was not really one at all."[5] Joseph began to collect around himself a group of right-wing, free-market economists like Alan Walters and Alfred Sherman, in the new Centre for Policy Studies, which became the breeding ground for Thatcherism. Meanwhile, there were others who were not going through a self-flagellating public conversion but who were nonetheless discontented and in search of a new role. One such was Clarke's former mentor, Geoffrey Howe, latterly the Minister for Trade and Consumer Affairs and now a member of the Shadow Cabinet. He was unhappy about the speed at which the incoming Labour government had repudiated the employment legislation he had painstakingly drafted, wounded by the suggestion that his handiwork had been the cause of defeat, and interested in the new Keith Joseph line that the real enemy of economic growth was not shop stewards, businessmen or the oil-producers, but government spending. Heath had, by chance, made Howe spokesman for Health and Social Security, the biggest-spending government department, only recently vacated by Joseph. He also chaired the party's Social Security Committee.

Kenneth Clarke did not waste time renewing what had been the most useful political contact of his career so far; he was elected secretary of the Committee in April. That summer, all the political parties were engaged in rushing out policy statements in time for the general election that they knew could not be far away. Howe and Clarke worked jointly on a statement on social security, which was put out in August. It was not to be expected that they would break new ground. Although the intellectual drift in the Conservative Party was towards private self-reliance in place of the welfare state, this was no time to be underbidding in the contest for the votes of pensioners. Clarke made that mistake in the first statement he made in his new capacity, when he attacked Labour's promise to increase the state pension annually in line with average earnings as a piece of "sheer overbidding" and "merely an election slogan, which I believe began as a gleam in the eye of Jack Jones of the TGWU".[6] He was vindicated in one sense, in that the earnings rule was abolished in 1979 and is never likely to be reinstated by a Conservative government. Even Labour changed the ground rules to avoid having to meet the increase in full during the financial crisis of 1976. However, once it was in place, Clarke was quick to demand that the rule should be applied also to the better off, whose pension rights were affected by their savings.

There were times, in fact, when the Tory opposition seemed to have only one policy on pensions, that whatever was available for the mass of pensioners who lived off their state pensions must also be there for the few who had another source of income. In 1974, about two hundred thousand people of pensionable age still had regular and substantial earnings, and consequently lost their full entitlement. Others who had investments or savings were taxed on their income. The Labour Party's opinion then was that pensions and other state benefits were a safety measure to protect the poor, not a perk for those who could afford to provide for themselves. Clarke, interestingly, was one of those who fought hard for what are known in the jargon as "universal benefits", payments made by the state to everyone within a given sector of the population regardless of need. He believed that everyone who had reached the appropriate age should be paid their full state pension, whatever their circumstances. Before it was Conservative Party policy to abolish the earnings rule, he put the case for doing so in a pamphlet co-written with Christopher Mockler, a researcher at Conservative Central Office.

At the beginning of 1975, he led what amounted to a successful ambush, when the government tried to put through what seemed like an uncontroversial bill uprating pensions for the coming year, and Clarke threw in an amendment scrapping the earnings rule. He spoke very passionately about the "burning sense of injustice" that thousands of pensioners experienced over what they regarded as a "tax imposed at a penal rate".[7] More important than the quality of his rhetoric was the fact that he and other Tories working in his field knew at the time that a significant number of Labour MPs privately agreed that the earnings rule should be scrapped, and carefully planned their tactics with a view to coaxing as many as possible to rebel. When the vote came, on 29 January, they won over fifteen right-wing Labour MPs, including the future television interviewer Brian Walden – enough for victory. The government had no choice but to give way. It was, perhaps, the high spot of Clarke's five years in opposition. Certainly, he must have been pleased to see it billed in his local press as "Clarke's Big Triumph".[8] He also received a backhanded compliment from the social services minister, Alec Jones, who accused him of using the seductive arts of a former government whip to coax the Labour rebels over to his side.[9]

Generally speaking, Conservative MPs are not very interested in state pensions as a political topic. It is immensely complicated and does not promise much as a route for self-advancement. Barbara Castle's 1974 Social Security

Pensions bill, which introduced the State Earnings Related Pension – known as SERPS – went through unopposed and almost undebated, as most of Her Majesty's Opposition and most of the government's supporters bunked off. "The decision about the future of our pensions system was taken with less than a dozen members out of a possible 635 present in the chamber", Norman Fowler observed.[10] Yet Clarke, who was an ambitious young Conservative MP, had volunteered to get stuck into this specialized field, and applied himself with such energy that he was able to take ministers on in highly detailed arguments, and to defeat the government on minor legislative points. In addition to the victory over the earnings rule, he secured a better deal for disabled pensioners, and for those living with children who were earning money. He also fought energetically, though unsuccessfully, against a proposed increase in national-insurance contributions for married women; for abolition of the so-called "married women's option", which allowed women who had never been in paid employment during their married lives to benefit from their husbands' pension rights; and against the sharp increase in national-insurance contributions by the self-employed, introduced in 1974. During these long debates, he never mentioned his family background, in the way that he was fond of doing when discussing education or the mining industry; yet it may have been that which motivated him.

In the early part of 1974, both Clarke's parents were still alive (and, no doubt, pleasantly surprised by their eldest child's rapid rise to prominence). His father was approaching retirement age, but being self-employed he was likely to carry on working anyway. His mother had not been in paid employment for over thirty years. They were exactly the sort of elderly people hardest hit by the rules: wealthy enough to lose their pension rights, but not wealthy enough to be able to shrug it off. They were to be penalized for working hard all their lives. If he had lived longer, the older Kenneth Clarke would have been one of the first to benefit from the abolition of the earnings rule which his son had adroitly steered onto the statute books.

The other "universal benefit" that came into existence in these years was child benefit, a cash payment to every mother based solely on the number and ages of her children regardless of her circumstances. It replaced a child tax allowance which, by definition, was paid to the family breadwinner. Clarke repeatedly attacked the Labour government over child benefit, not because they introduced it but because it was delayed until 1977 as an economy measure. He was loud in his support for the principle of transferring money "from the pay packet to the handbag",[11] and in his condemnation of Denis Healey and other Labour Treasury ministers who "are not in touch with the changed attitudes towards woman and motherhood".[12] In one attack, he accused Healey and Callaghan of being "terrified" of the reaction from male-dominated trade unions when the news sank in that the money would be paid to the mother.[13] On this issue, he was enlightened and ahead of his time. The stand he took is interesting in the light of the subsequent controversy over universal benefits. In 1987, the Thatcher government embarked on a process of killing off child benefit by not uprating it for three years. Thatcher's intention, as she confirmed later, was to go back to child tax allowances.[14] That phase ended with Thatcher's fall, but by the time Clarke became Chancellor of the Exchequer the future of universal benefits was seriously questioned again both on the left, by Labour's Commission on Social Justice, and by the Tory Party right. In that argument, Clarke and John Smith were fundamentally on the same side, in wanting to retain universal benefits.

During Clarke's two years as opposition spokesman on social security he was seldom to be found defending the taxpayer against the Labour government that the Conservatives have maligned ever since for being extravagant with public money. Almost the only exception is the one already mentioned, when Clarke opposed the policy of uprating pensions annually in line with earnings. He also spoke eloquently on the importance of privately funded works pensions schemes, and hinted that he believed the retirement age for women should eventually be raised to sixty-five to put them on an equal footing with men.[15] However, in neither was he making a concrete proposal to save public money. Norman Fowler, who succeeded Howe as principal social-security spokesman, also claims that "there never was such a responsible Opposition"[16] because of the occasions when they might have opposed the government but did not. They allowed SERPS to be introduced unopposed because the pensions industry had come to the conclusion that any legislation was better than the see-saw effect of reform being put on the statute books by one party and erased by the other before it could be implemented. They also said nothing when the £10 Christmas bonus for pensioners was abolished, or when Denis Healey abruptly changed the basis for upgrading old-age pensions. On these occasions, therefore, they sacrificed easy opportunities to embarrass the government.

On child benefit and on pensions, Clarke was plainly trying to force extra money out of the Treasury. At the same time, by campaigning against the proposed national-insurance increases, which he claimed were unfair on married women and the self-employed, he was seeking to deprive the government of some of the means to fund the welfare state. As the Conservatives exalted in their victory on the abolition of the earnings rule, they brought an angry Chancellor of the Exchequer, Denis Healey, to his feet, to complain that he was having to master a "wave of nausea" over their "hypocritical humbug", and to ask that there be "no more hypocritical claptrap from the opposition benches in future about the need to keep public expenditure under control".[17] He had a point, in that the Howe–Clarke team acted like normal opposition politicians, demanding more government generosity and opposing the means of paying for it.

A change came over the Conservative Party in February 1975, when Edward Heath, having underestimated the strength of feeling building up against him, lost to Margaret Thatcher by 130 votes to 119 in the opening round of a leadership election. This was not, of itself, a victory for the right. "The overwhelming reason for her victory was that backbench Tory MPs were sick of Heath and ready to vote for almost anybody except him. For the most part this reaction was not ideological but personal."[18] Clarke was not one of the band of devotees who worked hard for Heath's re-election, but he voted for him and became involved in his campaign in a small way, which only reminded him of the obstinate isolation that helped bring Heath down. He says:

> I went to one dinner where some of my contemporaries who didn't know Ted Heath – which tells you volumes in itself, since they had been MPs for five years – were to be introduced to him, a chat and all the rest of it. The dinner was a complete fiasco. Ted wouldn't really address a word to anyone much, certainly not backbenchers of whom he had never heard. I did join in, trying to steer the conversation so that he would talk to Ivan Lawrence, and he wouldn't. It just summed up what was wrong with him. Completely hopeless! ... They would have elected anybody who wasn't Ted Heath.[19]

It was a sensational result nonetheless. Heath had no choice but to quit, but the scale of his defeat also meant that any candidate like Willie Whitelaw, who entered the second round standing for loyalty and continuity, was running at a serious disadvantage.

In moments of crisis, opinion in the Conservative Party can move very quickly. As soon as the result was announced, MPs were scurrying about deciding what to do next. Opinion hardened even among those opposed to Thatcher's candidacy that she was going to win anyway. One group on the left of the party decided to cut their losses by running Jim Prior as a candidate, not because there was any hope that he would win, but because it would establish him as a strong man in the Thatcher Shadow Cabinet. Word of this reached friends of Geoffrey Howe, who decided to do the same for him. His supporters expected him to stand for a simplified tax system, more discipline in public spending, a hard line on trade unions, but a relatively liberal social policy. On the Tuesday night of Heath's defeat, there was an informal gathering at Geoffrey Howe's Lambeth home. Almost everyone present was a lawyer, and a good number had degrees at Cambridge University and a connection with the Bow Group, including Howe himself, Ian Gow, Elaine Kellett-Bowman, Leon Brittan, Norman Fowler, and Kenneth Clarke. The master of ceremonies was Anthony Buck QC, who had been at Cambridge with Howe. He was a former defence minister best known on the left for his tolerant views toward any regime that opposed communism, be it apartheid, General Franco or the Greek colonels. It apparently took until late into the night to persuade Howe to stand, but on the morning of 5 February he declared his candidature. Supporting him was, as Clarke later put it, a form of "intelligent abstention", since the only real contest was between Thatcher and Whitelaw, which Thatcher won by 146 votes to 79. Howe tied with Prior for third place, with 19 votes.

However, given its objective of turning Howe into a major player in the post-Heath Conservative Party, the campaign was astoundingly successful. Although Thatcher never warmed to him personally, she came to rely on him in the years up until 1983 more than any other politician, with the possible exception of Whitelaw. When the line-up in her first Shadow Cabinet was announced, the big surprise was that, in choosing a shadow chancellor, she passed over the loyal Keith Joseph and the other eligible former Cabinet ministers to give the job to Howe. It was one of her shrewdest appointments. Then, in another conciliatory gesture, she gave Howe's former job as social-security spokesman to another member of his tiny camp. This was Norman Fowler, who at thirty-seven became the youngest member of the Shadow Cabinet, and the only one without any government experience. Clarke was not promoted and, incidentally, was not the youngest member of the Conservative front bench any more, since it now included Norman Lamont and Malcolm Rifkind, the latter only twenty-eight years old. However, Clarke had no reason to be aggrieved at this stage, because the pensions bill was still grinding its way through the legislative process, so it made sense to leave him where he was. He also had a boss in Norman Fowler whom he knew well, and who concentrated on the health service, leaving social security almost entirely to Clarke.

Nonetheless, the arrival of a right-wing leader seems to have suddenly reminded Clarke that the proper role for a Tory spokesman is to champion the taxpayer. The pensions legislation was finally completed in July, and when the Commons returned from its summer break Clarke launched into a new campaign, very different in tone from his championing of pensions and child benefits. He now put the "scandal" of false claimants defrauding the social services at the top of his priority list. In part he seems to have been inspired by the *News of the World* – "that great journal of our time", as he called it – which had been running a regular "scrounger of the week" feature. "I know one is not meant to say that there is a great deal of abuse", Clarke told the Commons, in the mock-daring tone rather frequently used by those who know that they are picking on easy targets with no risk of retaliation. "The fact is that a lot of fraud is easy and is not carried out with any great sophistication and yet escapes detection."[20] On the face of it, if this fraud was escaping detection then Clarke had no way of knowing that it was happening at all. The best evidence he produced at the time was the increase in claims for sick pay. "It is not that the health of the nation is deteriorating: it is that sick pay is easy to abuse", he claimed.[21] A month later, figures were published showing that the Department of Social Security had called in 120,591 claimants for interviews the previous year, of whom 55,000 stopped drawing benefit. Clarke claimed this proved that there was abuse on a massive scale, although equally it could have meant that social-security inspectors were good at stopping suspicious claims. Anyway, he called for the number of investigators to be doubled.[22]

On one occasion, he singled out runaway fathers as the source of an unnecessary burden on the state and urged the social-security department to chase after them for maintenance, making attachment-of-earnings orders and threatening them with prison where necessary.[23] None of this really came about until the Child Support Agency was opened nearly twenty years later. With considerably less justification, he also singled out the Irish as a large part of the problem, coming over to Britain for no other purpose than to sign on, and he called for social-security officers to be given the power to refuse an Irish family any form of state assistance other than a one-way ticket to Eire.[24] This was at a time when the memory of atrocious pub bombings was fresh in the minds of the public, and one of the most dangerous IRA terrorist units ever to operate on the mainland, the so-called Balcombe Street gang, was at large. In the previous few months, the courts had convicted eighteen people for terrorist offences, jailing most of them for life, on highly specious evidence that was overturned many years later. These included the so-called Guildford Four and Birmingham Six. Barristers from Clarke's own chambers, though not Clarke himself, were involved in the Birmingham case. All in all, it was a time when it did not take much bravery to insult the Irish. It was an unusually cheap shot by Clarke, who usually refused to pander to tribal prejudice.

It is difficult to escape the conclusion that he was beginning to look over his shoulder at the new party leader, wondering if she was really as light-weight and transient as smart opinion at the time thought she would be. In October, he was part of a parliamentary delegation to Delhi led by William Whitelaw, whose loyalty to his former rival was so great that she was moved to say that "everyone needs a Willie". On his return, Clarke told a party meeting in his constituency that "Mrs Thatcher is a woman who has fought her way to the top in a man's world, and her appeal for freedom and enter-prise, her objection to the further growth of government, and a demand for the return to the basic principles of Toryism has struck a responsive chord in a very large proportion of the British people."[25]

Very soon, one of Clarke's closest friends discovered the new leader's habit, which would become more marked over the years, of ruling by iron whim. While the Commons was in recess in January 1976 a telephone call came through to Clarke's law chambers in Birmingham from an anguished Norman Fowler, ringing to say that he had suddenly been dropped from the Shadow Cabinet and offered the lesser job of shadow transport minister. The expla-nation he had been given was that Mrs Thatcher felt obliged to give belated recognition to John Biffen, who had fought from the back benches against what were now regarded as the discredited parts of the Heath programme;

but this story did not entirely hold up, because she also sacked the defence spokesman, George Younger. Insult had been added to injury when Fowler turned to the chief whip, Humphrey Atkins, who told him, in so many words, that he should not have been given so senior a job in the first place. The news was strictly hush-hush, because the person who was to replace Fowler and the person he was replacing were both abroad, and knew nothing about it. Fowler's immediate reason for ringing was to sound Clarke out on whether he ought to accept his new job, or resign. "Ken's advice was that the party would take the view I had been roughly treated and I would have their sympathy whether I went or stayed. If I stayed, however, I would have a debt in the bank to be repaid at some future date."[26] It was a principle which Clarke applied through each disappointment in his own career.

Clarke had only a few months working with the new head of the social services team, Patrick Jenkin, during which there was little in the way of government legislation to handle, and his attention was clearly on another issue, far less important than pensions, which nonetheless brought him more prominence than anything else he did in the whole of the 1970s. By the luck of the draw, he had an opportunity to introduce a private member's bill during the 1975–76 parliamentary year. He used it to make himself the subject of conversation in every bar in the land by tilting his lance at Britain's licensing laws. They were, Clarke told the Commons, "among the most complicated, archaic, uncivilised and restrictive parts of our legal system", an anachronism which survived only because "they are taken for granted and nobody has seriously questioned their supposed use". The laws originated in wartime, when in their embarrassment and distress after the bloodsoaked fiasco of Neuve Chapelle, the British authorities cast about for someone to blame, and their thoughts turned to the munitions workers who, plainly, had been drinking themselves legless all day and every day and turning out poor quality shells. Licensing hours did nothing to combat genuine alcoholism: they were "just an inconvenience to the social drinker", claimed Clarke.[27]

At the end of February 1976, then, Clarke put forward a bill which would have allowed pubs to stay open from 10.00 a.m. to midnight every day, and would have introduced continental-style licensed cafés. Most controversially, he also proposed that pubs should have family rooms where children were allowed, even if unaccompanied by an adult. It was the spectre of fourteen-year-olds spending the day in the pub, away from adult supervision, that was the main focus of opposition to his bill. Behind the bill, the influence of one of the most successful pressure groups of the early 1970s, the Campaign for Real Ale, can be detected. In March, CAMRA applied to Nottingham magistrates for drinking hours in the city of Nottingham to be extended from 10.30 to 11 p.m., which was when the pubs closed in several rural areas of the county. Then only a few years old, CAMRA still had an anti-establishment aura about it, as if it were sixties radicalism in a new form. Its best-known campaigner was a former editor of *Socialist Worker*, and there was an anti-capitalist element in its condemnation of the big, monopolistic breweries that dictated the nation's drinking habits. There was also the danger that CAMRA might degenerate into a refuge for people with florid complexions, slurred speech and limited ambition, yet it managed to be a disciplined and effective consumers' organization.

There was a risk involved for a career-conscious Tory MP to be associated with such a campaign. In Nottingham, CAMRA's application was turned down by the Licensing Committee, after opposition from the National Association of Licensed House Managers, Nottingham Licensed Victuallers Association, and a group of city-centre licensees, who warned that it would aggravate violent drunkenness.[28] Nationally, Clarke's bill also ran up against determined opposition from publicans, and from those who had religious or moral objections to drink. The publicans claimed that longer opening hours would oblige them to hire more staff, forcing up the price of drinks. Moralists feared the impact that a place where drink was consumed might have on the very young, a point which Clarke attempted to meet by proposing that no one under fourteen should be allowed to buy anything in a bar.

In parliament, the committee assigned to detailed deliberation of the bill turned out to be unusually lively. The bill's opponents decided that they would kill it by filibustering. The committee's first session was treated to a speech lasting two hours and fifty minutes, from Sir Bernard Braine, a right-wing Tory MP who chaired the National Council on Alcoholism. More of the same would have meant that the bill fell on the technical grounds that its line-by-line examination had not been completed before the summer recess. Clarke quickly demonstrated, though, that he could give as good as he got in procedural wrangling. He interrupted numerous times to demand that Sir Bernard be silenced for wandering off the point. Some sharp words were exchanged. He and his supporters broke with precedent by deciding that their committee would prolong its sessions into the afternoon, something which no committee had done for ten years.[29] Their final session went right through the night, ending at 4.00 a.m., allowing them to return to the floor of the House of Commons on a Friday morning to report an end to the bill's committee stage.

Even then, procedure threatened to block the bill from getting any further, because MPs had the Scottish Divorce Bill on which to deliberate. In one of those absurdities which the arcane rules of the Commons encourage, the anti-drinking lobby settled down to spend a whole day discussing Scotland's divorce laws; but they were so uninterested in the subject that when a vote was unexpectedly called halfway through the morning, no tellers were in place, and the Scottish Divorce Bill went through on the nod. Kenneth Clarke went back to his seat from the lobby which adjoins the debating chamber before the other side had had time to think of any more time-wasting tricks. One of his opponents, the Tory MP Michael Neubert, accused him of moving so fast that "Springheeled Jack would have been left gasping."[30] It was a short-lived victory, though, because in came the heavy artillery, in the guise of another juggernaut speech from the relentless Sir Bernard. In vain, Clarke protested to the Speaker that the debate was being sabotaged by "a long diatribe about the demon drink".

One more chance came Clarke's way in July. This time the debate was almost entirely one-sided. Although Clarke's supporters were present in large numbers, they obstinately refused to say anything because "to speak would be to aid the filibuster". In his own contribution, Clarke managed at one and the same time to accuse his opponents of being "hysterical" and "ridiculous" and to appeal for less "personal abuse".[31] His bill fell, because the parliamentary rules make it almost impossible for a backbench MP to get a measure through unless the government chooses to support him.

History does not record what Mrs Thatcher thought of this campaign on behalf of the nation's drinkers. Perhaps she saw it as a straightforward defence of the free market, or perhaps she concluded that her pensions spokesman was underemployed. That was certainly the opinion in the whips' office. Clarke's friend Jim Lester was now a whip, and feared that if Clarke was not moved soon he would become typecast as the only Tory who understood pensions, and would stay in one job permanently. Clarke thought so too, and eventually approached Mrs Thatcher and asked for a change. He got a rather stiff lecture on the fact that she had not enjoyed spending the entire period of the Heath government at the education department, but had had to knuckle under without complaining.[32] Nonetheless, she acceded to his request and, at the start of the next Commons session, Clarke was moved to a more promising position as a shadow minister for industry. He held the job for two-and-a-half years, until the general election. Since he was now talking about economic policy, it is possible to draw a clearer picture of whether and how far he shifted with the tide. There were three areas of industrial policy in which the future Thatcher government would depart from past practice: trade-union legislation, incomes policy, and state aid to industry. Heath's policies had been to seek cooperation with the unions, to impose a pay policy applicable to the private sector, and to subsidize important sections of Britain's manufacturing base rather than allow them to go bankrupt. If Clarke wanted to pass the Thatcherite is-he-a-believer test, he needed to show that he was now against all of the above.

Clarke's attitude towards shop-floor militancy appeared to harden as soon as Labour was in office, and the new Employment Secretary, Michael Foot, set about repealing large sections of the Industrial Relations Act, including those which imposed compulsory strike ballots and cooling-off periods, but retaining the sections on union recognition, and extending them to closed-shop agreements. There was no need for Clarke, as the party's new pensions specialist, to become involved in the emotive issue of the closed shop. Indeed, as a practising barrister – and a member, therefore, of one of Britain's most restrictive closed shops – with trade-union clients, it might have been prudent to keep out of it. Instead, he jumped in without even taking the elementary precaution of studying his brief thoroughly. Clarke was in full throat, speaking up for workers allegedly "sent to Coventry" for defying the closed shop, and accusing the Labour government of taking "subservience" to the trade unions to "ridiculous lengths" and "legalising wrecking activity on a scale we have not seen in the commercial life of this country" by "supporting a union's right to persecute", when he was interrupted by Employment Minister Albert Booth, who challenged him to name one victimized worker. The best reply Clarke could muster was that "if he imagines that my inability at once to name an individual example proves that no such cases have occurred ... few members of the public will accept it."[33]

It may have sounded at the time as if Clarke was trying to win points with the Tory right with some crude and ill-informed union bashing. It later turned out that there was a good reason to be worried about the effects of closed-shop legislation in his own constituency, which he may have known about at the time, although he did not say so. In those days, the UK's largest coal-fired power station was at Ratcliffe-on-Soar in Clarke's Rushcliffe constituency. There was also a smaller coal-fired station nearby, at Wilford. Half of the 480 power workers in the larger establishment, and 50 out of about 300 at Wilford belonged to the tiny Electricity Supply Union, which was not recognized by the TUC. About half of the 290 ESU members belonged only to that union, whilst the rest had dual membership with one or other of the unions that were party to the closed-shop agreement. The ESU became headline news during 1975, when six of its members at a Yorkshire power station were sacked for not belonging to a recognized union. The so-called Ferrybridge Six became the most celebrated victims of the closed shop in recent industrial history. Consequently, nearly 150 of Clarke's constituents had reason to fear for their jobs. They were, he later told the Commons, "long-standing trade union members, and most of them have been Labour voters all their adult lives", and rather than become martyrs for a cause in which they did not believe, almost all quit the ESU during 1975.

Even as he relayed the details of this case history to the Commons, during the passage of a subsequent government bill in January 1976, Clarke was careful to preface it with some conciliatory remarks, which make interesting reading given his subsequent role as an employment minister in the Thatcher government. He said:

> We know the value to the trade unions of the closed shop agreement because it can be a valuable addition to bargaining power, and we know the value to many major employers of satisfactory closed shop arrangements with the obvious and sensible negotiating unions. I also appreciate the legitimate anger of trade unionists about the pure "free rider", the man who determines to opt out of union membership and avoid paying his dues while intending to take advantage of union negotiations on his behalf. In those circumstances a proper closed shop can be a valuable addition to industrial relations.[34]

When Heath first introduced an incomes policy in 1972, he faced a small but determined back-bench rebellion, orchestrated by John Biffen, Nicholas Ridley and others. Margaret Thatcher, then a minister in the Heath Cabinet, is supposed to have approached them one evening to say how she wished she could join them in their battle.[35] Once the policy had been tried and had failed, the climate of opinion in the Conservative Party turned against any further attempt by the state to regulate the pay of anyone who was not a government employee. The title of a 1977 pamphlet jointly written by the *Financial Times* journalist Samuel Brittan (brother of Leon) and the future Cabinet minister Peter Lilley, *The Delusion of Incomes Policy*, speaks for itself. John Biffen's role as a prophet of the new thinking was recognized when he was made shadow secretary of state for industry in November 1976, with Kenneth Clarke and Norman Lamont as his deputies.

There was also opposition to incomes policies among the trade unions and on the left wing of the Labour Party, not because they interfered with the free market but because they were a constraint on union bargaining rights. Nonetheless, in summer 1975, the Labour government embarked on an attempt to impose a £6-a-week limit on all pay awards. Clarke, who was not yet an economic spokesman, reacted by welcoming Labour's "conversion to statutory pay policy", which he believed should have been introduced twelve months sooner.[36]

Government policy eventually ran up against particularly strong opposition from skilled workers like the British Leyland toolmakers, who objected to the erosion of differentials between their pay and that of unskilled labourers. Almost two years later, therefore, Clarke warned that "it is not possible to go into an engineering factory in the kingdom and find skilled men who are not furious about the form of pay policy that has been imposed on them."[37] However, opposing the form and consequences of a particular pay policy is not the same as rejecting pay policies per se. Even an unreconstructed Heathite like Peter Walker, whom Mrs Thatcher had sacked from the Shadow Cabinet, supported the BL toolmakers. Only months away from a general election, Clarke said, with uncharacteristic circumlocution, "I do not argue that the government should not take a view on pay."[38] That, when compared and contrasted with Mrs Thatcher's definitive conclusion that "incomes policy, in addition to restricting people's freedom, was invariably the prelude to a wages explosion",[39] helps explain why Clarke was dropped from the industry team as soon as the election was over. What he now says is that his real objection to what the Labour government was doing was that they were operating a statutory pay policy in secret, by calling it voluntary but then blacklisting firms that breached it, denying them valuable government contracts.[40] It is indeed the case that he ran quite an energetic campaign against blacklisting at the time.

Clarke also appeared to be taking a stand against state subsidies for industry with his persistent attacks on the so-called "Benn cooperatives", small factories in Kirkby and Meriden which would have gone out of business in the early 1970s had the then Industry Secretary not stepped in and provided government funds for them to continue under the collective ownership of their own workforce. Clarke came close to saying that they should be allowed to go bankrupt, rather than absorb any more money.[41] However, he was picking on an easy target, because the Labour Cabinet's commitment to the project was weak and weakening. Both cooperatives closed before Labour left office. On cooperatives as a general principle, Clarke made sympathetic noises, forecasting that a Conservative government would "look forward" to working with the "modestly conceived" Cooperative Development Association which Labour set up in 1978.[42] Tory ministers did in fact work with the CDA, before they closed it down in 1990.

More generally, there was a question of what was to become of the "consensus" politics that had operated since the war but was now breaking down as the Keynsian economic theories that had underpinned it appeared to fail. Margaret Thatcher's opinion of consensus politics soon became well established: it was

> the process of abandoning all beliefs, principles, values and policies in search of something in which no one believes, but to which no one objects; the process of avoiding the very issues that have to be solved, merely because you cannot get agreement on the way ahead.[43]

Contrast that with the words of Kenneth Clarke, uttered three years earlier, just as "Thatcherism" was beginning to emerge as a political philosophy and before it was obvious that the way to get on in government was to swing to the right:

> I call myself a Butskellite and I continue to use that phrase even though it has gone out of fashion for the time being. I remain a believer in consensus politics.[44]

The context of this remark was a parliamentary debate on the merits of proportional representation, an issue which cut across traditional political allegiances. Edward Heath and the circle of advisers associated with him, including Chris Patten, were on the whole sympathetic to the case for reforming the House of Commons. Clarke was as hard-line as the Thatcherites, but his argument in favour of the first-past-the-post electoral system was an unusual one.

> The main pressure that our first past the post system exerts is that it tends to pull politicians and politics towards the centre. The victor ... is the man or woman who strives to occupy the middle ground. Victory has always gone to the political party that succeeded in getting close to the middle ground.[45]

He went on to accuse the government of James Callaghan of having "uniquely" deserted the middle ground. One other utterance stands out as an extraordinary comment from someone who would subsequently rise to be a Cabinet minister in a government that displayed an almost maniacal zeal for right-wing reforms:

> A party will win support if it can commit itself to the minimum of repeal of what its predecessors did and the minimum of institutional change and reform, if it can show it has been made responsible by the experience of government.[46]

Anyone who thought that the future Thatcher government would settle for the "minimum of institutional change" was obviously going to have trouble fitting into it. Small wonder, then, that on the day Margaret Thatcher became prime minister, Clarke's political career very nearly terminated.

CHAPTER FIVE

MINISTER FOR ROADS

The Callaghan government collapsed in dramatic style on 28 March 1979, when it lost a motion of no confidence in the House of Commons by just one vote. The day had been one of frenetic excitement, but when the vote was over, it all suddenly descended into anticlimax. However, Kenneth Clarke and his friend Jim Lester had a contingency plan to keep themselves on a high a few hours longer. They sneaked off to Ronnie Scott's jazz club, where they were tracked down by Olivia Zeligman from BBC Radio 4, who invited them to comment on the vote and the impending election. The interview went out over breakfast the following morning, complete with the background effects of jazz music and clinking glasses. Lester says he had more public reaction than from any other radio interview he has ever done.[1]

Five weeks later, the election was over and Margaret Thatcher was installed in Downing Street and drawing up her government. Clarke was expecting a post as a minister of state, one step down from a Cabinet minister, which would have matched the level of seniority he had reached within the party and which Mrs Thatcher had told him he would get.[2] The most logical step would have been to allow him to carry on as deputy to Sir Keith Joseph, the Secretary of State for Industry. But Mrs Thatcher did not trust the civil servants at the industry department. She suspected it was infested with the corporatism of the Heath, Wilson and Callaghan years, and would be giving away money to ailing industries unless determined action was taken to stop it. She was relying on Sir Keith to do "the vital job that no one else could have done of altering the whole philosophy which had previously dominated the department."[3] Kenneth Clarke, with his Heathite notions on state intervention and workers' cooperatives, was not the type of person needed at Sir Keith's side. Before he knew it, then, Clarke had been dropped from the industry team, every minister-of-state position had been filled, and there was a real possibly that the West Midlands court circuit would be retaining his services after all. However, 10 Downing Street is not the only address at which the fate of ministers is decided. Number 12, home of the chief whip, is a rival power centre, which the Thatcherites never really conquered, and for years the whips quietly operated their own system of promoting ministers from the mainstream of the party despite Mrs Thatcher's efforts to push it to the right.

In addition to the goodwill of the whips, Clarke had his old Cambridge contacts to see him through. In this instance, the person who came to his rescue was Norman Fowler. Although he was politically no more Thatcherite, Fowler was always able to keep on the right of the prime minister by being eager to please and too mild in manner to be any threat to her authority. When Fowler inquired at the whips' office about who was available to serve as his deputy, he was surprised and a little bit shocked to find Clarke's name on the list. Fowler's status was that he was half in, half out of the Cabinet: he was a head of department, who could attend all Cabinet meetings with the same speaking rights as other members, but, because of a fixed limit on the number of ministers paid the full Cabinet salary, his formal status, and salary, was that of a minister of state. It followed, then, that his deputy would be another step down the hierarchy, a parliamentary under-secretary, or PUSS as they are known in Whitehall slang. In choosing his PUSS, Fowler expected to be left only with the scrapings that the more senior department heads had left behind. When he saw a chance to work with his old Cambridge chum, he of course jumped at it with alacrity.[4]

So, for two days Clarke waited to hear from Downing Street, but the only news he heard was about jobs being handed out to other people, some of them less experienced and – in his opinion, if in no one else's – less capable than him. Finally, just when he was beginning to fear that he was bound for the back benches,

> She rang me up and said "Kenneth, I'd like you to go to Transport as Departmental Secretary to Norman Fowler." Involuntarily I said "Margaret, but I don't know anything about transport." She said, "My dear boy" – which was the frosty address she always used – "My dear boy, you'll soon pick it up." So I went.[5]

However, he took the precaution to gather around himself a group of junior ministers, who have assembled about once a month throughout the parliamentary calendar every year since 1979, to eat in one of the House of Commons dining rooms and chat about their departments and about politics generally. This is the Amesbury Group, named after the road in which Clarke lived. There is a proliferation of political dining clubs of this type in the parliamentary Conservative Party. The Amesbury Group has always been for ministers; any member who loses his/her post in government is automatically excluded. At first, it was junior ministers only, so Clarke himself had to quit when he joined the Cabinet in 1985, but the rules were subsequently amended and he was allowed to rejoin. In the event of a Clarke challenge for the leadership of the Conservative Party, the general staff of his campaign will no doubt be provided by the dining club he set up in 1979.

The original cast was made up of junior ministers from right across the government: Kenneth Clarke (transport), Lynda Chalker (social services), Barney Hayhoe (defence), Douglas Hurd (foreign office), Tom King (environment), Jim Lester (employment), John MacGregor (whips' office), John Moore (energy), Malcolm Rifkind (Scotland), Sir George Young (health). Lynda Chalker, who took over the running of the group in 1985, and Barney Hayhoe had both shared Clarke's recent experience of a nail-biting wait before they learnt whether they had been dropped from the front bench. There was one odd man out, John Moore, who later became a born-again Thatcherite. The other names read like a roll call of Heathites wondering if they had a future under the new leadership. "It was a bit of a Heathites-in-exile", says Clarke.

> But I didn't believe in the king across the water. I didn't think Heath would ever come back. The main aim of the Amesbury Group was not to be Heathites in exile: it was to keep us all in touch with mainstream politics. From my days in the whips' office I had formed the view that if you weren't careful, being a junior minister could make you more cut off than any other job in parliament. I formed it deliberately so that there could be a meeting place for reasonably like-minded junior ministers, and we could all remain political. We could share views on the government, and actually talk about policy and just keep in touch.[6]

"We were compatible people", says Jim Lester. "It was no good anyone being uptight. Even John Moore was all right in those days: he went different when he went to the Treasury."[7]

There was much for the Amesbury Group to discuss. The first years of the Thatcher era were frenetic and unpredictable. A central figure in the most controversial events was Clarke's mentor, Sir Geoffrey Howe. The new Chancellor of the Exchequer was a late convert to Thatcherite economics, or monetarism, and in his dull, mumbling way, he proved to be the most important ally she ever had, while their partnership lasted, and thereafter the most dangerous enemy she ever made. He set the tone of his Chancellorship in his first budget, with a dramatic cut in the top rate of income tax, paid for by almost doubling VAT. This was but a prelude to the extraordinary budget delivered to the Commons in March 1981. According to Nigel Lawson, who was then number three in the Treasury team, Margaret Thatcher remembered the occasion as "her government's finest hour, her equivalent of the Battle of Britain, to which in her mind she was always harking back."[8] The sentiment was shared in Clarke's wing of the party with only marginally less enthusiasm. Clarke, for instance, thinks that "the finest budget of the 1980s was the 1981 Budget",[9] and was probably inspired by it when he drew up his own first budget twelve years later. This was the occasion when a government elected on a promise of lower taxes deliberately raised them, and raised them, moreover, in mid-recession, knowing that the effect would be to add to the millions already out of work.

It was done in reaction to a problem that would exercise Kenneth Clarke when he became Chancellor many years later: government spending, as measured by the Public Sector Borrowing Requirement, was judged to be too high. Sir Geoffrey Howe feared that the PSBR was edging towards £14 billion (about £30 billion at 1993 prices) that year. This was a lot smaller than the £50 billion deficit which Clarke confronted twelve years later; but in 1981, senior ministers believed in monetarist theories, which were then the fad among right-wing economists. Monetarists believed that the most important function of government was to protect the soundness of its currency by keeping its own finances under control. In 1981, the government had a genuine problem in that the pound was losing value, but it was a problem which they had themselves caused, seemingly on purpose. The outgoing Labour government had held inflation to single figures for sixteen months until April 1979. It started rising within two months of the Tory election victory, and was above 17 per cent by the end of the year; in May 1980, it peaked at 21.9 per cent, all as a result of deliberate government policy. By nearly doubling VAT, Sir Geoffrey Howe added to the price of consumer goods and services of almost every description. The nationalized industries were also instructed to put up their prices: the British Gas Corporation, for instance, raised its prices by 10 per cent more than the rate of inflation for three consecutive years. Rates, school meals, school buses and prescriptions all became more expensive. Simultaneously, John Nott and Norman Tebbit, at the Department of Trade, merrily scrapped the Price Commission and, with it, the very idea that the state should intervene to hold down retail prices. And out went all government restrictions on personal borrowing, like the rationing of mortgages.

All of these actions conformed to monetarist theory, because all except the rise in VAT were moves that reduced government indebtedness and hence controlled the money supply. Even the switch from the top rate of income tax to VAT, which was intended to give business executives an incentive to work harder by relieving them of punitive rates of taxation, ought to have created an "expectation" that prices would fall, according to a book on the early Thatcher years by the prime minister's personal economic adviser, Sir Alan Walters. He explained: "Price increases remove inflationary pressure; they do not add to it."[10] The first effect should have been to enable the government to bring down interest rates. Their actions in support of sound money were so ruthless that currency speculators around the world should have tripped over each other to buy sterling. Indeed, on the day after his Budget, Sir Geoffrey cut the bank rate to 12 per cent, bringing it down to the same level as it had been at when the Conservatives took power. Alas, there was a run on the pound, and within six months the bank rate was back up at 14 per cent, briefly touching 16 per cent before expectations of a reduced rate were at last fulfilled in summer 1982, seventeen months after the Budget.

The combination of high interest rates, high inflation, high taxes, high wage demands, and shrinking markets was deadly for the weaker parts of British industry. Between the 1979 election and the first quarter of 1981, output fell by 5 per cent, and manufacturing production by 17 per cent – the fastest drop ever. Even the monetarists had forecast that unemployment would rise, although they expected a "blip" rather than the permanent large-scale unemployment that resulted. The official figures, which were repeatedly adjusted downwards, rose from 1,089,100 in May 1979 to a peak in July 1986 of 3,133,200 – probably four times the 1979 level, comparing like with like.

The lowest level in fourteen Conservative years was 1,596,000, in April 1990. As the economy floundered, so did the government's popularity. Mrs Thatcher set a record in 1981 as the most unpopular prime minister since polling began, and it seemed a near certainty that she would be handing over in three years or less to Roy Jenkins of the SDP or even to Michael Foot. Clarke says "I remember thinking in the winter of 1981 that we had no chance at all of winning another election and I began to wonder whether the Conservative Party as a whole was going to stay in one piece."[11]

Then, in the spring of 1982, the economy recovered and, by coincidence, the Falklands War presented Margaret Thatcher with a victory as spectacular as it was unexpected. Sceptics like Sir Ian Gilmour, who almost steeled himself to resign from the Cabinet at the time, believe that recovery would have come anyway, because "economic activity never goes on falling indefinitely, and not even our government could have made permanent the catastrophic depression of 1979–81";[12] but what the Thatcherites believed, and a significant proportion of the electorate accepted, was that it was their determination to stick to their course during the difficult months that had dramatically reversed decades of decline. Their ideological assertiveness contrasted with the vacillations of the traditional leaders of the Conservative Party, who were appalled by Mrs Thatcher's dogmatism but had no idea what to do about it. In 1981, heads began to roll. Over the next two years a succession of grandees, all of them former public-school boys and most of them landowners, who had crassly allowed themselves to be labelled as "wets", were axed from the Cabinet to make room for the upwardly mobile, mostly grammar-school-educated corps of young Thatcherites. Several of Clarke's Cambridge contemporaries were among those to benefit – especially Leon Brittan, who entered the Cabinet as Chief Secretary to the Treasury in place of John Biffen, in 1981, and then made a remarkable leap to become Home Secretary in 1983. Norman Lamont became a minister of state at the Department of Industry in 1981.

Meanwhile, Kenneth Clarke remained second in command in a team of two, without either the formal title or the salary of a minister of state, in one of the least prestigious government departments. Having only just sorted out his family finances, he now had to give up his legal practice for good. Ironically, he acquired the title of Queen's Counsel in 1980, just too late to be able to attract a QC's fees. There was also much drudgery in his work. All over England there were communities who either wanted a new bypass to take through traffic away from their homes, or conversely were battling to prevent a new main road being constructed near them. All these problems came to Kenneth Clarke. "I find myself engaged in a crash course in the geography of England", he remarked soon after his appointment.[13] The first time he addressed the House of Commons from the despatch box, it was to read out a seventeen-minute speech on traffic conditions in Tarporley and Eaton, in Cheshire. The job regularly required him to be speaking at an hour like 2 o'clock in the morning on subjects such as Macclesfield's long-awaited relief road, or whether Manchester Road, Bedford should have a pedestrian crossing. It fell to him to make the last speech in the House before the Commons broke up for the 1979 summer break: a fourteen-minute discourse on why asbestos stripping in the British Rail maintenance depot at Ilford need not be regarded as a health hazard. Quite often, the parish-pump traffic issues on which MPs demanded answers were the responsibility of the local council, not the Ministry of Transport, but parliamentary rules said that a minister must be in the debating chamber each time, and for three years that minister was Kenneth Clarke.

Road safety, crash helmets, seat belts, reflectors on bicycles, driving tests, concessionary fares, road tax and fixed-penalty parking tickets were all within Clarke's sphere of competence. He paid a well-publicized visit to Islington, found eighteen cars parked in the streets without valid tax discs, and stuck a warning on each of their windscreens. Another day, he was out in Hyde Park for a photo call with the chairman of the GLC planning committee to publicize London's new cycle route, nicknamed the "ambassador" route. A year later, in February 1982, he similarly helped draw attention to the new cycle route along five miles of the old Bath-to-Bristol railway line. By and by, this photo call gained a certain minor historic significance, in that Clarke actually sat on a bicycle and pedalled, making it the last known public sighting of Kenneth Clarke taking physical exercise. Towards the end of his tenure in the job, he was at least given one interesting opportunity to travel, when he spent two weeks of the summer of 1981 in Chile, Argentina and Venezuela.

The humps across the surface of hundreds of residential roads in congested urban areas, which discourage motorists from using them as "rat runs" to avoid the rush-hour traffic, are attributable to Kenneth Clarke. The so-called "sleeping policemen" first appeared on British roads under legislation passed in 1974, but that allowed for them to be constructed for experimental periods only; when the experiment was over, they had to be removed and the road surface levelled again. Permanent humps are now permitted under a clause of the 1981 Transport Act steered through parliament by Kenneth Clarke.

The points system under which drivers guilty of repeated motoring offences have their licences taken away is another of the small reforms introduced by Clarke. Previously, the rule was that three endorsements on a driving licence in three years meant disqualification. He also introduced a couple of measures which were not particularly welcome to the commercial interests affected. He made buses and heavy goods vehicles subject to annual MOT tests in the same way as cars, and made black-cab drivers pay a realistic fee to cover the costs of issuing the special licences for them and their vehicles. Taxi drivers were used to paying just three shillings, or 15p, a rate unchanged since the 1930s, while the extant legislation covering cab licences applied only to horse-drawn vehicles.[14]

Amid these mundane matters, there were moments when even the Ministry of Transport became embroiled in the big political issues of the day. The government passed three blockbuster pieces of transport legislation in 1979–82. Each act contained a wide mixture of measures: most were matters of detail which were passed with little opposition, but there was always at least one proposal that generated political controversy.

Whilst Clarke was a transport minister, the government sold off choice morsels of British Rail that were deemed to be inessential to its core business of running trains. These included its twenty-nine hotels, Sealink UK, and various property interests. The government also introduced private competition in some of the more profitable bus routes, and privatized the National Bus Company. Each sell-off was opposed by the Labour Party.

One of the first enterprises transferred to the private sector was the National Freight Corporation, in 1980. This was one of the few sell-offs that had actually been promised in the general-election manifesto, and came so early in the Thatcher era that it was not even called "privatization". At this stage, ministers were engaged in "denationalization". Whatever the name, it had the same effect as almost every item in the privatization programme: prosperity for some, and for others the dole. The winners included Norman Fowler, who subsequently became a director of the private company he had helped to establish. Among the losers were the staff at the Roadline depot in Townsend Lane, Liverpool, where 250 jobs were axed within two years of "denationalization", to add to the 51,000 already registered as unemployed in the city of Liverpool; but, as Clarke explained to the Commons "with great regret", there was nothing to be done. "The fact is that the NFC has taken the decision, not the government. There is no question of the government intervening."[15]

However, these exchanges did not really give Clarke a chance to show off his talents as a parliamentary bruiser, which was to be the quality that eventually earned him promotion. In the first place, it was up to Norman Fowler, and then his successor David Howell, to supervise the detail of the legislation, clear it with the Cabinet, and introduce it to parliament. Secondly, the quality of the Opposition left something to be desired. The last Labour Transport Secretary, William Rodgers, and his former under-secretary, John Horam, left in 1981 to become founders of the Social Democratic Party. The new opposition team, Albert Booth and John Prescott, were from the Labour left. It was relatively easy, therefore, to attack the previous government's record, because there was no one deeply committed to defending it. Nevertheless, as the other half of a two-man team, Clarke was obliged to defend every item in each of the three transport bills. The manner in which he did so is illustrative. He treated the various denationalization measures as if they were almost apolitical, as if there were enterprises which belonged in the private sector, and others which, pragmatically, did not, and it only required a calm application of common sense to work out which was which. Of National Freight and Sealink, he said: "I have never been able to see the advantages to a business of the kind we are talking about being in the public sector, where, for instance, all investment counts as public sector investment."[16]

In these days, he did not sound like someone taking part in a crusade to "roll back the frontiers of socialism", an evocative phrase used by Thatcherites, but not by Kenneth Clarke. On the contrary, he warned:

Conservative and Socialist politicians are never more boring than when they are involved in an arid debate based on instinctive reactions to the idea of nationalisation or denationalisation, and to the idea "Public sector good: Private sector bad" or vice versa.[17]

That was in June 1980. The next year, events began to speed up in a way that must have given Clarke pause for thought, as Mrs Thatcher took a grip on her recalcitrant Cabinet. Her most important adversary was then seen to be Jim Prior, at the Department of Employment. There was a head of steam building up in the Conservative Party for a confrontation with the trade unions. What was to be almost an annual ritual of passing new legislation to restrict the rights and powers of organized labour had already begun, but Prior was insisting on taking it step by step, as if he still lived in the Heath era, when the Conservatives would legislate by reaching consensus with the TUC. Preparations were already being laid for the big battle that lay ahead, against the miners. One small step was a set of regulations laid before the Commons by Kenneth Clarke when the threat of another coal strike was looming in January 1981. They permitted 17-year-old soldiers to drive heavy goods vehicles, which they would not have been allowed to do in civilian life – not just routinely, but specifically so that the government could detail them to break strikes. However, at this stage even Thatcher preferred to settle with the NUM rather than engage in a conflict for which the government was unprepared.

In this atmosphere, the Department of Transport found itself being targeted by wilder sections of the Tory right for continuing to subsidize the London and Mersey docks, which were regarded as hotbeds of union militancy and restrictive practises. The back-bench maverick Tony Marlow accused Norman Fowler of wanting to "bail out the most notorious industry that this country has ever known." The attack was a little on the wild side, considering that the government had already arranged for the two dock authorities to axe 2,470 jobs in a little over a year and was embarking on a new enhanced redundancy scheme which would cut the workforce by another 2,460 in two months. Still, in his reply, Clarke said he had "considerable sympathy" for the idea of cutting off subsidies altogether, but pointed out that these were not ordinary commercial enterprises but "great port authorities which carry out conservancy and other statutory duties".[18]

During 1981, Mrs Thatcher struck twice. In January, one Cabinet minister was sacked, another allowed to retire. At a lower level, Clarke's friend Jim Lester was sacked, in her opening move against the Department of Employment. The replacements at the Cabinet table were both Cambridge contemporaries of Clarke's: Leon Brittan was promoted to Chief Secretary to the

Treasury, in place of John Biffen, who moved sideways; and Norman Fowler's title was upgraded to Secretary of State for Transport. In September, three more ministers were sacked and several others, including Jim Prior, were demoted.

One of those who was demoted was David Howell, formerly the Secretary of State for Energy, who had been the youngest member of the original 1979 Cabinet. A languid, cerebral Old Etonian, who had been through Cambridge University and the Bow Group a few years ahead of Clarke, he was full of ideas when out of office but painfully cautious and hesitant when there were decisions to be made. All in all, he was not Mrs Thatcher's type, although he was always loyal to her, in or out of office. She blamed him for the humiliation of February 1981, when she discovered that the government was facing a confrontation with the miners that it was likely to lose, and was consequently forced to pay them off, so she moved him and gave his job to Nigel Lawson. The other minister who unintentionally benefited from Howell's misfortune was Norman Fowler, who was moved to the Department of Health and Social Security, in order that Howell could be relegated to the job of Transport Secretary.

Brittan and Lawson, incidentally, had been in parliament only since 1974, a detail that would not have escaped the attention of anyone who had been there since 1970 or earlier and still wanted to be regarded as Cabinet material. The rising stars from the 1970 intake were now Norman Tebbit, Norman Fowler and Cecil Parkinson. Kenneth Clarke, who had been the first in his year to be given a government job under Edward Heath, was to remain in a political sideline, still second in command in a team of two, but now with a boss who had lost his own self-confidence and the confidence of the prime minister. However, one of the attractions of politics is its unpredictability. If Clarke was down in September 1981, it was only a matter of months before he was back up again. Within less than three years, he was being talked of as a future prime minister. The change in fortune came about through a mixture of good luck and a shrewd ability to make the most of an opportunity.

His first chance to shine came from the headquarters of the Greater London Council, just across the River Thames, where the newly elected Labour administration headed by Ken Livingstone had carried out a manifesto commitment to cut the city's tube and bus fares, at considerable cost to London ratepayers. The decision was challenged in court by Conservative-controlled Bromley Borough Council. Unexpectedly, the Law Lords ruled in December 1981 that the decision was illegal because of the "fiduciary duty" of councillors to look after ratepayers' money. On the face of it, this was a political gift to the Conservative Party, except that the policy of cheap fares was very popular with London commuters who might hold the government responsible if there was a sharp rise in the price of their season tickets. Howell's dilemma was made the more difficult by the ambiguity of the Lords' judgement, which could be interpreted as meaning that the GLC had already been breaking the law by subsidizing fares while it was under Conservative control, and that fares might have to be trebled, or worse, to comply with the law. Moreover, the £125 million cost of the first few months of the Fares Fair policy had to be heaped upon the rates.

Howell acted like a man who genuinely wanted to find a way out of the problem. Being the MP for Guildford, in the commuter belt, he privately accepted the case that London needed more investment in its transport infrastructure, as became apparent after he had been sacked from the government.[19] He agonized; he displayed what Livingstone's biographer called "signs of political stage fright",[20] and eventually offered a compromise which was humiliatingly turned down by the GLC leader, who was not interested in softening the impact of what he regarded as a politically motivated ruling by the judges. Clarke, however, was in the happy position where he did not have to find an answer to the problem, because it was not his job and his constituents were not affected by London fares; his role was to defend the government's corner. He quickly saw that the best tactic was to ignore the ball and go for the players, namely Livingstone, some leading GLC members like Dave Wetzel and Valerie Wise who were attempting to organize an illegal fare-dodging campaign, and the Labour front bench, who had considerable qualms about identifying themselves with their colleagues in County Hall. Clarke dismissed the GLC leadership as "politicians who took sensible and lawful policies to ridiculous extremes. They demonstrated not only left-wing policies, but sheer incompetence and financial mismanagement",[21] and taunted the Labour front bench with the undeniable fact that they had not believed in subsidies to public transport as generous as London's "until Livingstone, Wetzel and Wise moved them to a rather eccentric and oddball position".[22]

This sort of personal knockabout may not have added much to the quality of democratic life, but it reminded his own side that Clarke was not "wet" in the way that the word was applied to the ex-public-school landowning element in the Cabinet, who were too grand to engage in political fisticuffs. Clarke himself would use the word "wet" to describe other Conservative politicians, even if they were friends, like Chris Patten, but was reluctant to accept it when applied to himself. "I may be a liberal with a small 'l', but I do object to being called a wet liberal", he said in 1980.[23] The only senior "wet" to whom he owed any political debt was Francis Pym, who had given him his first job in the whips' office, but their association was not close. The others were separated from him by age and class background.

In a portent of battles to come, one of the issues that had come between Thatcher and the "wets" was Britain's relationship with the rest of the EEC. At this stage, Mrs Thatcher was not the mistress of her Cabinet. For instance, the Foreign Office refused to adapt its long-established ways to the new right-wing stridency. When the prime minister resolved to indulge her anti-European prejudices with a highly publicized campaign to reduce Britain's contribution to the EC budget by no less than £1,000 million, she did so against the sullen reluctance of the diplomatic corps. Her Foreign Secretary, Lord Carrington, and Ian Gilmour, who spoke for the Foreign Office in the Commons, regarded her behaviour at the conference table as little short of uncouth. The eventual compromise of a £760 million rebate for Britain was agreed only after a stand-up row between Thatcher and Carrington, which produced threats of resignation on both sides. Sir Ian Gilmour's view is that Thatcher's belligerence achieved nothing beyond antagonizing other European leaders, while the real negotiating took place backstage. The episode drove Sir Ian, the Third Baronet of Liberton and Craigmillar, to the conclusion that "foreign policy was a tool of party or personal politics. However badly things were going in Britain, Mrs Thatcher could at least win some kudos and popularity as the defender of the British people against the foreigner."[24]

As a declared pro-European, Clarke might have been expected to side with the Foreign Office on this one. On the contrary, in a speech to East Midlands Conservatives, he used the episode as ammunition against the Powellites and the Labour left, who wanted Britain out of the EEC altogether, in that it gave the lie to claims that a pro-EEC Tory government would fail to protect Britain's interest. "They have discovered that Mrs Thatcher's government is no pushover", he crowed.[25] In time, he would demonstrate that he was not a "pushover" either, given a suitable opponent he could kick around. This was the quality that would eventually commend him to the prime minister.

Eventually, but not yet: for the time being, the most important asset Clarke possessed was his political connections, particularly his twenty-year friendship with Norman Fowler. Fowler had been having an impossible time with his health minister, Gerald Vaughan, a friend of the Thatchers who believed in abolishing the NHS and replacing it with continental-style medical insurance. Vaughan's most notable achievements in office were that he had caused the law on abortion to be tightened, whilst making sure that the laws on tobacco advertising were not. In protecting the interests of the tobacco companies from anti-smoking legislation, he received the personal encouragement of Denis Thatcher. In March 1982, Mrs Thatcher moved him to another job of equivalent status. It was Fowler who asked to have Clarke moved over to replace him. She is reputed to have been "dubious" about his promotion,[26] but nonetheless she was persuaded. Fowler's memoirs, which are vague on the background, give a clear idea of the case he put up in support of Clarke's appointment. Industrial action was on the horizon, with all the main health unions including the Royal College of Nursing against the government, and Fowler wanted someone to fight his battles for him:

> He [Clarke] illustrates the difficulty of trying to divide Conservatives into "wets" and "dries". Many of his views categorize him as a wet ... but just as clearly he is a tough politician who speaks his mind sometimes in a blunt way. Once or twice we put these qualities to good use. An aggressive visiting delegation would be dusted down by Ken in his best James Cagney style, leaving me looking untypically reasonable and friendly in bringing the meeting to a conclusion. Ken Clarke is an exceptional man to have with you in a battle.[27]

CHAPTER SIX

HEALTH MINISTER, 1982-85

There is nothing "wet" about the hostility Kenneth Clarke has displayed towards public-sector unions. He made his reputation as a political bruiser during the bitter health dispute of 1982, by finding the words to send the pickets into impotent rage. Other ministers insisted on defying picket lines and visiting hospitals via the front door, but no one did it with the macho style of Kenneth Clarke. His behaviour may have done nothing to improve staff relations within the National Health Service, but it did his standing in the Conservative Party the world of good.

This is not to say that in Conservative circles he rated as a hardliner on the politics of health care. In the summer of 1982, after the euphoria of victory in the Falklands, the government was riding on a wave of over-confidence. Inside the party, the big question was not whether the health workers should be better paid, but whether the National Health Service, free at the point of delivery for everyone who needed it, should continue at all. Clarke's predecessor, Gerald Vaughan, was not the only one who believed in privatizing health care. The Chancellor, Sir Geoffrey Howe, issued apocalyptic warnings that unless the National Health Service and the welfare state were made "more responsive to market forces", income tax would have to rise from 30p to 45p in the pound, and VAT from 15 per cent to 25 per cent.[1] One proposal, in a paper written by a Treasury think-tank, which Howe and Leon Brittan put to the Cabinet in 1982, was that compulsory private insurance should take the place of free health care. For an estimated saving of £3 billion out of the 1982–83 health budget of £10 billion, Mrs Thatcher's Treasury ministers were, apparently, prepared to abolish the National Health Service.

This report was leaked to *The Economist*, presumably by a dissident Cabinet minister, setting off a reaction which demonstrated even to the woman who had saved the Falklands that there were certain things which public opinion prevented her from doing. Faced with what Nigel Lawson called "the nearest thing to a Cabinet riot in the history of the Thatcher administration",[2] with the grandees Lord Hailsham and William Whitelaw heading the charge, she had no choice but to give way, which she did with visible ill temper.[3] Two weeks later, she made her famous promise to the Conservative annual conference that "the National Health Service is safe with us". After the 1983 election, she took revenge on the think-tank responsible by abolishing it.

Kenneth Clarke had no part in this particular episode, even though he was Minister for Health and the Treasury ministers involved were his friends. Challenged about the report by Labour MPs, he dismissed it as a "dead duck" and an "absurd irrelevance".[4] Norman Fowler is adamant that "these proposals had come forward without any consultation with any health minister, and indeed without any of us knowing that such a study was taking place",[5] a fact confirmed in Mrs Thatcher's memoirs. She says she learnt two lessons from the episode: that no controversial proposal should be taken to the Cabinet without consulting the relevant minister first, and that she was surrounded by enemies who would stop at nothing. At no point does she say that the idea was wrong in itself.[6]

As a health minister, Clarke would demonstrate that he was prepared to take a hard line on some of the lesser issues, like prescription charges or denying free health care to foreign nationals. But he has never equivocated on the core question of whether health care should be provided free of charge by the state, and throughout his political career he has been prepared to defend that political principle in front of hostile audiences. Towards the end of his first stint in the health department, at a fringe party at the 1984 Conservative annual conference, the Federation of Conservative Students planned to disrupt his speech with a demonstration in favour of privatization of the NHS. On this occasion, though, his young opponents seemingly lost their nerve, because the only disturbance during Clarke's speech was the clatter of a disappointed television crew dimming its lights and packing up its equipment, over which he submitted a furious complaint, which produced a public apology from Central Television.[7]

The fact that Clarke saw himself as a friend of the NHS no doubt contributed to the ideological conviction with which he attacked the health unions. At times, he appeared to question whether they ought to be allowed to strike at all, because "in something so vital as patient care, there is no room for industrial action."[8] In one instance, he was prepared to see a particular group of health workers have their right to union representation taken away. For several months, the spectre of closure hung over Tadworth Court Children's Hospital in Surrey, which was an extension of the celebrated Great Ormond Street Hospital, until it was eventually taken over in April 1984 by a charitable trust chaired by the Tory MP Tim Yeo. Part of the agreement, which Clarke defended in a letter to the Labour MP Alf Morris, was that its employees could retain their union membership, but the trust would not allow their unions to negotiate for them.[9]

The health workers, especially the ancillary workers who kept hospitals running but who had no direct involvement in patient care, had reason to feel aggrieved. The government was making a pay offer to the nurses and other health professionals of 6.4 per cent or more; but the lowly porters, gardeners, cleaners, kitchen staff and the rest were told they must settle for 4 per cent. The unions wanted 12 per cent, which Clarke dismissed as "ludicrously unrealistic", on the grounds that it would cost an extra £1 billion a year[10] – although it was less than the increases that the government was offering the highest paid public employees: nearly 19 per cent for judges, and more than 14 per cent for top civil servants. After the experience of the Heath years, the Cabinet resolutely opposed anything that looked like a pay policy, and therefore insisted that each group of public-sector workers must be treated separately. Pay rises in the health sector must be paid for by cuts in some other part of the NHS budget, of which wages consumed 70 per cent of the total. In the circumstances, it was Norman Fowler who persuaded his Cabinet colleagues to rule out a 9 per cent pay increase recommended by the Doctors and Dentists Review Board, offering 6 per cent instead. In June, the offer for nurses and ancillary workers was improved to 7.5 per cent and 6 per cent respectively, but this was rejected and action intensified.

Once again, as in the winter of 1978, the public was given images of strikers disrupting the care of hospital patients. Clarke, for instance, visited Leeds General Infirmary in July, and was reported to have met a distraught mother who had been taking her child in to be treated for acute appendicitis, when the ambulance halted at the picket line and she was forced to carry the child the rest of the way. Under the last Labour government, incidents of this sort had brought immeasurable political benefit to the Conservative Party. They could do so again, provided public attention could be focused on the behaviour of the strikers rather than the underlying issue of health-service pay. Clarke, consequently, did not mince words as he shared his impressions from the visit with waiting journalists. The strikers were "noisy and belligerent"; he was "appalled at the lengths these people will go to";[11] they were being orchestrated by the health unions, COHSE and NUPE, which were relatively new on the scene, having "built up their membership on a reputation of extreme militancy".[12] Both unions, he claimed on an earlier occasion, were led by the "hard left" whose extremism "has shown clearly in the way they have struck inflexibly to this ridiculous claim throughout and threatened to back it up with vicious strike action against patients."[13]

The new minister really came into his own in August, when Fowler was abroad on holiday. As the man temporarily in charge, Clarke went on a highly publicized week's tour of hospitals in Croydon, Derby, Doncaster, Newcastle upon Tyne and Liverpool. In Derby, he attempted to meet union leaders at the South Derbyshire ambulance headquarters while 350 ambulance drivers were out on strike. Three of the strikers, from the public-sector union NUPE, barricaded themselves in the boardroom, and the meeting had to be moved to a nearby doctor's surgery. The next day, at Doncaster Royal Infirmary, the canteen staff refused to serve him so much as a cup of coffee and he had to retire to a nearby pub for lunch. Clarke told journalists that the demonstrators were "larking about", and that their actions might have been funny except that they were "abandoning patients to do it".[14] The following day's lunch, at Walkergate Hospital, Newcastle, was also called off when canteen staff refused to serve him.

The climax of the week came at Walton Hospital, Liverpool. This was at the beginning of the period when the left in that city was establishing a reputation for being ready to go that bit further than anyone else, and Clarke's demeanour on the previous days' visits seemed to present them with a challenge. NUPE's regional secretary Colin Barnett promised:

> We are going to leave that man with a bloody nose. The next result of his visit to the North West undoubtedly will be an escalation in industrial action because he insulted the intellectual capacity of the people who took action. The problem is he doesn't think before he opens his rather big mouth.

Certainly, Clarke's reception was lively. He was jostled, pinioned against a wall, and hit over the head with a rolled-up newspaper. Several policemen's helmets were sent flying, and one officer lost a clip-on tie. When the minister was at last inside, lunching with hospital executives, demonstrators hammered on the windows. Afterwards, he made a few choice remarks to journalists which did nothing to defuse the situation. He opined: "It is all rather silly. I don't understand how singing and chanting or even roughing up visitors makes a pay claim acquire more validity. It is done purely for publicity ... these idiots clowning about at the hospital gate don't have the slightest effect on my opinions."[15] On the same day, he gave an interview to the *Daily Telegraph* which was interpreted as a threat to call in the troops if the strike persisted.

While the week's events did wonders for the minister's reputation as a tough talker, public opinion remained surprisingly unaroused, as if there was little to choose between a militant hospital porter and an outspoken Conservative minister. Fowler and Clarke did not really add a sense of urgency when they took their family holidays abroad, as usual. They met at Bordeaux airport on the day after Clarke's Liverpool visit, as one family flew in and the other flew out. Clarke recounted to his boss how he had been chased across the tarmac at Heathrow by half-a-dozen photographers, who would have boarded his plane had the captain not denied them permission.[16] On their return, Clarke's family suffered the further inconvenience of a burglary at their Birmingham home. Two young men later appeared in court, and apologized through their solicitors, saying they had not known whose house it was. A third member of the gang, then still at large, was said to feel "morally obliged to burgle wealthy people's homes".

By now, any Clarke visit to any NHS premises was treated by the local shop stewards as a challenge. The unions were ready to put on a mass demonstration at West Bridgford health centre, in Clarke's constituency, when he was due there in September. The visit was cancelled because of "urgent government business".[17] NUPE was ready with two coach loads of demonstrators for a ministerial visit to nearby Saxondale Hospital a week later, but that was also called off. "He's got cold feet", claimed the chairwoman of NUPE's North Notts district.[18]

The "key moment" in the story of the strike, from the government's point of view, was on 16 September, when the health-union representatives were expected at the ministry to reopen negotiations. The public talks were to have been preceded by secret meetings at Fowler's Fulham home, but the unions failed to appear, announcing at the last minute that they were boycotting the negotiations. Their reason for doing so was the same as the government's reason for wanting to meet urgently: the TUC had declared what was in effect intended to be a one-day general strike on 22 September in support of the health workers. The action was only a partial success, and opened the way for a counterattack. The government could now claim that its real opponent was not the nurses and other professional groups with a strong hold on public sympathy, but the TUC. That was Clarke's line of attack in the Commons the following month. The health workers were "the poor bloody infantry" while "the Labour Party and the trade union movement wanted to hitch all kinds of unpopular causes on the back of what they perceived to be a popular health service cause … They are content to see the health workers driven on in the dispute throughout the winter for much wider political motives."[19] In fact the strike ended in December, with both sides claiming victory.

After those first nine months, the rest of Clarke's time as a health minister was relatively peaceful. The department was based in offices at the Elephant and Castle, which he heartily disliked. It was an inconvenient two miles' journey through dense traffic from Westminster, and the only place where ministers could slip out for lunch was a nearby Italian restaurant that was frequently filled by staff from the Labour Party's national headquarters up the road. In the House of Commons, he was obliged to go through the routine of debating the future of the health service, a repetitive ritual in which opposition figures would produce statistics to prove that the NHS was being starved of money, to be answered with counter-statistics to bear out the government's claim that no administration had ever been so munificent in its spending on health. This pointless argument was invariably punctuated with personal insults. The reason it was all so meaningless was that, after the scare of the Cabinet leak, Thatcher simply refused to touch the NHS with any form of legislation other than on peripheral issues for the entire 1983–87 parliament. Consequently, the only way that Labour could get the matter raised in parliament was to have a general debate on the government's record. This they were obviously eager to do, health being Labour's strongest issue. Neil Kinnock made his debut as a young party leader by leading off a health-service debate; Clarke replied to it with cruel mock flattery: "We all welcome him to his post. We are confident we will hear that speech again and again."[20]

However, to reach an authoritative judgement on the government's record, there had to be some agreement on how to interpret the raw statistics, which of course there was not. Clarke repeatedly claimed that there was one simple, effective way to measure the government's commitment: calculate the percentage increase in the total NHS budget since the last year of a Labour government, compare it with the Retail Price Index, and if health spending had risen by more than the rate of inflation – which it invariably had – it followed that the Conservative government was more generous in its spending on health than Labour. Alternatively, he offered figures for health spending as a proportion of gross domestic product, which went up in the years 1979–83, a not entirely surprising fact, given how much GDP had dropped during a government-induced recession; or figures for health spending per head of population, which also went up from £143 in 1979 to £268 in 1983. The other side claimed that this simplistic formula did not allow for the fact that health costs rise faster than average retail prices because of expensive advance in medical techniques; that the NHS was servicing an ageing population; that if an above-average wage settlement had to be met from a fixed NHS budget the amount left to pay directly for patient care was correspondingly reduced, and so on.

There was a rare occasion when reality impinged upon the abstruse argument of how to measure health spending when Hart District Council, in Hampshire, threatened to take Clarke to court to force him to provide more funds to help Frimley Park Hospital in Camberley cope with the implications of a huge new housing estate to which the Department of Environment had given planning permission, in the teeth of local objections. The council claimed that, without the extra funds, the hospital would be unable to comply with the National Health Act. But generally, it being impossible to arrive at any sensible agreement even on the basic facts, Clarke livened up a series of sterile debates with personal invective. At various times he accused Neil Kinnock of talking "tendentious political nonsense",[21] Michael Meacher, the shadow social services secretary, of uttering "the most blithering nonsense"[22] and on a subsequent occasion of "causing increasing annoyance by wheeling out the same speech and the same motion so regularly",[23] shadow health minister Frank Dobson of "knockabout, spartist rubbish with his fiddled figures in the middle",[24] and Labour generally of employing the "big lie technique" to support the "preposterous proposition" that a Conservative government was cutting the NHS.[25] Once, when he spotted Rodney Bickerstaffe and Albert Spanswick in the Commons gallery, he claimed: "The General Secretary of NUPE and the General Secretary of COHSE are sitting there watching their creatures perform."[26] That caused such an uproar that the Speaker had to intervene to restore order, whereupon Clarke remarked insouciantly "It seems I am being provocative."

Another annual event was the government announcement that, yet again, prescription and other NHS charges were to rise. In the same month that Clarke took office, optical and dental charges were raised to three times their 1979 level. In his first year, the cost of a prescription rose to £1.40, seven times its 1979 level. He was also plunged straight into a political argument over a decision to deny free health care to overseas visitors, unless they came from a country that had a reciprocal arrangement with Britain. This provoked fears at the time that Asian immigrants would be forced to produce proof of their citizenship at their hospital bed or pay for their treatment. Clarke claimed that the measure was actually aimed at Americans, Australians, Arabs and others who could afford to pay, and accused the "No Pass Laws to Health" campaign, formed to opposed the measure, of having a "particularly ridiculous title".[27] More generally, he defended the rise in charges on the grounds that the NHS badly needed the money. Income from charges rose from £149 million to £392 million in the years 1979–83, and Clarke repeatedly claimed that without it, either health care would suffer or taxes would have to go up. The rest of his defence, typically, was attack, in which he was not wholly consistent: in one breath he accused the Opposition of being "cynical in the extreme"[28] by pretending that a Labour government would not levy charges on patients; in another, he conceded that it had, in fact, held prescription charges down to 20p for several years, but claimed that was "foolish and irresponsible ... a bad decision, taken for politically expedient reasons".[29]

Clarke's opposition to the privatization of health care as such did not inhibit him from encouraging business entrepreneurs into the health service, to take over some of the ancillary services or even as administrators. In 1983, for example, he instructed health authorities to obtain estimates from private firms for laundry, cleaning and catering. When Orpington District Health Authority cancelled their contract with a firm called Hospital Hygiene

Services, on the grounds of "appallingly low" standards, Clarke rebuked them for not consulting his department first, whereupon he was accused by John Edmonds of the GMB of "a rather nasty abuse of political power in favour of commercial profit making interests."[30] He was also accused of trying to make political appointments to senior regional posts in the health service. While he was minister, the fourteen chairmen of the regional health authorities were reappointed or replaced. In each case, the appointment was undoubtedly Clarke's, since Fowler had his hands full with other departmental business. He always claimed that he was politically impartial about it, and could point to chairmen with known links to the Labour Party whom he reappointed. He also had no compunction about choosing an active Conservative, where he could find one with appropriate qualifications. In the West Midlands, he appointed James Ackers, an industrialist who lived in Fowler's Sutton Coldfield constituency, whom Clarke had known well for almost twenty years. Ackers had helped with the research on a Bow Group pamphlet co-written by Clarke in the 1960s, on regional government.

In 1965, Clarke and Ackers were also co-authors of a little pamphlet produced by the Birmingham Bow Group entitled *What's Wrong With General Practice*, which attempted to set out a solution to a shortage of doctors that was then afflicting the health service. One of their proposals was that every patient who visited a doctor should be charged a fee which could be recovered later by applying at a post office, as a way of deterring anyone from wasting doctors' time. Clarke frequently referred to Ackers as a personal friend and continued to defend him and praise his contribution to the health service after it had ended in highly controversial circumstances ten years later. Government auditors described the way in which the West Midlands RHA had managed its services organization as a "shambles" in which at least £10 million of NHS funds had been wasted. One senior officer had privatized part of the service without even telling the authority what he was doing, and then left with a lump-sum payoff of over £80,000. Another officer loaned £300,000 of NHS money to a firm in financial difficulties without telling the authority. For all his business experience, Sir James Ackers, as he now was, had had little idea of what was going on, and retired eighteen months before his contract expired.[31]

However, the fact that Ackers was his friend did not mean that Clarke gave him an easy time. Once the chairmen were in place, all fourteen authorities set about filling the newly created posts of general manager. The first twelve to make appointments all chose candidates who were already working as NHS administrators. At this point, Clarke and Norman Fowler reportedly became "desperate" to see at least one new manager brought in from private industry. When the West Midlands RHA, on which there were more Conservative than Labour members, announced after an open competition that they had unanimously agreed to appoint Kenneth Bales, an experienced health administrator, Clarke wrote to James Ackers, saying he was "unable to approve the appointment". Nonetheless, the health authority stood its ground, and Bales's appointment was confirmed. It was then reported that pressure from Clarke dissuaded the last remaining RHA, East Anglia, from promoting its administrator, James Stewart, to the position of general manager.[32]

Far from being on the defensive over this, at the very time when it was going on Clarke was leading an attack on Labour's Michael Meacher for allegedly trying to interfere with the composition of health authorities for political reasons. Bizarrely, the argument ended up in court. It arose over a circular sent round to Labour members of health authorities, advising them to convene privately before each health authority meeting, to plan their tactics. It so enraged Eric Moonman, a former Labour MP and chairman of Islington district health authority, that he resigned from the Labour Party. Clarke accused Meacher of trying to introduce a "whipping or caucus system", and was quoted as calling it a "shabby political exercise", although he had no evidence that Meacher was the author of the circular.[33] The word "shabby" subsequently reappeared in a piece on Michael Meacher by the *Observer* columnist Alan Watkins, along with the word "louse". In 1988, Meacher sued the *Observer* for libel and lost, at great personal expense. One of the factors that helped sink his case was the brief appearance in the witness box of Kenneth Clarke, by then a Cabinet minister.[34]

As much as Clarke's fellow Conservatives loved his knockabout style while it was aimed at the trade unions or Labour MPs, in his dealings with them they naturally expected decorum and deference. A minister may disagree with a senior back-bench MP from his own party, but he should do so with respect. But part of Clarke's appeal is that, once he is on his feet, he so loves an argument and is so easily carried away by his own cleverness than he can be quite merciless in debunking the gentlemen sitting behind him. An example was the obscure debate that raged during the mid 1980s over whether it was right to put fluoride in the water supply. The argument in favour was that it had a proven record for protecting teeth. There was, however, a remarkably vociferous civil-rights lobby, heavily supported on the Tory Party right wing, which said that it infringed individual liberty to force everyone to drink fluoride simply to protect people who were too feckless to use toothpaste. In 1985, a woman from Glasgow took Strathclyde Regional Council to court and, after a hearing lasting two hundred days, won a ruling against them that they had exceeded their powers. The government's answer was to alter the law with a Water Fluoridation bill which, with more political expediency than logic, laid down no national policy, but gave local councils the power to decide whether or not local water supplies were to be treated.

This provoked an extraordinary confrontation in the Commons, pitching Clarke against some formidable figures from the Conservative back benches, including Ivan Lawrence, then the vice-chairman of the Commons Select Committee on Home Affairs, who set what was then a twentieth-century record with a speech lasting four-and-a-half hours, in an attempt to block the legislation by a filibuster. Clarke dealt with the opposition, whom he accused of stretching "libertarian arguments to an almost absurd degree", by taking the mickey.[35] He parodied their claims by suggesting that fluoridation would "damage most of the parts of our bodies plus those who inherit our genes, would kill our mice, damage our rats, poison our deer and rot our pipes and sewers". Rebuked for describing the legendary Glasgow litigant as "a lady with no teeth", he retracted and called her "non-dentate". Even the dour Ivan Lawrence admitted: "It was a great feat of advocacy to laugh our opposition out, but on cool reflection the joke will not be funny."[36] Several other Tories were visibly angry and offended at being mocked by the minister.

More seriously, Clarke was also prepared to mix it with two of the better-paid professional groups in the health service. Opticians were offended by a clause in the cumbersomely named 1983 Health and Social Services and Social Security Adjudications bill which ended their monopoly over the sale of spectacles and partially lifted the ban on advertising by opticians. Having had their eyes tested by a qualified optician, customers would then be free to have the lenses made up and to buy frames wherever was cheapest. Subsidized NHS frames were to be abolished. The legislation aroused fears on the Labour side of a return to the bad days when the poor bought their spectacles off the shelf at Woolworths, being unable to afford an eye test. The most serious opposition to the measure came from opticians and Tory MPs who took up their case, especially Dame Jill Knight, whose husband Monty Knight was a prominent optometrist. Even against such formidable opposition, Clarke could not resist a chance to be funny. He regaled MPs with how, on taking up his job, he had plunged into a long-running discussion on the possible introduction of a new NHS ladies' frame, which he suggested should be called the Kenneth Clarke Memorial Frame.

> I am told that it is selling fairly well, although it reminds me of the kind of spectacles that typists wore ten years ago if they getting into the prime of life behind their typewriters. I concluded that it was farcical for a Minister to be involved in gazing at racks of frames and trying to choose a government approved type to be made available to ladies.[37]

On a more serious note, he accused the opticians of producing "convoluted" arguments to try to make it seem that they were fighting for their patients rather than their pockets, and argued that professional restrictive practices had no better claim to government protection than the trade-union closed shop. He answered fears that a part of the NHS was being abolished with the categorical promise: "We are keeping in the National Health Service what should be kept there – free eye sight tests for everyone regardless of need."[38] Five years later, it was Kenneth Clarke, as Secretary of State for Health, who abolished free eye tests.

Meanwhile, Clarke seemed to make a habit of falling out with the British Medical Association, which represented more than two-thirds of the country's 86,000 doctors. The same bumper health bill that antagonized the opticians also proposed to curb the growth of private deputizing services, which were being paid to relieve NHS doctors of their night-time calls. Clarke proposed that doctors working alone or in two-handed partnerships should be restricted to using deputies three nights a week and alternative weekends. Practices with three doctors or more would have to provide their own cover. In this, he had the support of the Opposition. The Labour Party feared that by night the general-practitioner service was being "quietly privatized". However, doctors were not far behind solicitors and barristers in the number who had become Tory MPs, and this rebellion was more than Clarke could handle. Overruled by the Cabinet, he had to make a public confession that he had been too "rigid and inflexible", and to promise that what had previously been firm rules were now "general guidelines" within which Family Practitioner Committees would be able to operate flexibly. Awkward though it was for Clarke to have to climb down in public, it did not do his reputation outside parliament any harm, especially in the Tory press, in which he was cast as the tough guy overruled by weaker spirits. The *Mail on Sunday* reported a "stab in the back" by Norman Fowler, "leaving Kenneth walking on thin air".[39] One Tory MP and former general practitioner, Dr Alan Glyn, claimed that the whole problem had arisen because Clarke had appeared to want to close all deputizing services down, to which he replied: "There was a failure of communication between myself and certain sections of the profession … I accept my share of the blame."[40]

Still the failures of communication between the minister and the BMA kept happening. They had public arguments over the potential medical effects of nuclear weapons, over the length of NHS waiting lists – about which Clarke publicly accused them of getting their facts wrong – and over prescription charges. In April 1984, the public was appalled by the case of a 32-year-old mother who died of cancer, having not been warned when a cervical smear test some years earlier revealed the onset of the disease. Two other women were ill after similar blunders. It was an occasion when public opinion demanded that the government do something, and Clarke did: he ordered health authorities to use computers and to ensure that women were called in for early-warning tests – but without allocating them any extra money. The BMA complained that they should have been consulted.

The first serious falling out between the government and the BMA began in November 1984, when, in an effort to reduce the NHS's huge annual drugs bill, Norman Fowler published a list of drugs which he proposed to ban doctors from prescribing on the health service. The government claimed that each drug on the list was an expensive brand name for which there was a cheaper substitute, and that the exercise could save £100 million a year without harming patients. They ran up against a well-orchestrated campaign by doctors and the pharmaceutical industry, backed by expensive advertising. When the issue came before parliament early the following year, Clarke was in no mood to mince words, accusing doctors of running "an unethical and unscrupulous campaign by alarming their patients" and "combining political campaigning with medical advice".[41] This confrontation marked the beginning of a development which would accelerate when Clarke returned to the health department as Secretary of State: the estrangement between GPs and the party that most had supported since the beginnings of the NHS. In mid 1985, the *Health and Social Service Journal* reported: "For some months now the crockery has been flying and the air has been thick with recrimination between the government and the BMA. Mutual loathing seems to have replaced the natural empathy that used to bind that most conservative of professions and the Tory party." Clarke understandably played down the rift, saying: "I am not conscious of any breakdown of relations with the BMA. We have had a couple of disagreements with them over recent months, that's all."[42]

By now, Clarke had a spreading reputation as a man who had been under-promoted. During the 1983 election, the *Sun* ran a jubilant piece headed "Goodbye to the Old School Tie" and introduced "Maggie's new breed of bright, talented, articulate ministers who have risen to the top on their own talents" which featured four Cabinet ministers – Brittan, Parkinson, Fowler and Tebbit – plus Kenneth Clarke.[43] "Crossbencher", in the *Sunday Express*, compared Clarke with Norman Fowler – "First at the Transport Department … now at the DHSS, it has been the sharp-minded Ken who has fielded the awkward questions in the Commons, Ken who has shone on TV, while the chief has hummed and hawed and landed him in one scrape after another."[44]

Far more significant than the comments of gossip writers was the judgement of his peers. In June 1985, *The Times* approached 85 of the 102 new Conservative MPs, elected two years earlier, asking whom they would choose as Mrs Thatcher's successor. Unsurprisingly, Norman Tebbit emerged as favourite, with Michael Heseltine as runner-up. However, when the MPs were asked to assume that she stayed on beyond the general election and to name her long-term successor, their clear favourite was Kenneth Clarke.[45]

This would not have pleased the prime minister. She had not had her own anointed successor since the fall of Cecil Parkinson. Tebbit would soon cross an invisible line, changing from being a trusted ally to a potential rival. As to the minister for health, she had agreed to make him a Privy Councillor in the previous new year's honours list, on the same day as another former Heath acolyte, Kenneth Baker. Promoting him to her Cabinet was quite another matter. In April 1985, Alan Clark noted in his diary: "It was reassuring to hear that the Lady cannot stand Kenneth Clarke, and it is for that reason that he has been so long excluded from the Cabinet, which apparently (but not in my estimation) his merits demand."[46] But Mrs Thatcher could not forever ignore the sort of support that Clarke had accumulated in the newspapers and the parliamentary party. No doubt she was heavily advised by the whips that she would look churlish and would make enemies for herself unnecessarily among the younger MPs if promotion for Kenneth Clarke was not included in her next Cabinet reshuffle. As she reflected later: "There are some people it is better to bring in because they would cause more trouble outside. Peter Walker and, to a lesser extent, Kenneth Clarke are examples."[47]

The newspapers were full of speculation about a reshuffle, obviously inspired by Downing Street, on the morning of Monday, 2 September, when a call came through to Kenneth Clarke in the Midlands, summoning him to Downing Street. As he hurried south, he must have known that his moment had come. A few words on the telephone would have been enough if the prime minister's intention had been to leave him where he was. A move sideways, to another minister of state's job, would have been left until later in the day, after the new Cabinet had been announced. There was no doubt that, at forty-five and after fifteen years in parliament, Clarke had reached the top table. It was not a startlingly fast rise. After all, his Cambridge contemporaries Norman Fowler and Leon Brittan had been Cabinet ministers for four years. Some of the 1974 intake, like Nigel Lawson and Douglas Hurd, had beaten him to it. Compared with the early career of, say, Peter Walker or Labour's David Owen, Clarke's had been almost sluggish. Nonetheless, it was fast enough to preserve his reputation as a man who was going places. No doubt, as he waited in Thatcher's outer office, he permitted himself some pleasant speculation about which department was to be put into his hands – little knowing that the prime minister still had a trick up her sleeve.

CHAPTER SEVEN

"LORD YOUNG'S REPRESENTATIVE ON EARTH", PART ONE: THE PAYMASTER GENERAL

When Kenneth Clarke arrived at Number 10 on the first Monday of September 1985, the first surprise was that the prime minister was not alone. Also present in her upstairs study, and looking very pleased with himself, was a man whom Clarke had never met before, though he knew him by reputation. He was Lord Young of Graffham, an amateur politician who had been on the fringes of government for the past six years, having very good connections with the Thatcher circle. Clarke was familiar with the outlines of his career: he had grown up in Thatcher's Finchley constituency, after his parents escaped the poverty of London's East End, and had been able to call on the help of a very extended family to get him, first, into the legal profession, and then into the management of General Universal Stores, one of whose directors, the present Lord Wolfson, had married his cousin. When Clarke was learning the arts of government in the early 1970s, David Young was not even an active Tory. He had been a Labour voter in the 1960s, but was now beginning to make serious money by taking advantage of the London property boom. He hit upon a direct route into Thatcher's circle of intimates quite by accident: the partner in one of his property deals had been an ambitious businessmen named Jeffrey Sterling, who had since become Chairman of P & O Steam Navigation. Sterling introduced Young to Alfred Sherman at the Centre for Policy Studies, who then introduced him to Keith Joseph, who encouraged him to take part in the exercise of redefining what it meant to be a Conservative. Having been an unpaid adviser to Keith Joseph and later to Norman Tebbit, he became chairman of the Manpower Services Commission and of the National Economic Development Council, a life peer, and was brought into the Cabinet in 1984 as Minister without Portfolio, still unpaid. Young had never run for office, made a political speech, or been tainted in any way by association with Edward Heath. In short, he was exactly the kind of self-made right-wing amateur Mrs Thatcher wanted to have around. His presence must have alerted Kenneth Clarke at once that something was going to spoil his day.

Mrs Thatcher explained. She had decided to enhance the role of the Department of Employment, which, under three Secretaries of State – Jim Prior, Norman Tebbitt and Tom King – had been responsible for trade-union legislation and schemes to alleviate unemployment, but would now, additionally, take over small businesses and tourism. Lord Young had kindly agreed to enter full-time politics as Secretary of State for Employment, but, since he would be based in the Lords, he would need a minister with a gift for presentation and mastery of the Commons despatch box to be his representative there. That was the job she wanted Kenneth Clarke to do.[1] It was not much of an offer to make to someone who was now being taken seriously as a future prime minister by the up-market newspapers on the left and the right. That autumn, the *Daily Telegraph* reported that Clarke was "widely tipped as a future Conservative leader",[2] and on the same day, the *Guardian* said he was "the man tipped by almost everyone for high office under any imaginable Conservative Prime Minister."[3] A politician who could attract that sort of critical acclaim could reasonably have expected to be given a government department to run, rather than being moved from the number-two slot in a large department to a rather smaller one, so that he could protect an inexperienced chief whom he had never met and whose political philosophy differed from his. The last Cabinet minister put in an equivalent position had been Ian Gilmour, who was deputy to the Foreign Secretary Lord Carrington; but he at least was working with someone of similar background and vast political experience. It was not a happy precedent, and it was not long before Gilmour was sacked.

As if to make things worse, the next member of the employment team, after Clarke, was another devoted Thatcherite, Alan Clark, whose feelings about his near-namesake are set out in his diaries, in epithets like "butterball" and "pudgy puff-ball". In one entry, he whimsically regrets that one so fat is unlikely to have a nervous breakdown. In another, he complains that Clarke "actually *sued* the manufacturers of Trivial Pursuit because they had muddled us up",[4] which at first reading sounds remarkably thin-skinned and petty, because the diaries do not say what the "muddle" was about. One of Clark's most famous remarks was made at a private function soon after his appointment as an employment minister, responsible among other things for race relations, when he is reputed to have referred to British blacks as coming from "Bongo Bongo Land". A pocket addition of Trivial Pursuit wrongly attributed the remark to "Health Minister Kenneth Clarke", who understandably objected.

That was the bad news. The good news was that Lord Young had generously agreed to continue working without pay, as he had done since 1979, allowing the prime minister to circumvent a rule which limited the number of ministers to whom she could award salaried Cabinet posts. Clarke's job would carry the title of Paymaster General, a post which had been defunct for several years and which would come to occupy his time for about one day a month, but which carried a seat in the Cabinet and a commensurate salary of £44,969. It meant that his pay had risen by almost £24,400 in two years. With no source of income outside politics, and two children at private schools, the money alone would have been a serious inducement to stay and make the most of what he had been offered. Clarke, anyway, was not the type to suffer from hurt pride. According to David Young, "He looked a bit shocked when he found out his new job, but cheered up immediately as soon as he realised that he was in the Cabinet ... It says a great deal for him that in all the years we worked together he never complained or made a mistake."[5] He would be Lord Young's "representative on earth"[6] for the next three years.

In the previous six years, the function of the Department of Employment had been to produce one piece of legislation after another restricting the freedoms of trade unions. At least, that appeared to be what Mrs Thatcher required of it, although during her first eighteen months in office she became convinced that it was a nest of wets and backsliders. Clarke's friend Jim Lester, who was a junior employment minister, was one of the first members of her government to be sacked. She also put a block on the career of an eminent civil servant in the department, and cleaned out the entire ministerial team, headed by Jim Prior, sending in Norman Tebbit, who carried on his predecessor's policy with added verbal aggression. However, the brief conversation with the prime minister established that she now wanted something more than union bashing from her employment team. The unemployment statistics were too high, and she wanted action. Lord Young promised to come up with something within eight weeks.

The next day, the four ministers who made up the employment team divided their responsibilities. Clarke was given charge of industrial relations, health-and-safety legislation, the Manpower Services Commission, and the Enterprise and Deregulation Unit. The issues of racial and sexual equality were sensibly taken out of the hands of Alan Clark, who went back to looking after job centres and employment schemes, and passed on to Peter Bottomley. Here Clarke at least had one colleague whom he could trust, a fellow member of the Bow Group and the Amesbury Group. Since the mid 1970s, Bottomley had been part of the informal circle who deviated from normal Conservative behaviour by fighting the Labour Party on its home ground, social policy. He had been Clarke's leading supporter on the back benches during the campaign to push the Labour government into speeding up the introduction of child benefit, and had served for a year as Norman Fowler's parliamentary private secretary at the DHSS. Bottomley's interest in social security was inspired by his wife, Virginia, a psychiatric social worker who was elected to parliament in a by-election in 1984. He was also one of the few Tory MPs who boasted of being a paid-up member of a major trade union, the TGWU. Unfortunately for Clarke, Bottomley was not around for long. Having been very outspoken on the importance of ending job discrimination against blacks, he was suddenly moved to another department in January 1986, without being replaced. His departure meant another shuffling around of responsibilities, with Young taking upon himself the supervision of the Manpower Services Commission, and giving Clarke responsibility for equal opportunities.

Clarke's friend Jim Lester says: "I think it was the only job that Ken was ever offered that he was really unsure of. I remember him ringing me up and saying 'help' over the telephone. He has never had a very high opinion of trade unions. It was not a field that he was comfortable with."[7] Clarke invited Jim Lester into the department as his "ad hoc adviser", a bold appointment in that his friend's political misfortunes had not ended with his sacking in January 1981. In 1983, the right succeeded in ousting him from the chairmanship of the party's backbench Employment Committee after only five months. The trade unions had not known that Lester was their friend: as an employment minister, he had promised to punish the workshy and curb union immunities, and had introduced the legislation which set a £12-a-week limit on benefits payments to strikers; but the right thought he was "wet". In 1985, he was the moving spirit behind the Tory Campaign Action to Revive Employment (CARE), as well as being around the department offering advice, but since the job was unpaid and unapproved by the prime minister, he never had a secure place around the table with the ministers. When Clarke was asked by a local newspaper whether he had consulted the prime minister about Lester's appointment, he replied that he had not, adding: "I think I am entitled to take advice from whoever I wish."[8]

In the latter part of 1985 the British trade-union movement was heading towards its greatest defeat in recent history, when the miners were forced back to work after a strike lasting more than a year. When the strike ended, the Coal Board was able to continue with the relentless rundown of the industry. One of the pits closed in July 1985 was Moorgreen colliery, where Clarke's father had worked. Naturally, Clarke wasted no time in joining the attacks on Arthur Scargill and the leaders of other unions who had backed the NUM. "It requires little courage to stand in Scargill's paid picket lines, but it requires guts to go through them",[9] he said at the autumn Tory Party conference, a place where attacking Scargill also required little courage. At a subsequent conference of Conservative trade unionists, he urged TGWU members to take their leaders to court for failing to comply with recent legislation on the conduct of elections. Later he would pull out some surprises, as when he appeared at the TUC annual conference, the first minister to do so for five years, and when, during the bitter print dispute centred on News International's new plant at Wapping, he found generous words of praise for the union leader Brenda Dean and directed some mild criticism at Rupert Murdoch.

Clarke displayed more imagination than the average dark-suited and forgettable Conservative employment minister, but it would be wrong to be misled into thinking that he had become "wet" on trade unions. If anything, he was more "Thatcherite" than when he was an industry spokesman in opposition. On trade-union rights, he had not fundamentally changed. At heart, one suspects, he would have liked to see all unions behave as the electricians' union, the EEPTU, was behaving, collaborating with employers to improve productivity and eliminate militancy. "The EEPTU lives in today's world, where we are trying to get competitive industries and improve people's job prospects", he enthused;[10] whereas, by contrast, "the TUC and labour movement is extremely old-fashioned and backward looking: its veneration for a slowly vanishing society can sometimes be taken to extremes."[11] He actually believed, in a paternalistic way, that militant trade unions served their members badly.

The dispute at Wapping was provoked by Rupert Murdoch's decision to close down the offices of the *Sun*, *News of the World*, *The Times* and *Sunday Times* in Bouverie Street and Gray's Inn Road one weekend in January 1986, and move them to a cheaper site, operating up-to-date technology, in London's docklands. He took advantage of a rash decision by the print unions, the NGA and Sogat 82, to call their members out on strike in protest, by sacking all 5,500 of them, without compensation or redundancy payment. New production workers had already been hired to replace them, from the EEPTU. With the new printworks in operation, barbed wire up around the site, the government delighted to give moral support, and the Metropolitan Police briefed and ready to control the pickets, there was almost nothing the unions could now do except conduct protest marches.

Throughout, Clarke maintained that the government was not involved in the dispute, but was even-handedly ensuring that it was conducted according to a sensible set of rules. Those rules led to the sequestering of Sogat's funds, because the union had called on its provincial members to black News International titles without balloting them. On the face of it, this was an example of union leaders attempting to deny their own members the right to vote, and being punished for it. However, had there been a ballot and had the members voted to carry out the blacking, the law as it had been rewritten by the Thatcher government would probably have blocked them in some other way. The provincial employers could have followed News International's example and sacked all their workers without compensation for breaking their contracts. Alternatively, News International could have obtained an injunction preventing the action on the grounds that it constituted unlawful secondary picketing, because at the start of the dispute, the conglomerate had created a new company, News International Distribution, which was distinct from the companies that had sacked the printers.

None of this gave Clarke pause for thought. The only conclusion he drew from the dispute was that new legislation was needed to prevent unions taking disciplinary action against members who crossed picket lines. His analysis of the cause of the dispute was that:

> Fleet Street fat cats in the print unions reversed the traditional economies of employment. They priced themselves into a position where presumably Mr Murdoch judged it worth while to start again from scratch.[12]

However, in the middle of the dispute, Clarke spoke at a lunch with the House of Commons press gallery, which included a small number of journalists who had refused to make the move to Wapping, alongside others employed by Murdoch. Here, he surprised his audience by the tone of his remarks, which was rather different from the lionizing of Murdoch by Thatcher and her circle. Clarke looked forward to the defeat of the print unions in the hope that afterwards more newspapers would be able to survive at lower costs without being controlled "by proprietors from the Old Commonwealth", and suggested that "Rupert Murdoch's personal public relations could do with a little improvement." He went on to praise the leader of Sogat 82, Brenda Dean, as "the most persuasive spokesman on the left in the union movement for some time".[13] Politically, his remarks did not deviate from government policy; but what they seemed to imply was that the spectacle of thousands of print workers separated by barbed wire from the enterprise that had fired them without compensation was unhelpful to the Conservative cause.

It appears that Clarke genuinely believed that the concentration of ownership of Britain's national newspapers by a small number of mostly multinational companies could be blamed on the unions. "Overmanning and excessively high costs", he claimed, were "the greatest inhibitions to a wide range of ownership."[14] Around 1986, with the launch of the *Independent*, *Today*, *News on Sunday* and, subsequently, the *Sunday Correspondent*, it did appear that the slashing of print costs would open up the market; but some months after the Wapping dispute, Lord Young had to make a hurried decision about whether the Monopolies and Mergers Commission should be brought in to examine a proposal by Murdoch to add one more title to his stable, the ailing daily newspaper, *Today*. Unsurprisingly, the sale was allowed to go ahead, a decision which Clarke was required to defend in the Commons. He did so without any sign that he disagreed, claiming that the competitiveness of the newspaper was basically unaffected because *Today* was in the middle of the market, alongside the *Daily Express* and *Daily Mail*, where Murdoch owned no other title, and that "it is not the government's duty to look for other buyers".[15] Within a few years, all the new titles had either been taken over by a large conglomerate, or had closed.

Clarke's appearance at the fringe of the TUC conference in October 1986 caused a stir, in that he was the first Cabinet minister to do so since James Prior in 1979. He timed his visit to coincide with the overwhelming vote in support of the recently drafted TUC/Labour Party policy document, *People at Work – New Rights and Responsibilities*, which had already been condemned as a blueprint for "delivering the country back into the stranglehold of the trade union bosses".[16] In a press conference afterwards, Clarke claimed that it had been a rather easy policy to persuade unions to adopt. "They have swallowed a lot of sugar with no pill inside."[17] However, the real interest was not in what he said, but in what he was doing there in the first place. According to the *Daily Telegraph*:

> Some onlookers interpret Clarke's visit as a sign that the government wishes to show a more understanding face to the unions, while others more cynical are suggesting that the minister can do his Cabinet career no harm at all by being on hand (and probably on television) giving on the spot reactions to the arcane doings of the brothers.[18]

Right at the start of his career as an employment minister, Alan Clark had confided to his diary about the dreary grind of the job: "Faster than I can digest them great wadges of documentation whumped into my 'In' tray. The subject matter is turgid: a mass of 'schemes' whose purpose, plainly, is not so much to bring relief to those out of work as to devise excuses for removing them from the Register."[19] With a general election less than three years away, and mass unemployment the most visible blight on the government's record, the demand for more and better "schemes" was pressing, and would take up a good deal of Kenneth Clarke's time.

His first difference of opinion with Lord Young came on day two. Before their arrival, civil servants had been working on importing an American idea called Job Clubs, to which small groups of the long-term unemployed were brought together during regular office hours, provided with free postage, telephones, advice and back-up services, and set the task of filling in ten job applications a day. Lord Young immediately rejected the idea as "dangerous", but was persuaded by Clarke to go ahead with it. Within a little over six months, forty-four Job Clubs had been started, and two-thirds of those taking part had found work "within a reasonable time".[20] By the time the general election was approaching, Clarke was able to boast that there would soon be four hundred and that "we are well on course to have a thousand in a few months' time."[21] The clubs were, of course, catering for tiny numbers who made no significant impact on the overall unemployment totals. For instance, the Sunderland Job Club, which Kenneth Clarke singled out as one of the most successful, dealt with 145 claimants in its first fifteen months, of whom 105 found jobs. Even so, they were important to those who took part in them and created a modest flow of good publicity for the Conservative cause. Lord Young generously acknowledged that Clarke had been right, adding "so much for my political instincts!"[22]

Clarke's first appearance in the Commons in his new post revealed other plans for reducing the unemployment totals. They were not primarily Clarke's ideas: his role was to defend them in the Commons hot-house at the same time that Young was announcing them in the well-mannered and sedate atmosphere of the Lords. One of Young's first moves was to introduce a rule that everyone who had been claiming unemployment benefit for a year or more would be called in to the appropriate Jobcentre for a "counselling interview". This scheme, known as Restart, was billed as a service to genuine claimants, who were to be provided with advice, encouragement and the offer of a place from a menu of government projects. It included a new "Jobstart allowance", under which anyone who had been out of work for over a year and was prepared to take a job paying less than £80 a week was offered a top-up of £20 per week for the first six months. "Our plans," said Clarke, "are concerned with the social consequences of unemployment and the dignity of those seeking work."[23]

Restart had a less genial purpose, which the government was not keen to emphasize at the time. It was to be the cheap solution to the problem of how to cut the unemployment figures quickly. Lord Young's memoirs are very frank on this point. As if in answer to the accusation that his political instincts were weak, he makes it plain that he wanted a quick purge of the unemployment register before the general election, and believed that the prospect of being cross-examined by social-security inspectors would induce large numbers to sign themselves off, either because they were cheating by working in the black economy or because they were old enough for early retirement. A more drastic and long-term means of reducing unemployment would have been to import from the USA some form of Workfare, under which the long-term unemployed are offered a job on a government scheme with the threat of losing their benefit if they turn it down. Margaret Thatcher and Nigel Lawson were both in favour of it. Surprising though it may seem, it has its defenders on the left, among those working with the unemployed; but a genuine Workfare scheme, providing worthwhile and rewarding work, would be extremely expensive and complicated. "Unfortunately, an alliance between Norman Fowler, as Social Security Secretary, and David Young ... produced so many alleged practical difficulties that the idea was dropped", Lawson complains.[24]

Even the relatively modest cost of Restart was too much for the Chief Secretary to the Treasury, John MacGregor, who was battling to achieve a 2p cut in the basic rate of income tax in time for the general election. The dispute went to the so-called "Star Chamber", which consisted, in this case, of Margaret Thatcher, Nigel Lawson and Norman Tebbit, who assembled in the prime minister's study to hear both sides of the argument. Naturally, the argument presented by Lord Young had nothing to do with the interests of the long-term unemployed and everything to do with public finances and electoral calculation. He told them that if he was allowed to go full steam ahead, he could manipulate the jobless figures so that they fell below the figure of three million, psychologically important in the midst of an election campaign.[25] Nonetheless, he was told he would have to be content for the time being with nine pilot schemes, involving a little over nineteen thousand of the unemployed being called in to answer questions. By March, Clarke felt able to claim that the scheme had provided "help" for 90 per cent of those interviewed, and may have been responsible for the fact that unemployment had fallen by 1.1 per cent in the areas covered by the pilot schemes, compared with a fall of 0.1 per cent nationally[26] – which sat oddly alongside a calculation by the Unemployment Unit that just 1,117 out of 19,112 had been placed in work. However, the Treasury had obviously been convinced that Restart was cost-effective, and it was allowed to proceed at a cracking pace. The Manpower Services Commission took on two thousand extra staff in order to conduct forty thousand interviews a week, so that the entire list of 1,250,000 long-term unemployed could be worked through by March 1987.

Unemployment peaked at 3,279,594 in July 1986, at which time Kenneth Clarke remarked, with that special aptitude shown by Conservative ministers over the years for blaming others, that it was "largely a self-inflicted problem" caused by wage increases which were not matched by productivity increases and hence had "absolutely no justification".[27] By November the figure had fallen for three successive months, producing the largest drop in the headline figure for thirteen years, in what was clearly not just a statistical blip. Restart is likely to have been part of the explanation. Restart was supplemented late in 1986 by the introduction of a new questionnaire, which cost £16 million to introduce and required the hiring of another 1,400 staff. If nothing else, Lord Young and Kenneth Clarke were committed to creating jobs for benefits officers. The most significant question in this new form was "Can you start work today?" Anyone who replied that they needed twenty-four hours or more to make the necessary arrangements risked having their benefit cut because, as Clarke explained to the Commons, "unemployment benefit is a daily benefit and … a person is entitled to to it for those days when he is able to start work."[28] He added that it only required two applicants out of every hundred to drop their claims on being confronted with this form to turn it into a money saver rather than a cost.

A different type of scheme that allowed the government to claim to be doing something about unemployment involved the much-publicized inner-cities initiative, which, if it achieved nothing else, allowed Clarke to prove himself as an effective departmental infighter. Mrs Thatcher showed her concern about the dereliction and hopelessness of inner-city ghettoes in three spasms: one after the riots of 1981, the second during the run-up to the 1987 general election, and the third immediately afterwards. It was a matter of dispute about which department should coordinate inner-city policy. The first time, when Michael Heseltine was Environment Secretary, it was an environmental question; when Kenneth Clarke was an employment minister, it was an employment issue; by the time he had moved on to be an industry minister, it was an industrial issue. Each time, the job went to the minister with a gift for what Mrs Thatcher called "presentation", rather than to someone she trusted politically – a reliable indicator that she wanted the government to be seen to be doing something, rather than to take serious political decisions.

At the beginning of 1986, Mrs Thatcher's leadership was in crisis because of the extraordinary dispute over the future of Westland, a small helicopter firm based in Cornwall, which provoked two resignations from her Cabinet. The first was that of the Defence Secretary, Michael Heseltine, who walked out of a Cabinet meeting on 9 January 1986, after his attempt to put together a European consortium to rescue Westland had failed. He had been undermined by the deliberate leak of a letter from the Solicitor General, Patrick Mayhew, criticizing his position, and had been told he must clear any future statements on Westland with the Cabinet Office. The second, on January 24, was the Secretary of State for Trade and Industry, Leon Brittan, who was forced to take the rap for the leaking of the Mayhew letter.

Westland began as a quarrel about foreign-policy objectives. Heseltine, as a pro-European, believed that Europe needed the capacity to construct its own military helicopters, whilst Thatcher was content to see Westland became US-owned. It ended as a scandal about propriety in high places, because to leak a law officer's letter is one of those offences which mean nothing to the general public but are regarded in Westminster as a gross breach of accepted conduct. If it had been a purely political quarrel, Kenneth Clarke could have been expected to sympathize with Heseltine, to whom he was ideologically much closer than either was to Thatcher. However, Heseltine chose to act individually rather than as a team player. Personally, he and Clarke were never close.

By contrast, Leon Brittan was one of his oldest acquaintances: a member of the Cambridge mafia, part of Geoffrey Howe's circle, now being treated abominably by the prime minister, who seemed to blame him for not protecting her reputation adequately, and by Conservative MPs and peers who were determined that he would be their fall guy. Brittan was vulnerable because he had risen very high, very fast, becoming Home Secretary at the age of 42 after less than ten years in parliament, before being suddenly demoted after losing the prime minister's good will. Another element that contributed to his fall was that anti-Semitism had never died in the Tory Party. Thatcher herself was impervious to it. Immediately before Brittan's downfall, there were five Cabinet ministers whose grandparents had fled the anti-Semitic pogroms in Tsarist Russia. According to Nigel Lawson, there was "an unpleasant whiff of anti-semitism"[29] about; Alan Clark's diaries record a dinner in the House of Lords at which Tory grandees spoke of there being "too many jewboys in the Cabinet".[30] Another joke going around at the time was that the Cabinet had too many "old Estonians".

Typically, in a month when ministers were cautious about accepting invitations to go on the air to defend the government, Kenneth Clarke went to the opposite extreme, turning up on almost every channel to fight the government's cause. He was not doing so out of excessive loyalty to Margaret Thatcher, whose premiership was at its lowest ebb since 1981; his personal reason for being so readily available was to speak up for Leon Brittan.

> I thought the government was getting itself in a hell of a mess and I thought we were inflicting on ourselves appalling trouble. I went on when perhaps others were less eager to go on. I thought the least Leon deserved was for some of his friends to go and explain what was happening.[31]

It was appealingly bold of him to come out in support of an old friend whose parliamentary career was wrecked, in defiance of the mouldering prejudice in some of the murkier circles of the Tory Party.

There was one occasion soon after Westland when it would have suited the government better if Clarke had been tactful about feelings that were running high on an issue which, at heart, he seemed to think was deeply unimportant. The question of whether supermarkets should be permitted to open on Sundays may not have been the biggest issue facing the government of the day, but it was the one on which, uniquely, the Thatcher administration was defeated in the House of Commons.

By mid 1985, the law on Sunday trading was unworkable and full of anomalies. The lists of items which could or could not be sold on a Sunday were absurd. A fish-and-chip shop, for instance, was allowed to sell any food except fish or chips, which could be bought only at a railway station. An increasing number of traders, such as garden centres, do-it-yourself shops or small corner shops were flouting the law anyway by opening for business with impunity. However, lined up against the proposal to liberalize the Sunday trading laws there was an unusual coalition comprising the shopworkers' union, which prevailed upon the Labour Party to oppose the change, and Conservatives with religious objections or simple fears that the traditional family Sunday would be ruined.

It was the sort of issue that the Commons traditionally treats as a matter of personal conscience, allowing individual MPs to vote as they wished without pressure from the whips. It fell to Clarke to explain why, on this occasion, the government had decided at the last minute to put a three-line whip on the bill. His point was that whatever else happened, the old 1950 Shops Act must be replaced by a new shops act. Once that was done, there would be the opportunity for any number of amendments to be introduced and voted on freely. Unfortunately, he was struggling to explain this when time was running out at the end of an eight-hour debate, with continuous interruptions from Labour and Tory MPs. Under pressure, he reacted as he usually did, by going on to the attack, suggesting to the assembled MPs that most of them were probably lawbreakers who shopped illegally on Sundays. He refused to give way to Tory MPs wanting to question or protest about the government's handling of the vote. A few minutes later, large numbers of them defied the whip, and the government was defeated. The Sunday trading laws were still in the same shambles when, seven years later, it fell to Clarke, as Home Secretary, to start the legislative process all over again. Shopping hours were finally reformed in 1994. Meanwhile, there was another, more serious issue on which Clarke had no compunction in making enemies on the party right.

In October 1985, there had been race riots again, in London and Birmingham. On the Broadwater Farm Estate in Tottenham a policeman was gruesomely murdered by a raging crowd. In public, ministers refused to accept that there was a correlation between worsening race relations and the high level of unemployment among blacks. When Labour MPs suggested such an idea, Clarke tartly replied that "it is an insult to the inhabitants of inner cities to believe that they react in criminal ways to the problems that all face."[32] Clarke's gift for presentation was now put to use in some of the areas of Britain where the ethnic population, unemployment levels and the crime rate were all high. The most obvious presentational problem was that the areas of greatest social need were administered by Labour councils. Ministers had spent years railing against their extravagance, introducing new legislation to give the government unprecedented power to order them to cut their budgets. They had also drastically cut the Rate Support Grant, taking millions of pounds of central funds out of the affected areas. Now someone had to explain why some of the money was being put back, without allowing that the government might have been wrong. Clarke did this in characteristic style, by going on the attack.

As to the government's plans, Clarke announced in February 1986 that there would be eight pilot areas – Notting Hill and Peckham in London, Chapeltown in Leeds, Highfields in Leicester, Moss Side in Manchester, St Paul's in Bristol, Central Middlesbrough, and Handsworth in Birmingham – where the government would send in task forces of two or three civil servants who would open up a shop front and endeavour to attract investment from private firms, in cooperation with the local council and voluntary groups. In April 1987, just before the general election, eight more inner-city task forces were set up, in Nottingham, Coventry, Doncaster, Hartlepool, Preston, Rochdale, Wolverhampton, and Tower Hamlets in London. Each task force was allocated a budget of £1 million. In Leicester, to take one example, this produced the Highfields Workshop Centre, which took thirty people, most of them Afro-Caribbeans, off the dole and into the repair of electrical goods and renovation of furniture. Clarke called his task forces a "bold experiment"; his opposite number on the Labour side, John Prescott, countered that it was a "mouse of a statement compared with the scale of the problem".[33] Certainly, £8 million spread around areas with a total population of 300,000, of whom more than one-fifth were unemployed adults, was not going to make a dramatic difference. In Middlesbrough, the least racially mixed of the eight areas but the one with the highest unemployment rate on the mainland, there were 11,401 dole claimants, which meant that the task force had an average of less than £90 to spend on each.

Small beer the scheme may have been, but it produced an interesting clash within the Conservative Party, in which free-market ideology collided with the government's intention of combating racial discrimination in the job market. The disagreement centred on a housing project in Handsworth, which had attracted a large amount of money in various forms of government grant. The issue was whether the private building firms carrying out the work should be allowed to bring their own, predominantly white workforce from outside, or be required to recruit from local Jobcentres, where claimants were mostly black. From the beginning, Clarke declared himself in favour of local recruitment,[34] and on a visit to Handsworth even spoke of the eventual emergence of a black middle class.[35] It will be remembered that, as an opposition spokesman, Clarke had campaigned hard against the blacklisting of firms which breached the Labour government's pay policy. Now, in effect, he was proposing to do the same to firms that imported white labourers into Handsworth.

According to contemporary newspaper reports, this provoked a furious argument inside the Cabinet, where his main opponent was the Environment Secretary Nicholas Ridley. As well as being a free-market ideologue, Ridley was seeking to prevent Labour councils from inserting political clauses into building contracts, for instance by blacklisting firms which hired non-union labour or worked on Cruise-missile bases. In October, it was reported that Clarke had emerged victorious from the conflict.[36] Clarke himself denied that there was a rift, saying that he supported Ridley on the issue of curbing Labour councils. In the event, a compromise was struck up by which councils were banned from imposing "contract compliance" under a bill published by Ridley in July 1987, whilst Clarke deployed the Race Relations Act to enforce contract compliance in Handsworth. As a result, the eighty-strong workforce that carried out the contract to modernize eighteen Victorian homes on Broughton Road, Handsworth included two dozen local men, aged between eighteen and twenty-four, who came off the dole to work with trained builders – a small but tremendously well publicized contribution to alleviating social stress in inner-city Birmingham.

Clarke's insistence on introducing what amounted to inverse discrimination, even on such a tiny scale, was too much for some Tories from the backwoods. Sir Nicholas Fairbairn, former Solicitor General for Scotland, accused him of being "plain racist" in his "discrimination" against whites, adding: "Mr Clarke should come to Scotland and the inner cities there, where he will find no blacks but a lot of Scots and a lot of unemployed".[37] But it was an opportune moment for Clarke to reinforce his reputation as a political infighter and human face of the Tory Party. A general election was drawing near.

CHAPTER EIGHT

"LORD YOUNG'S REPRESENTATIVE ON EARTH", PART TWO: THE CHANCELLOR OF THE DUCHY

Kenneth Clarke claims now that he does not know how he came by his reputation for being "combative". The best explanation he can offer is that politics is like a never-ending soap opera and its characters have to be simplistically typecast to make the plot easier to follow. "If you had told me when I started out in politics that I was going to be regarded as combative, or robust, I would have been very surprised", he says.[1] Be that as it may, this reputation was working to his advantage. Moreover, Clarke knew it was working for him, and at times his conduct gives rise to a suspicion that he was playing to the gallery. In the midst of the 1987 general election campaign, according to Lord Young, who by now was doubling up as vice-chairman of the Conservative Party, Mrs Thatcher was urged by her image adviser, Tim Bell: "'You've got to have the combative people – Kenneth Baker and Kenneth Clarke.' ... He went down a list of five or six people. 'We've got to concentrate on those for television, and use *only* those.' She accepted this",[2] but with one reservation: the next day, a Sunday, Mrs Thatcher fussily insisted that before Clarke was let loose on television screens, he must "smarten himself up". Soon afterwards, the nation was treated to Clarke's thoughts on Labour's industrial policy: "It isn't just foreign aggressors to which Neil Kinnock would show the white flag. It's now clear he has capitulated to his union paymasters as well."[3]

Clarke had been rather "combative" in the preceding weeks, after parliamentary debates had passed the point at which they were ever likely to shed light on the process of government and each day had become a party-political knockabout. In January 1987, the government put him up to give the closing speech in a parliamentary debate on the state of the economy when, strictly, it should have been made by Paul Channon, who had taken Brittan's place as Secretary of State for Trade and Industry. Channon was an old-style Tory nob who had effectively inherited his seat from his famous father, and who was eventually sacked for allowing Labour's John Prescott to make a fool of him too often. Clarke enjoyed mixing it with Prescott. During one perform-ance in February, he had been on his feet for more than half an hour when he was stopped by the Deputy Speaker to be reminded that he had done nothing but attack the Labour Party when he was supposed to be outlining government policy. He carried on regardless, accusing Prescott of talking "gibberish".[4]

Outside the Commons, Clarke addressed himself to the North–South divide. It was politically awkward for the government that its policies so far had widened the gap between the wealthy South and the deindustrialized North, so Clarke talked the problem out of existence. He conceded: "No one has ever denied that there is a disparity of opportunity in different parts of the country ... However, I do not agree that they [sic] are new or that they are increasing." Indeed, recovery was levelling out the differences, he claimed, by bringing unemployment down slightly more rapidly in the north than in the south. Hereafter, it was up to northern cities to pull themselves together. Although it might be "easier to attract new investment and jobs to Bracknell than to Gateshead, the answer is not simply to complain about it ... it involves changing Gateshead."[5] He even travelled to Manchester to chide "the pro-pensity of some northern people, who ought to know better, to accentuate a poor music hall image of themselves and the part of the world they come from ... The so-called North–South divide is a classic example of an un-necessary barrier which has perpetuated very tangible drawbacks to business investments."[6]

Meanwhile, with the unemployment figures heading down towards three million, Clarke felt able to predict that "the target of full employment is now well within our grasp."[7] Moreover:

There can no longer be any doubt that we are now enjoying extraordinary economic growth, so the real question facing us today is, will it last? If the experience of the 1960s and 70s is all we had to go by, I would have to answer no, but I believe that under Mrs Thatcher, Britain has seen such a change, and such irreversible change, that I can answer yes – yes, it can last. In the old days borrowing always threatened to get out of control. Today all that has changed.[8]

Only one thing seemed to stand in the way of this rosy prospect, namely the threat that Labour might be elected, and implement its policy of a national minimum wage. The figure that Labour proposed was £80 per week, a sum which Clarke's own department recognized as the approximate minimum below which it was arguable that the recipient would be better off claiming benefits. There were several million workers in specific service industries who were protected by minimum wages via twenty-six separate wages councils, which the government had been wondering whether it dare abolish. In the end, they had settled for legislation which tinkered with their powers, removing any minimum wage protection for teenagers for instance. In deciding to keep the wages councils, Clarke conceded that "I do not think one can apply the rules of the market to the employment of people." Even so, he claimed that Labour's proposed minimum wage would destroy six hundred thousand low-paid jobs.[9] This is not to say that he was giving any great credence to the possibility of Neil Kinnock being prime minister. Indeed, in April, he predicted that David Owen would emerge after the impending election as the Leader of the Opposition,[10] a forecast almost as inaccurate as his prognosis for the unemployment figures.

Clarke also opened fire on another favourite Tory target, the trade-union closed shop. His sentiments were a long way removed from what he had said in opposition, about the "value" of a closed shop to members and employers. On the contrary, he wrote in the *Sunday Express*: "The time has come to draw the remaining rotten teeth of the closed shop and remove the last traces of legal support."[11] It was immediately noticed that these were the words of a barrister who, when he was practising law, had benefited from membership of a closed and very self-protective professional group. He found it necessary to explain himself soon afterwards, in a speech to the Industrial Society: "I do not have to belong to the Bar Council to practise at the Bar. It is not actually a closed shop."[12]

After the general election, Clarke had better reason than ever to hope that he would finally be allowed a chance to be his own boss, in charge of a government department. Then he would never again have to face the sort of embarrassment that had afflicted him whilst he was campaigning in one par-liamentary by-election, where the Conservative candidate had formally intro-duced him to a party meeting as a minister "not in the Cabinet".[13] He was officially fourteenth in seniority in the post-election Cabinet. More impor-tantly, he was seen as having contributed to what had turned out to be an astoundingly good result for the Conservatives. According to the *Evening Standard*, "he is already being spoken of as a possible leader of the Conserva-tives when Mrs Thatcher finally sets off into the sunset."[14]

Once again, Thatcher had other ideas. Only two of the five outgoing Cabinet ministers had actually been in charge of departments, the others being the party chairman, the Lord Chancellor, and the Leader of the House of Commons. The party chairmanship is traditionally occupied by someone below Cabinet rank for the first couple of years after a general election, thereby freeing up one Cabinet salary. It was awarded to a grateful Lord Young, who had given his services to the government free for eight years. The sinecure of Chancellor of the Duchy of Lancaster – a title which, for some arcane reason, holds more prestige than that of Paymaster General – was also free; but as for the two vacancies for heads of department, Mrs Thatcher was determined that one should be filled by her fallen favourite, Cecil Parkinson, whom she judged to have served sufficient penance on the back benches for his behaviour towards his former lover. The other went to John MacGregor, so that his post as Chief Secretary to the Treasury became available to a new favourite, John Major. She also decided to promote Lord Young, by transferring him to the Department of Trade and Industry, which would take over responsibility for inner-cities policy, which was to be a government showpiece of the next few months; and she decided that, like it or not, he was keeping Kenneth Clarke as his deputy.

So Clarke packed his things at Caxton House, the headquarters of the Department of Employment, and moved round the corner into Victoria Street into a new office, doing a job which had not vastly changed, deputiz-ing for someone less experienced. Young had not wanted to move and did not want the working relationship to continue, not because of any personal differences with Clarke, but because he wanted to run his own show without having another Cabinet minister watching over him.[15] Clarke, obviously, would have liked to call it quits too and have his own department, instead of playing second fiddle in one which the prime minister liked to fill with ministers from her own wing of the party. His old adversary, Alan Clark, was already there, as Minister for Trade. The only other "wet" in the team of six, besides Clarke, was his new deputy, Robert Atkins, who, according to Clark, was "radiating bitterness and frustration"[16] because he thought he deserved a better job.

However, one of Clarke's great strengths was that he knew better than to radiate bitterness and frustration. One of the civil servants then employed at the DTI described his arrival, in place of the gentlemanly Paul Channon, as something of a shock.

> He could be a bully, and he had a certain way of conducting meetings. He would say "We're here at Point A, and we want to be there, at Point B, now you go away and work out how to do it." You didn't necessarily like the way he spoke to you, but you came away with a very clear idea of what he wanted.

The civil servants found him more formidable than Lord Young, which comes across in Young's memoirs: "The department quickly found out that Kenneth was drier in money matters than I was."[17] The DTI budget was held so tight that Clarke was invited to join the Star Chamber which sat in judgement over other departmental budgets. Nigel Lawson reckoned that of all the ministers who served in the Star Chamber in the years 1983–89, "the most effective ... were, in their different ways, Norman Tebbit and Kenneth Clarke."[18]

Clarke also saw the funny side of the absurd new status granted to him, Chancellor of the Duchy of Lancaster, a post dating back to 1399, previously held by Thomas More and Winston Churchill among many others. The County Palatine of Lancaster is the source of the Prince of Wales's vast private wealth. It owns 36,000 acres of agricultural land in Yorkshire and Lancashire, about 15,000 acres of woodland in North Yorkshire and South Wales, several hundred acres in Staffordshire, Cheshire and Shropshire, a castle in Pontefract, and valuable built-up land in Leeds, Leicestershire, Bradford, Lewes and London. The so-called "Savoy Estate", which includes a couple of acres off the Strand, in Westminster, is probably worth more than its entire agricultural holdings. It is administered by the Duchy Council, whose real head is the Vice-Chancellor, a High Court judge. The new Vice-Chancellor appointed in 1987 was none other than Sir Richard Scott, who would head the inquiry into the arms-for-Iraq affair seven years later. Clarke's role as Chancellor attracted a salary of £2,000 a year, "which is probably all I am worth";[19] and even that was docked from his Cabinet minister's salary.

Having been told that he was the minister responsible for the inner-cities programme, Clarke had to wage a long battle inside the Cabinet to hold on to it, against the Environment Secretary Nicholas Ridley. At the time, the government publicity machinery built up the "inner cities" as if they were the big issue of the moment. In retrospect, it is doubtful whether ministers ever took it all that seriously. Neither Mrs Thatcher, nor Nicholas Ridley, nor any other Cabinet minister who has published memoirs thought it mattered enough to be worth mentioning. The major government departments were absorbed in preparing highly controversial and complex legislation, like the health reforms and the introduction of the poll tax. This left them with a quiet period which they could fill up with a campaign that would generate publicity without costing much in government time or money. Phase two of the inner-cities programme fulfilled that function.

Nonetheless, Clarke would have lost face if someone else had been allowed to take over what was already seen as his project. According to Robin Oakley, the political editor of *The Times*, he and Ridley fought over who would deliver the "inner cities" speech at the autumn party conference. Ridley already had a local government speech to make, so he reportedly pushed for the job to go to a "neutral minister", leaving the question of who headed the inner-cities programme open.[20] Clarke won that round, but only in December, just a week before Christmas, did a brief government press release finally announce that his responsibilities had been extended to cover "coordination and presentation" of the inner-cities programme.

The following March, the great inner-cities initiative was launched at a glittering press conference featuring the prime minister and six Cabinet ministers. The fact that so many ministers were making themselves available to be questioned was a reliable sign that they had nothing worthwhile to say. Mrs Thatcher informed journalists that a new free phone line was being installed, to connect the public to Kenneth Clarke. "You say, where do you start? Well, you start with him." Unfortunately, unlike so many other members of the Cabinet, Clarke never quite lost his sense of the ridiculous, and jovially corrected the prime minister later by pointing out that the phones would be answered by operators not by him. When he said that, according to

James Naughtie, then of the *Guardian*, Mrs Thatcher "turned away with an expression suggesting that she had just sucked a lemon". Moreover:

> He was the only one of the ministers wheeled on by Mrs Thatcher who was not wearing the regulation dark suit. This, her expression seemed to say, was typical (and it was) ... He knows he irritates Her, but perhaps not why. In those circumstances, he has little choice. Hard work, a perpetual smile and a hope for better things. Mrs Thatcher says inner cities are important, so he knows he has an important job. Or has he?[21]

That afternoon, Clarke was in the Commons soldiering through a statement outlining twelve "initiatives" which made up the inner-cities programme, none of which was new or involved spending any substantial sums of money. Number 12 was to be a series of breakfasts with businessmen and other leading figures in the affected communities. Perhaps the most revealing remark Clarke made all day was when, in passing and without any obvious relevance to the matter in hand, he disparaged government White Papers, saying "it is usually published, read the next day and never referred to again by anyone."[22]

One document which seems to have suffered that fate was Clarke's attempt to sweep away some of the regulations that obstructed British business. While he was an Employment Minister, in May 1986, he produced *Building Businesses – Not Barriers*, which promised employers many things from a let-up in planning regulations and a review of VAT to a more personal approach from civil servants. John Prescott at once spotted the similarities between this and an earlier statement on the same subject by a Treasury minister, John Moore. "Was the same word processor used for the two statements?" he asked. "Remarkably I found that on 16 July 1985 there were 80 proposals in the White Paper and there are 80 proposals in this White Paper."[23] The main difference, however, was that Moore had forecast that his 80 proposals would create 8,000 jobs; Clarke was predicting a more modest 4,000. His campaign cannot have been an unqualified success, because seven years later Michael Heseltine, now President of the Board of Trade, launched another deregulation drive, claiming to have uncovered more than 500 expendable items on the statute book.[24]

The most important decision taken in the DTI during Clarke's period there was to sell off the state-owned Rover group to British Aerospace, itself recently privatized. The decision was entirely Lord Young's, including the details of secret "sweeteners", some of which subsequently ran foul of EC rules and had to be repaid. Clarke's role was to defend the deal in the House of Commons, which he did by means of the unfortunate forecast that after privatization "the company should be removed at long last from the spotlight of political debate and the political battlefield",[25] and that British Aerospace looked upon it as a "long term acquisition"[26] which would bring the troubled company a "period of stability". Nevertheless, just as a precaution, the government had inserted a clause in the agreement according to which British Aerospace would have to repay the taxpayer part of the proceeds were it to sell any part of Rover for a quick profit within five years. Unfortunately, the Rover deal produced years of political controversy, including Select Committee hearings and a ruling from the European Commission, and far from being committed to it as a "long term acquisition", British Aerospace sold it to the German car manufacturers BMW within months of the expiry of the five-year period.

Even if Clarke had known that Britain was to lose control of its last big motor manufacturer, it is unlikely that he would have acted differently. He had always backed the right of multinational companies to shift capital around the globe unhindered by national borders. When MPs objected to the proposed takeover of Rowntree, the confectionary manufacturer, by the Swiss firm Nestlé, he told them it was "chauvinistic nonsense" to think that the "alleged nationality" of a firm influenced the number of jobs it retained in the UK, and warned that "little Englander" attitudes could undermine the interests of British firms which had bought up approximately £12 billion of foreign assets during 1986 alone. "We are by no means a satellite economy", he said. "We are the major predator of overseas companies."[27]

It was this internationalism which had underpinned his support for the European project; but this did not commit him to supporting all the legislation or joint projects emanating from Brussels. Indeed, there were two notable instances of Clarke marching into European negotiations apparently spoiling for a fight. The first was over the beginnings of what later became known as the Social Contract, when European Commissioners were considering detailed legislation which would standardize certain employment legislation, allowing three months' statutory parental leave for employees with young children, and extending social-security protection to the wives or husbands of the self-employed. Four weeks before Mrs Thatcher was due to begin a six-month stint as EC president, Clarke loudly denounced the entire package as "piffle" and emerged from a ministerial meeting in Luxembourg complaining that it had spent two and a half hours on "an obscure directive on farmers' wives" – farmers being, in most cases, self-employed. He put forward counter-proposals, backed by Ireland and Italy, which offered the typical Thatcherite remedies for unemployment: deregulation and "flexible" labour relations.[28]

Later, after his move from Employment to the DTI, there was an extraordinary confrontation, which launched Kenneth Clarke into the politics of outer space. Ever since the days when the first man set foot on the moon, Britain's interest in space exploration had been minimal. Such as it was, it concentrated on satellite technology with clearly defined military and commercial applications. There were signs, though, that the policy might change after Geoffrey Pattie, one of the party's abler right-wing intellectuals, was appointed Minister for Information Technology in 1984. Rather daringly, for a minister in the Thatcher government, Pattie declared that investment in high-risk new technology could not be left to the market,[29] a view which was certainly supported in academic circles, and which had some backing from industry. A new British National Space Centre was opened in January 1985. When the European Space Agency met in Rome, in February, other European ministers were rather pleasantly surprised to find Britain's representative, Pattie, stressing a positive interest in space technology. He appealed for ESA backing for a new space-launch vehicle being developed by British Aerospace and Rolls Royce, known as HOTOL.[30]

At some point late in 1985, the government's mood changed, probably as an indirect result of the Westland saga. The very idea of a state-funded European space project sounded suspiciously like Heseltine's aborted helicopter consortium. Pattie no longer had a secretary of state capable of backing him up, and after the 1987 election he was sacked, with a knighthood for compensation. In July, funds for the space centre were unexpectedly cut, and its director Roy Gibson resigned in disgust.

It was here that Clarke stepped into the story. He had an informal agreement with Lord Young that he always handled negotiations with Europe. On this occasion he did so with an absence of finesse which was almost Thatcherite. He was due at a ministerial meeting at the Hague in November

1987 to discuss an ambitious programme including a manned orbiting module called Columbus, to be built by Germany, a French space rocket called Ariane–5, and a piloted mini-shuttle called Hermes, to be built by the French and launched on Ariane–5. Clarke set the tone in advance by berating the European Space Agency as a "highly expensive club with an over ambitious programme."[31] On another occasion, he accused them of indulging in "grandiose prestige projects that are of dubious scientific and economic value".[32] He then published an article calling for a "fundamental reappraisal" of the ESA, whose spending was scheduled to increase by 150 per cent by 1992, forcing the UK's annual contribution to increase by over £200 million, the equivalent of a dozen new hospitals a year.[33] During his two-day meeting in The Hague he was in a minority of one, which did not quieten him down at all. Undiplomatically, he accused the ESA of "growing like topsy", consuming money which would be better spent on other projects. According to the *Financial Times*, he had overridden the advice of his own officials, who had advised him to be conciliatory, and "in the end, the harassment tactics backfired and drove other countries closer together."[34] In the Commons his Labour "shadow", Bryan Gould, pointed out that he had failed in his stated objective of bringing about a reassessment of the European space programme;[35] but Clarke was not in the mood to apologize. He said: "I still think I'm right and they are wrong. If these countries want to frolic in space on their own then that's their affair."[36]

Perhaps his reason for charging in so aggressively was that, as someone who believed in Europe, he thought it particularly important to stop Europe from being wasteful; although in the short term, all he seems to have achieved was to reinforce Britain's reputation in Europe for being unreliable. Alternatively, he may have been playing to a gallery back home in 10 Downing Street. He never succeeded in convincing Mrs Thatcher that he was not a Heathite corporatist intent on using the state to intervene in industry, but he certainly tried. Whatever the motive, in the longer term he was vindicated. After the Cold War and German reunification, with Europe in recession, Hermes was scrapped, Columbus was left in limbo, and the time for expensive commitments to space exploration had passed.

In his days as a transport minister, Clarke had treated the issue of privatization pragmatically, even taking a sideswipe at "boring" Tories who started from the principle "private sector, good: public sector, bad". However, that had since become a tenet of ideological certainty which had gripped the government. Every departmental minister was expected to find something to privatize. Clarke found British Steel. Immediately after the 1987 Conservative Party conference, Clarke called in to Lord Young's office and told him that British Steel's half-yearly returns were about to show a healthy profit, and it only required a short, simple piece of legislation to convert it into a private company. There was, though, the political problem of finding space in the parliamentary timetable for snap legislation which would certainly provoke opposition from the Labour Party.[37] It was partly for that reason that Clarke proceeded with uncharacteristic diplomacy.

It was never publicized at the time that he met privately with John Smith, who was then Labour's shadow chancellor. Clarke regarded Smith with some respect as one of the pro-marketeers who had broken the Labour whip in order to secure British entry into the EC in 1972. He once said of him: "We agree on one or two political issues rather too often for our respective political good."[38] On this occasion, though, the meeting was tense. Clarke says: "I made it clear that I didn't see privatization of British Steel as an end in itself" but, nonetheless, "he got quite cross with me."[39] However, Clarke did ascertain that the best thing he could do to mute the reaction from the Labour side was to secure the huge Ravenscraig steel plant, near Motherwell, which was vital to the economy in that part of Scotland. He duly made an agreement with Bob Scholey, chairman of British Steel, that Ravenscraig would stay open for at least seven years after privatization. The Motherwell MP John Reid sarcastically and perhaps prophetically called it "a timetable for execution".[40] Nonetheless, in Lord Young's opinion it was that which "effectively disarmed the Scottish lobby".[41]

In December, British Steel announced a half-yearly profit of £190 million. Two months later, Clarke presented a parliamentary bill which would not technically privatize British Steel, but would convert it to a limited company wholly owned by the government, which could then be privatized without any further legislation. There was a mild risk attached, because this was the first privatization since BP, which had gone horribly wrong when the stock market collapsed in October 1987; but no one would have thought so listening to Clarke address the Commons. He claimed: "The nationalisation–privatisation debate is effectively over in this country."[42] His argument for privatization was that steel had made massive losses because no previous government had been prepared to face up to the harsh necessity of closing steelworks like those at Consett and Corby until the Thatcher government came along. The sale of British Steel was completed after Clarke had moved on, but there is no doubt that it was his initiative.

Clarke also barred the Post Office from expanding the services available at its counters to include the sale of insurance and travel documents and the handling of building-society accounts, although this had been accepted by the Monopolies and Mergers Commission and welcomed by small building societies who needed access to a high-street network. From a Thatcherite point of view, the Post Office's problem was that it was an efficient, successful state-owned business which employed 200,000 people, performed a valuable service, and made a huge profit. In short, it undermined the maxim that the private sector is best. Privatization of the Royal Mail had been ruled out by Thatcher herself, reputedly because of objections from the Queen. As a first step, however, Clarke arranged for the Post Office's successful business venture, Girobank, to be sold off. One business journalist, the *Guardian*'s Mike Smith, claimed that "in simplistic political terms, Mr Clarke does not want to be responsible for creating a dynamic, expansive public sector corporation. The result is that the Post Office is left in something of a hiatus."[43]

If Clarke had stuck rigidly by his Heathite origins, he would have sought an "industrial strategy" or even a "plan", uniting government, management and unions. Heath's former chief whip, Francis Pym, called for just that in a debate on unemployment in the House of Commons in 1986. Clarke's response was to make a joke of it, saying that it was like listening to his "former headmaster".[44] However, even a government which, in Pym's words, "spurns industrial policy as some sort of heresy", has to be involved in some strategic questions. Shipbuilding, for example, is so dependent on the military budget that, in effect, it is up to the government whether a shipyard stays open or goes into liquidation. Ships had been built at the mouth of the River Wear, around Sunderland, for hundreds of years. In the mid 1980s, Sunderland had one of the world's most technologically advanced shipyards, served by a highly skilled workforce. It is closed now and may never reopen, largely because of decisions taken by Kenneth Clarke.

In 1988, Clarke decided to privatize what remained of British shipbuilding, which consisted now of four regionally based companies, three of which were successfully sold and are still operating at the time of writing. The fourth was

North East Shipbuilders Ltd, which owned three yards employing about two thousand people around Sunderland. Since the government wanted to be rid of them, and they were running out of work, there was a clear threat that the yard could close, putting thousands of men on the dole in a city which until relatively recently had had one of the worst unemployment levels in Britain. However, in April 1988, Clarke visited Sunderland after one of his highly publicized breakfasts with business leaders, in nearby Newcastle, and convinced himself that the opening of a large Nissan car factory and other developments had basically secured the town's economic future, with or without the shipyards. The government had only just completed the sale of a shipyard in Govan, on the Clyde, to a Norwegian company. There was, therefore, one shipyard on the British mainland with a secure future, and in the tortuous negotiations that followed, Clarke acted as if that was good enough for him.

The prospect of an order for ships from the state-owned Cuban line, Mambisa, persuaded NESL managers and the local Sunderland MP Bob Clay that the yard could be saved. The order required subsidy by the British government, which was not at all unusual in the shipping industry. But Clarke simply refused to treat the Cuban order as a serious proposition, and insisted that the yard would have to be privatized and that any new order would have to manage without subsidies. The yard eventually closed in December 1988 – after Clarke had moved on to another Cabinet job – and 2,000 men were made redundant. With cruelly bad timing, this happened just as shipbuilding appeared to be recovering from a worldwide slump. Unexpectedly, two foreign bidders, from Greece and Germany, stepped in with offers to buy the yard and reopen it. Neither required subsidy. At this point, the final blow to Sunderland's hopes was delivered by Sir Leon Brittan, now the European Commissioner in charge of competition policy, who claimed that the British government had promised not only that Sunderland would close, but that it would not be reopened for shipbuilding for at least five years.[45] Even when the five years had expired, in January 1994, it emerged that the yard could not be used even to repair ships for yet another five years without permission from Brussels, for which the British government had no intention of asking.[46]

What had happened, in short, was that far from allowing market forces to operate, the state – in the form of the Department of Trade and the European Commission – had intervened to force the closure of a well-equipped and potentially profitable shipyard in an area of high unemployment. Whoever was responsible for sealing Sunderland's fate, it was not Tony Newton, who took over from Clarke at the Department of Trade in July 1988, and devoted six months to what appeared to be a genuine attempt to keep it open.

The yard's death knell had implicitly been sounded in the last statement Clarke made to the Commons as a DTI minister, when he warned that "it would be wrong for me to disguise ... the fact that there is a very large question mark over the future of the Sunderland yards."[47] In retrospect, he makes no bones about it:

> It would have closed quicker if I had stayed. I always thought that the Cuban order was a mirage. The Cubans would have taken ships off us if we had given them away, but they were in no position to pay for any ships. In the medium term, the best thing for Sunderland was to stop hoping that the shipyard was going to rise again. Sunderland needed to forget shipbuilding and acquire another economy. Washington New Town and Nissan was the future.[48]

However, despite outward appearances, Clarke says that he has not fundamentally changed his opinion about privatization as a general policy.

> I never did get terribly passionate about the question of ownership. It was something I never got frightfully worked up about. I was extremely impressed by the success of the management buyout of the National Freight Corporation, which turned the company into a rip-roaring success. One of the benefits was to depoliticise management. It should not be left to political parties to argue about how to run industries like British Rail. I think in every case privatisation has lifted the performance of the industry.

The charge laid against Kenneth Clarke by his old Cambridge contemporary Nick Budgen is that he was fired by a particular set of ideas when he was a government whip in the early 1970s and has never moved on.[49] There may be an underlying truth in that, but like any other professional politician, Clarke has had to adapt to prevailing political fashion, and in the late 1980s, when it was very fashionable to be a free-marketeer, he shifted to the right. It paid off. In July 1988, he was appointed Secretary of State for Health.

CHAPTER NINE

HEALTH SECRETARY

Unfortunately for Kenneth Clarke, the Cabinet reshuffle came at the start of what is known as the silly season. With the Commons away on a long summer vacation and the government doing well, there was nothing to keep politics interesting, unless a story of some kind could be generated from nowhere. Kenneth Clarke and his health team turned out to be it. They ought to have known better. Mrs Thatcher had filled her new health team with ministers celebrated for their skill at presentation: Clarke, David Mellor and Edwina Currie, who between them must have had as much skill at headline grabbing as any ministerial team ever assembled in Westminster. (Despite their political differences, Mrs Thatcher paid tribute to Clarke in her memoirs as "an extremely effective Health minister – tough, ... direct and persuasive."[1]) But during their first few months, while Clarke was working on what was to be the biggest reform of the National Health Service since its foundation, they attracted nothing but bad publicity, much of it trivia dressed up as political controversy.

First, there was the question of whether Clarke himself was the right man to educate the public on healthy living. Part of the minister's job is to persuade people to take exercise, stick to a suitable diet, give up self-destructive habits like smoking, and generally do what they could to avoid becoming an unnecessary burden on the health service. Yet here was Kenneth Clarke, measuring 5 ft 10½ inches and weighing 13½ stone, a habitual smoker, a lager drinker, who had once admitted with appealing frankness, "I don't take any exercise of any kind myself, apart from the occasional walk."[2]

"Kenneth Clarke looks like an advertisement for health disease. He is fat. He drinks beer. He smokes. He takes no exercise ... Having Mr Clarke as Health Minister is rather like having a convicted burglar as Lord Chief

Justice", said the *Sun*.[3] "Piglet, as Kenneth Clarke is known to his children, waddled through the Department of Health front door and posed while the photographers fiddled for their wide angled lenses", said *Today*.[4] The coverage exaggerated his weight to 15 stone and reduced his height by an inch and a half, and gave him a wholly inaccurate medical history of heart trouble. In fact, Clarke's constitution refused, like Winston Churchill's, to do the decent thing and give way under a lifetime of abuse. Into his fifties, he had never been in hospital. The most serious complaint he had ever had was a leg muscle pulled in 1987 during a cricket match.[5] In September 1988, he answered some of the speculation about his fitness by joining twenty other members of Rushcliffe Conservative Association in a ten-mile sponsored walk, which raised £3,000 for party funds.[6] This was all in marked contrast to the previous Health Secretary John Moore, a fitness freak up early every morning using his exercise bicycle, whose health broke down under the strain of the job.

A serious point could be made, though, about Clarke's smoking habit. After all, it costs the National Health Service £610 million a year to treat patients for illnesses and diseases resulting from smoking.[7] The fact that Clarke was addicted to tobacco might have provoked less of a reaction had he been less brazenly unapologetic about it. Having given up cigarettes years earlier, restricting himself to small cigars, he was less culpable than Labour's former chain-smoking Health Secretary, Barbara Castle. However, Mrs Castle at least appreciated that smoking was a health issue and delegated the task of doing something about it to her non-smoking and medically trained deputy, David Owen. Owen fought a hard departmental battle to have tobacco designated as a product to be controlled under the 1968 Medicines Act, a small enough measure in itself, and a compromise between the competing claims of cigarette makers and anti-smoking campaigners, which anyway never reached the statute book because "the tobacco industry mobilised their supporters among the MPs and they used their considerable influence over the legislative programme to ensure that it was postponed indefinitely."[8] He could have added that one of the MPs who campaigned hardest against anti-smoking legislation was Kenneth Clarke.

One Friday in the late 1970s, Clarke took the trouble to stay in London to help lead the opposition to a private members' bill sponsored by the Labour MP Robert Kilroy-Silk, who wanted tougher restrictions on tobacco sales.

Clarke was not only opposed to that, but used the occasion to denounce a government order, announced by David Owen, under which cigarette manufacturers would have to seek approval for any new substitutes or additives in their products. Clarke claimed it was unnecessary to use the law, because the industry was prepared to conform to the new policy voluntarily. He feared the order could "pave the way for a more stringent statutory regulation". The particular horror he foresaw – although no minister had said anything about it – was a ban on tobacco advertising, which would be a disaster for such sports as motor racing, cricket, angling and tennis, and would kill off the Conductor of the Year award. He also suggested that cigarette advertising might be good for public health, if it encouraged smokers to switch away from older and more dangerous cigarette brands. He went on:

> I can understand the exasperation growing on the part of the tobacco industry, which is manufacturing a lawful product. They are involved in impossible negotiations. They are being asked to give only one concession, but then we go on to the next one. There is no finality … They are entitled to ask how much further they will have to go … To do good to people who do not wish to have it done to them seems to me to have no justification.[9]

Actually, there were instances when Clarke had backed legislation which would "do good to people who do not wish to have it done to them". As a former transport minister, for example, he had supported a change in the law which compelled motor cyclists to wear crash helmets, despite religious objections from Sikhs. There were no Sikhs in his Rushcliffe constituency, but there were a substantial number of people employed at the large Player cigarette factory in Nottingham. This sponsored Nottingham's annual tennis tournament, which claimed to be second only to Wimbledon in the British tennis calendar. Consequently "the well-being of the area I represent is very much affected by the well-being of the tobacco industry."[10]

Clarke was undeniably consistent in defending smokers' rights. It was reported that the Health Secretary's aides and advisers wanted to turn their new headquarters in Richmond House, Whitehall – the old offices at the Elephant and Castle, which he hated, having been bequeathed to the Social Security department – into a smoke-free work environment by compelling smokers to indulge their habit outside shared offices. They were overruled by

Clarke in person, who was unmoved even by their protestations that smoke could ruin the new light pastel coats of paint which had brightened up their walls.[11] It was not until Virginia Bottomley's reign that Richmond House became smoke free. By then, Clarke had taken his smoking habit to the Home Office. There, the Home Office's Establishments division marked the approach of National No Smoking Day, in spring 1993, by declaring its Queen Anne's Gate headquarters, in central London, a no-smoking zone. This brought forth a retaliatory memo from the Home Secretary informing his officials that "No decisions will be taken without ministers' approval … and I make the rules."[12]

One initiative he inherited from John Moore in 1988 was an advertising campaign entitled "Look After Your Heart", which concentrated on the dangers of smoking and cholesterol. The next major television advertising campaign was to begin immediately after Christmas, when television slots could be bought relatively cheaply. The government had also recently taken to promoting No Smoking Day, during which addicts were encouraged to curtail or drop the habit for twenty-four hours. The term "passive smoking" had only just entered the nation's vocabulary, helped by a report published in 1987 by the government's Independent Scientific Committee on Smoking and Health. Like it or not, his department was already committed to doing a limited amount of good to people who might not want it done to them. However, there was a simple administrative answer on hand, which was to delegate the anti-smoking campaign to Edwina Currie, an asthmatic who had never smoked a cigarette in her life and had no compunction about lecturing others on the subject.[13] Until December, this is what Clarke did. Then David Mellor was suddenly sent in her place to handle negotiations on EC directives about health warnings on cigarette packets. The official British view was that minor decisions like this should be decided at national level rather than in Brussels, and Clarke was reportedly "furious" at Mrs Currie for taking a pro-EC line. The argument ended with Britain, in a minority of one, being overruled and having to knuckle under. Clarke was unapologetic: "Irritating though it is, this is not of earth shattering importance."[14]

Generally, though, Kenneth Clarke understood how to delegate. From the moment he had a department of his own to run, it became apparent that he was not going to be one of those insecure and hyperactive managers, like Margaret Thatcher, who could not bear to leave others alone to get on with their jobs. In August 1988, barely a fortnight after his appointment, he set off abroad, as usual, for the month's family holiday which had been a fixture throughout his working life. Since he attached so much importance to his own family's summer break, he could hardly demand of either David Mellor or Edwina Currie, both of whom had teenage children, that they reorganize theirs. Consequently, for part of August, the administration of government health policies was delegated to the civil service. In itself, that may not have been a bad idea. Unfortunately, Labour's Robin Cook was far too sharp to let the opportunity slip by. The absentee health team became the next silly season special, with tabloid newspapers scrabbling over one another to track Clarke down to his Mediterranean hideaway, in scenes reminiscent of the previous year's battle to be the first newspaper to rescue Blackie the Donkey from the Spaniards. The *People* offered a £500 reward for a sighting of the "so-called Health Minister". Clarke claimed that bribes of up to £10,000 had been offered to anyone who would reveal his whereabouts. The police were called to the hospital where his daughter, Sue, was working, to prevent journalists from harassing her. Gillian Clarke's elderly mother was also approached.[15] Eventually, the *Daily Mail* tracked him down to a farmhouse in the hills in Northern Spain, where he reputedly kept in touch with Whitehall from a roadside call-box.[16]

When the summer was over, Clarke's department was plunged into another controversy which occupied far more acreage of newsprint than any other, although it concerned the obscure subject of salmonella poisoning in eggs. Health officials had become alarmed by the rising graph of instances of food poisoning. There had been a steady increase for five years, until 1988 when it seemed to achieve vertical take-off. During the first ten months of that year, there were 23,038 cases in England and Wales, compared with 12,322 for the whole of 1982. Almost the entire increase could be attributed to 10,544 reported cases of *Salmonella enteritidis* PT4, a new variant of salmonella which, apart from its highly unpleasant effects on individuals, had the worrying property that it could live inside eggs without doing any harm to the hen, enabling it to spread undetected. In one celebrated example, it infiltrated a reception at the House of Lords for the London Magistrates Associate, laying low a large number of peers and JPs.

Although the story had its funny side, in excess of five hundred cases a week of people affected badly enough to take their complaint to a doctor or to hospital was too serious to be ignored. In July, the health department warned NHS catering managers against using raw eggs. In August, the Chief Medical Officer turned that into a warning to the public at large, with special emphasis on vulnerable groups like pregnant women and the elderly. Later, the alarm spread to include eggs that had been only lightly cooked, which produced another official warning in November. None of this need have embroiled the health department in political controversy. Its task was only to alert the public; the Ministry of Agriculture had to take on the difficult question of whether egg producers should be compensated for the slump in their business. That is until the focus of attention suddenly switched from the salmonella epidemic to what many people in Westminster regarded as a much bigger pain in the gut: the junior health minister, Edwina Currie.

Since she first took office in 1986, under Norman Fowler, Mrs Currie had shown an exceptional talent for making front-page news out of health education. Her expressed belief was that it was more important to achieve coverage in the *Sun* and the *Daily Mirror* than in the *Guardian*. In this, she excelled. Soon after her appointment, she visited Newcastle-upon-Tyne and, whilst she was there, made a few remarks in front of a television camera implying that the cause of the North's health problems was not poverty but ignorance, which caused northerners to drink, smoke and eat crisps in excess. Years later, she admitted that these remarks were made off the cuff when she was in a foul temper because her visit had been badly arranged,[17] but at the time, she flatly refused to back down when challenged. This became a mark of her ministerial career: an occasional outburst which caused waves of offence, followed by a flat refusal to apologize or explain.

During the 1987 general election, she told a surgeon who tackled her on the government's underfunding of the NHS to "fuck off". In March 1988, she delivered some succinct advice to teenage girls, via the magazine *Family Circle*: "Don't screw around and don't smoke".[18] In September 1988 she met the fears that elderly people would die of hypothermia because of high fuel costs in the coming winter by advising them to stock up on woolly socks, hats and longjohns, and have their hot-water bottles ready. The following morning's *Daily Mirror* featured a mock-up picture on its front page of Mrs Currie in woolly underwear, looking like Scrooge.[19]

All this made her astonishingly famous. Although she was on the most junior rung of the government, with only two years' experience, she was one of about five Conservative politicians at most who could genuinely claim to be a household name. One opinion poll showed that five times more voters could identify Edwina Currie than Kenneth Clarke. A local newspaper then carried out a straw poll in Nottingham, and found that even in the Health Secretary's home territory she was almost five times as famous as he was. Clarke's response was: "I'm glad I'm not as instantly recognisable as Edwina Currie. It means I can go to pubs and football matches without being bothered."[20] This would have made her a vulnerable political target even if she had had strong family connections and old-school charm. In fact, her offhand manner added to the number of her enemies. She was riding for a fall, and – improbably – it was the salmonella outbreak that brought her down. During a television interview, early in December 1988, she repeated the standard line that whilst millions of eggs were being safely consumed every week, some were a danger to the public, adding the fateful words: "We do warn people now that most of the egg production in this country, sadly, is now infected with salmonella."[21]

The effect of those words, broadcast on the main Saturday evening news, was to send egg sales spiralling downwards, while the blood pressure of Conservative MPs with egg factories in their constituencies rose. One Tory MP stood up during Prime Minister's Question Time in the Commons to make a public demand that Currie be sacked. Throughout this clamour, Currie kept stubbornly silent. This was in character: in the past, she had always refused to apologize or explain; but this time, she had offended a body of opinion wealthy and well-connected enough to take revenge. Within ten days of her remarks, she had been forced to resign.

Kenneth Baker, who would shortly be appointed Conservative Party chairman, later interpreted this strange episode as "a sort of turning-point" in the history of the Thatcher government, "where everything that happened subsequently seemed to go wrong", and heaped the blame upon Kenneth Clarke, who "could have resolved the matter either by forcing Edwina to retract or modify her statement, or saying something himself; but, for whatever reason, the smack of firm government failed to descend".[22] Certainly, no one on the Conservative side emerged very creditably from this episode. Mrs Currie's words had been badly chosen, and contributed to a drastic drop in egg sales which threatened to put several poultry farmers out of business. For example, 239 people were laid off by a chicken factory in Monklands, near Glasgow, in

February; the management blamed Edwina Currie. It would be surprising if Clarke had not heard complaints too from poultry farmers in his constituency, who had lobbied him on this or that from the day he entered parliament. As a brand new MP, with the first written question he had submitted to a minister and on the first occasion when he used a parliamentary device known as an adjournment debate to speak on a topic of his choice, he was lobbying for Nottinghamshire's poultry farmers. At that time they were badly hit by an infectious disease nicknamed "fowl pest". Whenever a single case was detected, the entire stock had to be slaughtered to prevent contagion. This happened on 140 occasions in Nottinghamshire in 1970. The unlucky farmers, according to Clarke, were not insured, not compensated, and were not receiving the public sympathy they deserved. He wondered aloud why this should be true of poultry growers but not dairy farmers. "Whether cattle evoke greater sympathy than chickens I do not know. Perhaps there is something about their eyes that evoke sympathy", he mused.[23] Unusually for the time of night, Clarke had an audience of six MPs, including Norman Fowler, all anxious to speak up for the poultry farmers.

Without doubt, almost every Tory MP with a rural constituency was hearing the complaints of poultry farmers in 1988 about how the salmonella scare was ruining their businesses. With a few careless words on prime-time television, Mrs Currie turned herself into a convenient focus for their anger. However, it was not her job as a health minister to represent the financial concerns of farmers, and Clarke obviously felt that jealousy and anti-feminist prejudice were also factors working against her. His advice to her, as he confirmed at a subsequent hearing by the Commons Agriculture Committee, was to keep her mouth shut. He then displayed just how concerned he was about the affair by allowing himself to be photographed watching Notts Forest lose 1–0 at the City ground in Nottingham. After Currie's resignation, he defended her as an "extremely valuable member of the team" and accused other MPs of being "a little envious of her natural gift for obtaining publicity".[24]

All in all, this was an uncomfortable incident in the life of the Thatcher government, but it is difficult to see it as anything more than that. Mrs Currie was so outspoken and hooked on publicity that there was always the risk that one day, as Labour's Robin Cook put it, her "embarrassment quotient" would exceed her "entertainment value". In the end, he surmised: "The government will let her insult pensioners, caricature northerners and threaten child benefit, but stubbing the toes of the National Farmers' Union is going too far."[25]

The impact of the salmonella-in-eggs affair on the public at large was much less than that of another parliamentary row rumbling at the same time, when the Cabinet decided to abolish free eye and dental tests. This caused what threatened at one point to be a serious rebellion on the Conservative back benches, involving up to sixty Tory MPs, which David Mellor did nothing to defuse by adopting a debating style that made Clarke look conciliatory. It was probably for that reason that Mellor was later moved to another job and replaced by Virginia Bottomley, an ally of Clarke's and an assiduous attender at Amesbury Group dinners, who would eventually become the public face of the health service. The new changes were hard to defend, since the economy was allegedly in such good shape that the government could afford an enormous reduction in the top rate of income tax. It was also made against the advice of the Chief Medical Officer. To have offered the excuse that it was being done under pressure from the Treasury and its Chief Secretary, John Major, would have been an admission of weakness, so Clarke went out of his way to deny it. He said:

> I have the greatest respect for John Major, who is a personal friend. We discussed [the funding of the NHS] for a long time. One meeting lasted five and a half hours. At the end of it, we had not settled very much so we had to start again. Throughout those discussions, I never reopened this question.[26]

Actually, according to a later account Clarke gave of the same meeting to a sympathetic journalist, he probably did reopen this question, because he and John Major apparently went through the "whole field" of health expenditure without either of them giving way. What seems to have happened is that Clarke had gone into the meeting thinking he could browbeat the inexperienced and inoffensive looking Chief Secretary into increasing the health budget to help him through a difficult period, only to find that Major was harder, and closer to Thatcher's way of thinking on public spending, than he had realized. Eventually, Major ended the meeting by losing his temper, or pretending to; they met again and struck a compromise in about ten minutes.[27] It did not include giving any ground on charges for eye or dental tests. Instead, Clarke defended charges from first principles, claiming that no one would be put off having their eyes or teeth tested because they had to pay; on the contrary, charges might increase uptake because of the general fact that people value only the things which cost money. The trouble with that argument is that it could apply to virtually any service provided by the NHS. Clarke's old university chum, Hugh Dykes, warned him that he might be "the victim of a long term Adam Smith design to impose charges in all sorts of screening services in hospitals, clinics and other institutions."[28] The measure scraped through the Commons by a margin of eight votes, as a much-diminished group of Tory rebels, including Michael Heseltine and former health minister Barney Hayhoe, voted against it. Getting it through the House of Lords required even more energetic government whipping. In total, 467 peers took part in the vote, the third biggest turnout in the twentieth century, giving the government a majority of just over forty.

Of all the measures that Clarke piloted through the Commons as Health Secretary, the one which roused the strongest emotions was the Human Fertilisation and Embryology bill, the first legislation in Britain on the relatively recent phenomenon of research conducted on human embryos. This was sensibly treated as a matter of conscience. MPs were free to vote for or against embryo research; the government merely insisted that there must be some legislation where none had existed before, so Clarke was not campaigning as a minister for any particular outcome. As an MP, though, he voted in favour of embryo research, having declared himself as an "enthusiastic supporter" of it. This was in line with his liberalism on most social issues. Abortion was already legal by the time he was an MP, but there were a number of attempts to reverse or restrict it, which Clarke consistently opposed. While the embryology bill was being debated, there was a series of votes on whether to amend the law which in effect made abortions after the embryo was twenty-eight weeks old illegal. Clarke voted with the majority, to set the new limit at twenty-four weeks.

A year after the conclusion of Mrs Currie's adventures, Clarke was grappling with a far more serious distraction. Britain's ambulance drivers had taken him on in a pay dispute that lasted almost six months. The union leaders were remarkably successful at keeping public opinion on their side. When they went out in the streets with collection buckets, the public showered money on them, according to the *Independent on Sunday*, "as though their cause had Bob Geldof in command".[29] The dispute arose from the different pay formulas applied to the three emergency services. The police had done well under the Conservatives: by 1989, a trainee began at a salary of £10,587 p.a., a qualified officer was paid at least £12,756, and a constable with fifteen years' service, £16,521. New recruits to the fire brigade did better in the early years, starting at £11,505 and receiving £13,180 when they were trained, although the rise after fifteen years' service was a paltry £583. Of the three services, ambulance drivers were worse off at every stage of their careers, since their pay began at £7,340, and rose to £10,093, with no extra reward for long service. In other words, an ambulance driver who had been responding to emergencies for over fifteen years was worse paid than the rawest young policemen or fireman on the scene. The reason was that, in the government's eyes, ambulance drivers were NHS employees, qualifying for the same pay awards as other health staff. For years, their pay had been settled by the so-called Whitley Councils, which predated the Thatcher government. However, during the Thatcher years, all the staff covered by Whitley Councils, who made up two-fifths of the NHS payroll and a third of its wages bill, had done badly compared with lower-paid workers in the private sector. The ambulance drivers had done better than other health service employees, such as the administrative and clerical staff whose pay fell 28 per cent behind inflation in the years 1979–87. Nonetheless, in the mid 1970s, ambulance drivers had been better paid than the average manual worker; but by the late 1980s, they were earning 8 per cent less.

By summer 1989, prices were rising out of the government's control, and homeowners were suffering from high interest rates, yet Chancellor Nigel Lawson had been able to cut taxes and declare a government surplus for two years in a row. Moreover, Clarke's proposed health reforms were now public knowledge, embroiling him in a propaganda war with almost the entire medical profession. He needed a pay dispute with 22,500 ambulance drivers about as much as he needed a hole in the head. In June, when the question of a pay deal with the National Union of Railwaymen came to Cabinet, other ministers around the table were surprised to hear Clarke pitch in demanding that the government take a stand, even at the risk of a prolonged rail strike. They ignored him, and granted the railwaymen an above-inflation award of 8.8 per cent.

Clarke did not have a special grievance against the NUR, but it was going to be a hard task to persuade the electorate that ambulance drivers, who commanded much more public sympathy than railway workers, should settle for less. After the ambulance drivers, other groups of health workers would submit their demands, probably using the ambulance settlement as a benchmark. Whereas British Rail had three ways of meeting a pay award – by adding the cost to fares, extracting extra money from the Exchequer, or cutting services – the NHS had only two. As the economy ran out of control, and the hatches were battened down on public spending, Clarke's chances of adding an extra 10 per cent or more to the health budget were nil. He knew very well that the Cabinet would force him to meet part of the cost of an above-inflation pay award by cutting other parts of the health budget. The prospect of presiding over ward closures and other such cutbacks at a time when large sections of the public suspected him of being engaged in privatizing the NHS was a grim one, and no doubt Clarke ground his teeth in frustration as the rest of the Cabinet left him to hold the line against public-sector pay increases.

The health unions cleverly calculated that this was the time to try to raise the pay of ambulance drivers to a level comparable to the police and firefighters. They rejected the government offer of a 6.5 per cent increase, which would not even have covered the rising cost of living. Early in September, members of all five ambulance unions – NUPE, GMB, TGWU, COHSE and NALGO – voted for industrial action in support of an 11.14 per cent pay claim. A week later they began an overtime ban. The government's weapon in previous disputes had been the general unpopularity of trade unions. In particular, the main ambulance union, NUPE, had handed the Conservatives valuable propaganda weapons during the "winter of discontent", with hot-headed branch officers threatening to refuse to treat patients or bury the dead. This time, the union compounded Clarke's problems by presenting a public face of moderation and reason. When it was all over, Clarke paid a rueful tribute to the principle negotiator, Roger Poole:

> They made the wise decision to lock [NUPE General Secretary] Rodney Bickerstaffe away somewhere so that he sustained six months of total silence, which I've never known, ever, when his own union is engaged in an industrial dispute. Roger Poole did the job very well indeed and is a more attractive personality.[30]

Instead of engaging in Scargill-style talk of class warfare, and calling for the government to capitulate, the unions put forward the modest suggestion that the dispute should go to arbitration, knowing that the most likely result would be a compromise somewhere between the government's 6.5 per cent and the union's 11 per cent. The arbitration service, Acas, in fact met on 9 October, but discovered they were wasting their time, because the government would not concede that any group of health workers could have their pay set other than by the management of the NHS. Even on the Tory side, there was sympathy for the idea that ambulance drivers were a special case. The London MP Jerry Hayes suggested a compromise under which the drivers would have accepted their pay offer for the current year, in return for having their own pay review body, separate from that of other health workers. Kenneth Clarke's retort was that "the health service cannot afford it."[31] He told parliament, during an emergency debate on the ambulance dispute, that arbitration would be

> an abdication of management responsibility. If any government were to endeavour to run the NHS on the basis that so long as any group take industrial action against the patients, that group will be given arbitration, they will reproduce the chaos they did indeed produce in 1979.[32]

Towards the end of October, the dispute threatened to turn nasty when the London drivers announced that they would refuse to use a newly installed semi-automatic call-and-recall system, but would rely on the radio-phone system that they had operated until eight months earlier, which was identical to the one operated in other big cities. Clarke reacted as if this were an act of sabotage. He seemed to suspect, in fact, that it was, and that the unions were resorting to the old open-call system because "all it requires is one microphone to be left open, accidentally, accidentally on purpose, who knows how, and the whole system is completely aborted."[33] The London ambulance drivers were suspended and the army called in to run a makeshift 999 service. Fifty-one ambulances from forty army and RAF units were based at police stations around the capital, with twenty-three other military vehicles kept in reserve. Clarke warned that he was prepared to do the same throughout the country if necessary. By the following January, in fact, there were 180 army ambulances deployed in sixteen English health districts, from West Sussex to South Yorkshire. The army had answered 60,000 calls in four months.[34]

Although Mrs Thatcher accused the ambulance drivers of taking "action against the sick",[35] public opinion stayed obstinately on their side. In the public mind, these were uniformed professionals on call at all hours to perform a life-saving and occasionally distressing or dangerous job, who ought not to be treated like ancillary staff at a hospital. Their case appeared to be strengthened in November, when the fire brigade was offered an 8.6 per cent increase. In the first two months of the dispute, doctors, tax officials and members of parliament all received better awards than the one offered to the ambulance drivers. Later, the police were awarded 9.25 per cent. For themselves, MPs agreed an inflation-beating 10.7 per cent increase. As Christmas drew near, even Richard Littlejohn of the *Sun* called for a settlement. He wrote:

> Go to any High Street today and you'll see a strange sight. People are queuing to sign the biggest single petition in British history and throw cash into buckets. Not for Ethiopia, not for Bangladesh or even for Children in Need. It is for the ambulancemen.[36]

Clarke replied three days later, claiming that any pay rise for the ambulance workers would have to be paid for by cuts from somewhere else in the NHS. Naturally, he did not go into the question of why a government which had only recently cut £2 billion off income tax for the highest paid could not afford to fund an award from general taxation.

In mid-November, the NHS Chief Executive Duncan Nichol was in a position to improve the pay offer to 9 per cent, spread over eighteen months. Even the tactic that had worked so well against the miners, of making a separate deal with a breakaway union, failed. Early in December, Clarke tried out the 9 per cent offer on the 3,000-strong Association of Professional Ambulance Personnel, which was outside the TUC. According to NUPE, the Association's membership was already suffering a haemorrhage as attitudes in the dispute hardened. Its leaders recommended accepting the deal, but a few days before the Christmas the members voted to continue the dispute.

Clarke's main argument against the drivers' claim was that the ambulance service was not solely or even principally an emergency service. According to his figures, nine-tenths of the journeys undertaken by ambulances were routine, such as ferrying housebound patients to and from hospital. Whilst 70 per cent of drivers were qualified to stem haemorrhages, bind fractures, resuscitate the dying and deliver babies, only one in ten was a fully qualified paramedic. A few weeks into the dispute, Clarke was talking in general terms about how there could eventually be a "two-tier" ambulance service, in which staff who dealt with accidents and emergencies were better paid than those who dealt with routine cases. The Northumberland service, which had been reorganized in the mid 1980s, was held up as a model to others. There, five ambulance stations, seventy-three vehicles and seventy-nine staff were cut, a separate service was set up under the control of the health authority to transport the elderly to day hospitals, and the rest of the work of ferrying outpatients – about 43 per cent of all journeys – was hived off to private taxi and minicab firms. The unions attacked this idea as "elitist" and "divisive".[37]

Early in the New Year, Clarke rehearsed his arguments in a letter to the 15-year-old daughter of a Nottingham ambulanceman who had written to him backing the union claim. Clarke told her: "The vast majority of ambulance staff have had no extended paramedical training at all. They are professional drivers, a worthwhile job – but not an exceptional one."[38] It was one of those sweeping, knockabout statements which the Health Secretary liked to make from time to time. If he had said it in the House of Commons, he might have got away with it. Addressed to a teenager, it was too much. The Association of Chief Ambulance Officers, representing eighty chief officers in Britain and the Irish republic, which had kept out of the dispute until now, announced that it could no longer "remain silent on this vital issue" and warned that a government which set out "to destroy or devalue the worth of any group as part of a pay dispute will reap the rewards of a disillusioned and disgruntled workforce".[39] The British Medical Association urged the government to "recognise the valuable contribution of all ambulance workers" and settle up.[40] Clarke's case was not helped by the fact that some chauffeurs were earning a good deal more than ambulance drivers, however unexceptional their contribution to the general well-being. The average ministerial chauffeur, for example, was being paid £15,000 a year, which was one-and-a-half times the rate for an experienced ambulance driver. There was one, indeed, who had earned £25,000 in a year after notching up "colossal" overtime.[41]

The importance of this sort of slip was that, with talks abandoned and the union leaders refusing to oblige the government by escalating their action to an all-out strike, the dispute had become a battle for public opinion, fought out in television and radio studios and in the columns of newspapers, often in the form of a personal dual between Kenneth Clarke and Roger Poole.

The *Daily Telegraph*, in an editorial urging that there should be no more concessions to the unions, warned that "Mr Poole's popularity underlines the real problem for the government. The public seems almost solidly behind the ambulance staff."[42]

Kenneth Clarke's difficulty was that the combative style for which he was famous worked best against opponents who paid him back in the same coinage. As a junior health minister, he had thrived on the personal attacks he had drawn from union leaders. Early in the ambulance dispute, he had done his best to get personal with Roger Poole, once accusing him of being on an "ego trip", but his antagonist persisted in being exasperatingly polite and reasonable. After the incident of the ambulanceman's daughter, Clarke decided on a change of tack. He sent Poole a note congratulating him on his "ingenuity". During a television interview, he was heard to refer to him as "Roger",[43] and he told the *Financial Times*: "I actually like him ... he is one of the more able, more attractive trades union leaders that I have come across."[44]

However, Clarke's efforts to seem reasonable led him straight from one disaster to another. That weekend's Sunday newspapers were full of stories attributed to a senior figure in the health department, alleging that Clarke was angry at the way certain Cabinet colleagues, notably the party chairman Kenneth Baker, had failed to back him in his hour of need. From details which emerged subsequently, it became clear that he had actually paid tribute to two members of the Cabinet, Geoffrey Howe and John Major, who had stood by him at the worst moments of the dispute. Later he would express gratitude, or at least relief, that Thatcher had also backed him. Yet, pointedly, he had not mentioned the party chairman at all. One newspaper, the *Observer*, reported that a serious climbdown was in prospect: the ambulance drivers would be offered more money if they would drop their demand for automatic annual awards. The reports must have ruined Clarke's weekend, which he was spending at home with his family. He made a personal appearance on lunch-time radio to admit that he was the senior source who had given an off-the-record briefing to the Sunday press; but he flatly denied he had attacked Kenneth Baker or promised extra money. However, he did offer to resume pay talks if the union side would say something "a little closer to the real world".[45] By Monday, it was clear that there was no give on either side.

This was the low point in the dispute for Kenneth Clarke. It was not now just a question of whether he could win, but whether he could survive the dispute without going the way of John Moore. He was being more or less openly criticized by fellow Tories for steering them towards electoral disaster through his intransigence. Although he denied at the time that he had any complaint against Kenneth Baker, he certainly felt hurt enough to complain to an interviewer three years later:

> You don't half discover who your friends are when you're in trouble. Nameless colleagues, who I've never had any time for distanced themselves rapidly from this difficulty and were really not at all helpful. One character in particular used to cheerfully brief journalists that it was all being handled so badly, he could have sorted it out.[46]

When the Commons returned from its Christmas break, one Tory MP voted against the government and ten others abstained after Labour had forced another vote on the dispute. However, in the end Clarke proved the point that if the government was prepared to ride out the unpopularity engendered, the other side must eventually have to give in. The ambulance drivers settled in February, having won a small improvement on what they had been offered almost a year earlier. By then, opinion polls were saying that the most unpopular member of the Cabinet, more disliked by the electors even than Mrs Thatcher, was Kenneth Clarke.

CHAPTER TEN

THE N.H.S. REFORMS

The British public has never been more afraid for the future of the National Health Service than when it was in the care of Kenneth Clarke. Suspicious minds really believed that health care was about to go the way of gas, water and electricity: out of the public sector, into the hands of private shareholders. This suspicion cost the Conservatives a parliamentary seat in the Vale of Glamorgan in May 1989, and was still prevalent enough two years later – by which time Clarke had moved to another department – for the government to launch an aggressive campaign in the hope that they could finally lay it to rest. It was fronted by the new prime minister, John Major, in person, who denounced what he called "the big lie Labour peddled to voters",[1] and promised "No privatisation of health care, neither piecemeal, nor in part, nor in whole, not today, not tomorrow, not after the next election, not ever while I'm Prime Minister."[2] Even the NHS chief executive, Duncan Nichol, whose position required him to keep out of party-political controversy, was moved to say that "the idea is unbelievable. I don't even give it house room."[3]

It was ironic that this idea should take hold in the public mind when Kenneth Clarke was Secretary of State for Health. He had never taken out private health insurance, although his view was that "if I had something wrong with me which for some reason it was more convenient to have done quickly, I'd have it done privately."[4] His nineteen-year-old daughter, Sue, was now working for the NHS, as a student nurse. He believed in the principle that health care should be available for everyone, free at the point of delivery, and was prepared to defend it against the Tory right. To take one example, Clarke spoke at a fringe meeting at the Conservative Party conference in autumn 1993, at which the right had turned out in force, in a rowdy and rebellious mood, and there was a noisy section of the audience that evidently looked forward to the abolition of the NHS. Clarke told them: "I do not believe in a pure market in health care. The reason you cannot have a pure market in health is because customers have no resistance."[5] At the onset of the health reforms, he proclaimed: "Anybody in the NHS who knows me knows that I am extremely committed to it. No hospitals will be leaving the NHS. We are not going to privatise it."[6]

With hindsight, it can be seen that a political battle did take place after the 1987 general election over the relative merits of private and state health care; but Clarke, personally, was not on the side of the Thatcherites. The health reforms that he pushed through were highly controversial, but their purpose was not to privatize health care. In fact, his appointment as Health Secretary meant that the right had already lost. One of the most vivid images from the 1987 general election was of Margaret Thatcher, questioned at a campaign press conference, baldly asserting that it was her right to visit the doctor of her choice at the time of her choice – an option open, of course, only to those who can afford it. One week later, she was back in office with a majority of more than a hundred, and in no mood to relent or retreat. She wanted as many people as possible to partake in the privileges and responsibilities of the middle class: home ownership, share ownership, private education for their children, and private health care.

There were two ways to increase the number of patients treated privately. The more drastic was the one proposed in the notorious Cabinet briefing in 1982: to abolish free health care at a stroke, except for people who qualified for state benefits, and introduce compulsory health insurance for everyone in work. Gerald Vaughan, the former health minister and friend of the Thatchers, now chairman of a private health company, was still promoting this cause,[7] but he was not the influential figure he had once been, and the trouble in which it had landed Mrs Thatcher in 1982 made it unlikely she would try a frontal assault on free health care again. The more subtle way was to use the tax system to stimulate private-treatment health care: make BUPA's subscriptions tax deductible, and ensure that those with money behind them can buy their way into better-equipped hospitals than NHS patients, and there would be no reason why anyone in good health and on a decent wage need ever use the state health service again. The danger of such an approach is that it would create an explosion in demand for private care which private hospitals and clinics would be unable to meet, so it would be necessary at the same time to alter the internal accounting system of the NHS to give its hospital managers an incentive to take in more private patients. It also needed a compliant Secretary of State.

Directly after the 1987 election, Norman Fowler was replaced by John Moore, one of Clarke's former gang from the Amesbury Group who had no known experience or interest in health issues, but had become a born-again Thatcherite during a period as Financial Secretary to the Treasury. He claimed that he had virtually invented the privatization programme while he was there. His sudden elevation, combined with Norman Tebbit's departure from the Cabinet, made him an obvious choice to be the next prime minister, assuming that Mrs Thatcher was in a position to determine the choice of her own successor. Someone as close to her as Nicholas Ridley, for instance, states it as an established fact that, having lost Cecil Parkinson four years earlier, "her second choice of heir apparent was John Moore."[8] In her own memoirs, she says: "I had not, contrary to much speculation, reached a firm decision that John was my preferred successor. I had simply reached the conclusion that he must be given wider recognition and greater experience";[9] nonetheless, she obviously expected him to deliver something that could not be entrusted to a "wet" like Norman Fowler or Kenneth Clarke. Moore was at once servile and highly ambitious. He promised a fundamental review of the welfare system to move people "away from dependency and towards opportunity", and promised that there were no "sacred cows".[10] If Mrs Thatcher was looking for a minister to usher in a new era of private medicine, she had picked the right man.

In the latter part of 1987, the health service appeared to be in crisis, with exceptional publicity being given to hardship caused by ward closures and other symptoms of underfunding. It is to be doubted whether the financial crisis was any worse than in previous years, but in a politically dull period after a general election, there was general gloom about the future of the NHS which seemed to demand government action. Mrs Thatcher let slip during a *Panorama* interview that she proposed to convene a small Cabinet committee – it was made up of just five ministers and two advisers – that would meet regularly to review the management of health care. The meetings began in January 1988.

A number of proposals for tax concessions for private health care ran up against the Treasury's traditional hostility to tax breaks of any kind. The problem was that it was much quicker and simpler to create the demand for private care than to satisfy it. The result, Nigel Lawson warned in a private note, was that the price of health care would shoot up, creating pressure for compensatory salary and wage increases. All that came out was that health-insurance premiums for the over-sixties became tax deductible in the 1989 Budget, at an estimated annual cost of £600 million. And Lawson subsequently claimed: "Had I known that, within weeks, John Moore would have been replaced by the robust Kenneth Clarke, I would not have made even this concession."[11] Since this was Cabinet policy, it fell to Clarke to announce and defend it, whether he agreed with it or not. He defended it on the rather odd basis that there were elderly people who had taken out private medical insurance during their working lives but now found that the premiums were beyond their means.[12] However, when a future Treasury minister, Tony Nelson, urged him to extend tax relief for health care to other sections of the community, Clarke gave away what he really thought: "I do not agree [with] the general case for tax relief" – because it was not for government to determine that some forms of personal expenditure were more "desirable" than others.[13]

That aside, the idea of reducing the cost of the NHS by bribing tax payers to use private health care died, and so did the political career of John Moore. His relationship with Mrs Thatcher became like Leon Brittan's:

> He framed the Health Service reforms exactly on the basis of what he thought she wanted. But she kept changing her mind. One minute she wanted to go further, the next she got an attack of the doubts, wanted to trim a bit. Each time the unfortunate John agreed, made the adjustments, came back for approval. The result was a total hotchpotch and she ended up thinking he was a wanker, and got rid of him.

That is the explanation attributed to Archie Hamilton, who was then Thatcher's parliamentary private secretary.[14] Moore also had the misfortune to be struck down by a serious illness late in 1987, and to be opposite one of Labour's most effective parliamentary performers, Robin Cook. Also, his status as Thatcher's golden boy inevitably created enemies for him in the Tory Party. One of his worst enemies was John Major, a member of the committee reviewing the health service, and the Treasury minister in control of public spending, who is said to have sworn to get him.[15] His fall came in two quick stages. In July 1988, when Moore's department was divided in two, he lived on in the lesser role of Secretary of State for Social Services. In 1989, he was sacked, an act of ingratitude which shocked even a devoted admirer of Mrs Thatcher like Nicholas Ridley. Nonetheless, Moore was doggedly loyal to his mistress, playing a willing but ineffectual part in trying to secure her re-election to the party leadership in 1990 and to preserve her legacy after her fall.

When she sent for Kenneth Clarke, Mrs Thatcher knew that there was no point in expecting him to fight for tax allowances for private health care. As always, he was promoted because he was good at handling hot political issues. With him in charge, there was a chance that the plans to create an "internal market" in the NHS could be put into effect without doing crippling damage to the Conservative Party's popularity.

If it had suited him, Clarke could have made political mileage out of being the minister who saved the NHS from depredation by the Tory right, in the same way that Michael Heseltine was quietly promoting himself as the former Environment Secretary who refused to introduce a poll tax. If he had, Clarke might have dispelled some of the public alarm about his health reforms, and made it harder for Labour and the health unions to launch a campaign to save the NHS from privatization; but with uncharacteristic modesty, he chose not to. He preferred to maintain the line that everyone in the government was solidly lined up in support of the NHS. At the time of his appointment, the economy was booming, Thatcher was dominating her administration to a degree unmatched for a generation, and Neil Kinnock's leadership of the Labour Party had hit rock bottom amid a messy dispute over unilateral nuclear disarmament. According to one contemporary press report, the prime minister was also holding informal lunches with right-wing junior ministers outside the health department, like Peter Lilley and Michael Portillo, to sound out their opinions on the health reforms.[16] It was no time to be making enemies on the right.

Conflict with the health unions was another matter. Clarke had been through it before, without doing his career any harm at all. There was no prospect of changing the management structure of the NHS without going through it again. So, to quote his own word, he "bulldozed"[17] the reforms through. Consultants, doctors, nurses, ambulance drivers, ancillary workers, and everyone else employed by the NHS were united as never before in opposition to the government's plans. Those plans emerged amid a blaze of publicity in January 1989, six months after Clarke's appointment. Unfortunately for Clarke, the publicity did not begin at the time or in the manner of his choosing, but when a draft of his White Paper was leaked by somebody inside the health department, enabling Robin Cook to have the case against the government's proposals broadcast before the state had even begun to spend the £1 million allocated to selling the proposals to the public. Naturally there were complaints from the Conservative side against Cook and his unnamed informant, but their case was weakened by a series of well-placed leaks over the preceding months which had obviously emanated from a source not far from Kenneth Clarke. He had even been challenged about this by Robin Cook in the Commons, earlier in January, and had implicitly admitted that the leaks were intended to draw Labour's fire before publication day. "At least the knee jerk reactions of the Labour Party are now out of the way. I hope we have cleared the ground for a serious discussion when the White Paper appears", he said.[18] *Working for Patients* duly appeared on 31 January 1989.

Having disposed of the idea that the crisis in the health service could be resolved by altering the manner in which it was financed, the working party had now opted for the solution of an "internal market". This expression meant what it said: health care was to be a service which had to be paid for; the "buyer" was to be given a choice of suppliers, so that institutions which provided cheap and efficient care would attract customers and thrive, while inefficient ones would lose business and, in extreme cases, fold. This idea was not entirely new. It had been introduced in small corners of the NHS during Clarke's previous stint as a health minister. For example, there was Tadworth Court, the prototype trust hospital, selling its services to councils and health authorities. There had also been a Department of Health circular in 1983 requiring hospitals to invite competitive tenders for cleaning, catering and laundry services. By 1987, this practice was widened to take in portering, transport, computer operating, and even certain clinical services like pathology. Even when the contracts were awarded in-house, the mere fact that they had had to tender in a sense separated the ancillary workers, as providers of a service, from the hospital, as purchaser.

However, these peripheral examples were relatively simple to put into practice because it was obvious in each case who was buying and who was selling. Kenneth Clarke and his working party needed to invent a "market" for a commodity which the state had undertaken to give away to everyone who needed it. If the patient wasn't buying and the NHS wasn't selling, who were to be the buyers and sellers in this market of Clarke's? This question had been pondered over for some years by Professor Alain Enthoven of Stanford University, who is mentioned in Margaret Thatcher's memoirs as a progenitor of the health reforms. He published an essay in 1985[19] envisaging a market for health care in which district general managers would purchase the services of NHS hospitals in their own districts, or in neighbouring districts, or of private hospitals, on behalf of patients resident within their district. This was one of those wacky right-wing ideas prevalent in the mid 1980s, reminiscent of the bizarre blueprints for a socialist society drawn up by nineteenth-century Utopians like Robert Owen and Fourier. As soon as Margaret Thatcher had come to hear of it, it was on the way to being government policy,[20] although there was no mention of it in the Conservative election manifesto.

When Clarke's working party considered Professor Enthoven's scheme, their only apparent objection was that it was too simple. A market with only one buyer per district was not a sufficiently competitive market. There were not many sellers competing with each other either, since the government did not dare use the tax system to encourage more private hospitals to enter the market. Consequently, two refinements were added. These two innovations were at the centre of the political storm that bedevilled the government for the next three years. The first was to give doctors in large general practices the option of controlling their own budgets. Having been allocated funds by the NHS, they would then be able to "buy" treatment for their patients from the hospitals of their choice. Initially, this scheme was open only to the thousand or so biggest general practices, with at least 11,000 patients each on their books. Before the end of the year, the requirement had been reduced to 9,000 patients, and the government was offering an initial lump sum of £16,000 to any practice prepared to take the plunge. Thus hundreds of new customers were introduced into the internal market. Whether they became budget holders or not, GPs were affected by the reforms in other ways. Patients were given greater freedom to choose their GP and, simultaneously, the method by which doctors were paid was altered so that they could earn more by persuading more patients to come on to their books. Also, the bill for drugs prescribed by doctors had become a problem again, having reached £1.9 billion in 1987–88. The NHS was paying more for drugs than for the salaries of the doctors who prescribed them. Consequently, GPs were to be given "indicative" budgets as an incentive to make them prescribe fewer or cheaper drugs.

The other startling innovation was to give hospital managers the option of leaving the NHS management structure and setting their hospitals up in business as self-governing trusts, selling their services to the NHS. The first freedom given to trust hospitals was that of negotiating separate pay deals with their staff, thus limiting the power of the big health unions. In addition, all NHS hospitals were given freedom to sell their services to different health authorities and to the private sector, and the system for allocating funds to hospitals was altered so that "the money follows the patient" and the more patients a hospital treats, the greater is its grant. The reforms also affected the top management. Clarke created a new policy board, onto which he coopted four eminent businessmen: Sir Roy Griffiths, deputy chairman of Sainsbury, Sir Graham Day, chairman of Rover, Sir Kenneth Durham, deputy chairman of British Aerospace, and Sir Robert Scholey, chairman of British Steel. Three of those four, of course, were best known for helping state-owned industries into the private sector. No nurses were included on the board. Later, the "head office" of the NHS was split administratively and geographically from the Department of Health, and relocated in Leeds.

The launch of the White Paper was quite unlike any other. In one day, in addition to reporting to the House of Commons and taking part in a press conference and the launch of a booklet, a video, speakers' notes and other information for NHS staff, Clarke put himself through a televised live link-up hosted by television and radio presenter Nick Ross, in which he answered questions from an audience of about two thousand health workers from around the country. The next day he set off on a three-day regional tour, starting with a public meeting in Birmingham with an audience made up principally of doctors whose reactions to the reforms was sceptical, at best. At the same time, David Mellor was meeting doctors in Newcastle.

Despite the proselytizing by ministers, the reaction of the health professions was overwhelmingly hostile. By mid-March, the House of Commons Social Services Select Committee had had fifty submissions from health authorities, community health councils, the pharmaceutical industry, the Royal College of Nursing, the British Medical Association and others, almost all of them critical. The BMA, which represented 32,000 family doctors, was already locked into a conflict with Clarke over plans to change doctors' contracts. These were not directly related to the health reforms, but the two issues quickly became intertwined to provoke the most serious conflict between doctors and the government of the day since the foundation of the health service. The BMA set aside £3 million for a publicity campaign to oppose the reforms. The dispute gathered momentum during February and reached its crescendo early in March, when Clarke stirred it up in characteristic style in an after-dinner speech to the Royal College of General Practitioners, by saying:

> I do wish that the most suspicious of our GPs would stop feeling nervously for their wallets every time that I mention the word "reform" ... The public interest requires that the Government and GPs do not spend their time in pointless battle.[21]

Those four words, "feeling for their wallets", went buzzing around almost every surgery in Britain. Having implied that members of an esteemed caring profession were motivated by sheer greed, Clarke compounded the offence in a radio interview the very next day by claiming that the average doctor was earning £55,000 a year. The BMA immediately countered with a statement which gave a detailed breakdown of where that £55,000 came from, and how much was made up of expenses to cover the cost of running a surgery. They claimed that an average doctor's net pay was a little over £31,000.[22] That week, one of the BMA's chief negotiators, Dr Tony Stanton, told a meeting of GPs in Oxfordshire in March: "It's all-out war. We must not give up the NHS without a fight."[23]

Indeed, they did not. In this dispute, the leaders of the BMA revealed that they had no compunction about taking on a Cabinet minister and the government's propaganda machinery in direct combat. A leaflet which the BMA produced for its members so angered Clarke that he wrote to every doctor in the country urging them not to display it in their surgeries. It was full of "scurrilous nonsense", he told the Commons: "It is a long time since I have encountered a trade union which is prepared to spend millions of pounds of its members' money on spreading untruths among its customers in that way."[24]

One fear provoked by the new concept of GP budget holders was that some doctors would begin to cull their list of patients to rid themselves of any who needed expensive treatment, while boosting their income by persuading the fit to sign up. There were a number of cases reported in the *Daily*

Mirror in which doctors appeared to have struck off expensive patients, but the government insisted that if they had done so, it was because they had misunderstood the terms of their contracts, under which they gained nothing.

Undeterred, the doctors took the fight to where they knew it would hurt the government most, to the Vale of Glamorgan, a supposedly safe Tory seat which had become vacant because of the death of the incumbent MP, and turned the by-election into something of a one-issue campaign. About one hundred and fifty local doctors were mobilized to sign a petition urging their patients not to vote for the Conservative candidate. One doctor entered the election as a "protect the health service" candidate. Kenneth Clarke put in a fleeting visit to the Vale of Glamorgan; but wisely he did not stay and refused to meet local doctors, hurrying back to London instead for a meeting with consultants from ten royal colleges, who were all opposed to his plans. Later, he implicitly admitted that health had been the issue that decided the by-election result, when he said: "I regard the Vale of Glamorgan as having been won in part by a campaign of untruths."[25] A Tory majority of 6,251 disappeared, and the Labour candidate won by 6,028. It was the govern-ment's first by-election defeat for three years. But having lost once they then made a habit of it: at the time of writing, the Conservatives have lost every parliamentary by-election since 1989. This was a symptom of a more general political development. Until the end of 1988, the Labour Party had appeared to be sinking ever more deeply into political crisis, whilst the Liberal Demo-crats had such serious problems that even their new leader, Paddy Ashdown, feared that they might never recover. It was only after the health reforms had been announced that the Conservatives were compelled to take the Opposi-tion seriously.

During the first half of 1989, Clarke went through nineteen meetings with doctors' representatives, which produced 110 hours of negotiations and thirty-eight discussion papers. In one revealing slip of the tongue, he described their professional body as the "British Medical Opposition".[26] In the end, he had to give way a little on the proposed new contract for doctors in the hope of mitigating their relentless opposition to the health reforms. It was, as the saying goes, no coincidence that the doctors won their biggest concession during a nine-hour meeting held on the same day that votes were being counted in the Vale of Glamorgan. They won better pay for night visits, an extra fee for each patient aged over seventy-five on their books, and recognition that visits to community hospitals and health-promotion clinics were as much part of their work as hours spent in the surgery. Nonetheless, Clarke was able to maintain that he had kept intact the principle that "the highest rewards go to the most hard-working doctors."[27]

Meanwhile, the government was encouraging as many hospitals and other health organizations as possible to bid for trust status. The decision was left to the managers. Neither the staff, nor the local population, had any say in the matter. Staff were to have no choice but to continue working for an organization that had been converted to a trust, although it would mean that they had lost the right to have their union negotiate national pay rates for them. A number of unofficial ballots of health staff were conducted, producing overwhelming majorities against trust status, but Clarke never accepted that people who worked for the NHS could be sufficiently well informed to know what they were voting about. "If the staff are given a description of NHS trust status which makes their blood run cold and their hair stand on end, one tends to find that in a subsequent ballot nine out of ten say they are against it", he said.[28] As to the idea that the local population might vote, in the same way that parents were being allowed to vote over whether schools should opt out of local authority control, Clarke dismissed that on the grounds that there was no "tightly knit group of users" qualified to determine the future of a hospital, whose patients "come from anywhere".[29]

Speaking to the Royal College of Nursing's annual conference, after their president, Maude Storey, had won a standing ovation for warning that the reforms would "change the culture of our hospitals irrevocably in favour of the conveyor belt", Clarke answered their fears in customary style, telling them that such talk was "frankly nonsense" and that there was no point in "putting great sums of money into campaigns against reforms which they know are going to happen anyway".[30]

The decision being thus left to managers who had most to gain from conversion to trust status, the government received a satisfyingly large number of expressions of interest – more than two hundred in the first five months, from hospitals, health authorities, ambulance services, psychiatric units and others, including some showpieces like Guy's and St Bartholomew's teaching hospitals in London. In the so-called "first wave", 57 units took on trust status on 1 April 1991. Two years later, their number reached 151.

There was another momentous reform, unconnected with the creation of an internal market, which was not in the January 1989 White Paper, but was included in the legislation that went through the Commons the next year. This was the introduction of an ambitious project called "care in the community", under which the mentally ill and mentally handicapped were to be taken out of institutions and allowed to rejoin society. The principle behind it was universally accepted. It had been the aim of successive governments since the early 1960s to close down the Victorian lunatic asylums and find a better way of caring for the mentally ill. In 1986, the Audit Commission for local authorities in England and Wales had carried out a detailed study of all the groups who needed long-term care – the elderly and physically disabled, as well as the mentally ill or handicapped – and produced damning conclusions which demanded fundamental changes.

The government appointed a commission headed by Sir Roy Griffiths, then the managing director of Sainsbury's, to find solutions. The Griffiths Report, published in March 1988, recommended that local authorities should be responsible for identifying all the people within their own areas who needed community care and ensuring they received it; but they were to be the planners and purchasers of care, not its providers. Social-security payments to those who needed community care were to be paid, in the first instance to the local council, who could choose to use the money to provide care in the recipient's own home rather than in an institution. Griffiths recommended that these funds should be "ring-fenced", a legal device that would compel councils to spend the money on the purpose for which it was provided. This was an important recommendation because community care, if handled properly, is not a cheap option. Indeed, there are certain economies of scale in keeping the mentally ill and others locked up under one roof; without "ring-fencing", there was a risk that people who needed attention would simply be let loose on the street and ignored. The NHS would no longer have responsibility for them, unless they needed medical care. Councils might decide that there were more important things they could do with the money than spend it on people who attract little public sympathy and have almost no means of defending their own interests.

The Griffiths report was greeted by a sixteen-month silence, probably explained by the fact that Kenneth Clarke and other ministers had their hands full with the NHS reforms. In July 1989 there came a White Paper, *Caring for People*, which, in line with the Griffiths report, announced that local council social-security departments would indeed take over responsibility for community care. Politically, this was a bold step. For ten years, central government had dedicated itself to diminishing the power of local government, abolishing councils where they could, and taking power and funds away from those that remained. On this occasion, right-wing pressure groups within the Conservative Party like the Adam Smith Institute and the "No Turning Back" group of MPs urged that the government establish new quangos for community care to cut out elected councillors altogether. Psychiatrists, as a professional group, were also opposed to the idea of government funds being diverted to councils with whom they had no experience of working. However, the Cabinet was persuaded that it must at all costs avoid another dispute involving the health service, and for the one and only time in its existence the Thatcher government surrendered money and responsibility to local councillors. The announcement inspired Robin Cook to congratulate Clarke on "persuading the Prime Minister that providing community care means swallowing her distaste for local government ... a major achievement which deserves full recognition". But, far from being flattered, Clarke retorted: "It is easy for you: you only have to see the words 'local government' in a White Paper to ring NALGO – when it's not on strike – and ask what to say."[31]

Despite that important concession, there were gaps in the White Paper. Griffiths had recommended that the government appoint a minister for community care, and retain for itself the responsibility of setting clear objectives and policies. These ideas were not taken up. Neither, ominously, did the White Paper say that funds for community care would be "ring-fenced".[32] Within a year, the government faced a political crisis even greater than the one provoked by the health reforms, when the first poll tax bills went out in England and Wales. By the summer of 1990, nothing took precedence over the government's need to extricate itself from the mess into which it had landed by changing the way local councils raised their revenue. Professionals in the field, anxious to see care in the community enacted, began to fear that ministers would block a proposal which would increase the amount of money spent by local councils; but a group who met Kenneth Clarke on 25 June came away reassured after he had told them that he was "not at the moment" persuaded of any need to delay.

Within three weeks, he had changed his tune. He announced to the Commons that the reform would be introduced in three phases between 1991 and

1993, instead of coming into effect in one move in 1991. Obviously, true to a tradition that ministers had honoured for ten years, Clarke tried to present this climbdown as being entirely the fault of local councils, for "not managing their services and their spending so that they deliver good quality services effectively"; but the longer he spoke, the more clearly the true reason for the delay emerged. He said:

> I accept that the overwhelming majority of directors of social services felt that they were ready to implement the new policies. I have no basis on which to challenge that. I accept that most voluntary organisations were ready to go ahead ... [But] it is impossible for us to turn a deaf ear to the concerns of charge payers.[33]

In short, whilst the poll tax was threatening the government's survival, the most vulnerable people in the community must wait. That statement was actually the last that Kenneth Clarke made to the Commons in his capacity as Health Secretary, and consequently his successors' share responsibility with him for the way in which care in the community worked out in practice. It took a dreadful killing, in December 1992, to alert the general public to the possibility that something had gone terribly wrong. A young musician named Jonathan Zito was waiting at Finsbury Park tube station when a complete stranger walked up to him and, without a word, stabbed him in the face, and then sat in a train with other passengers as if nothing had happened. The assailant was a schizophrenic named Christopher Clunis, who had been through ten hospitals, including psychiatric units at four major London hospitals, but had been allowed to roam the streets without anyone taking responsibility for his aftercare. Haringey social services, who found him a flat, were not told about his violent record. The victim's young widow, Jayne Zito, became an articulate and passionate campaigner for proper care for the mentally ill.

An official inquiry criticized the police and the health and social services, and warned that London's psychiatric wards simply did not have the capacity to take in the number of seriously mentally ill who needed permanent attention. "We are very concerned that these failures may well be reproduced all over the country, in particular in poor inner city areas", they warned.[34] It would appear that care in the community, which the report endorsed as the right policy, had been treated as a cheap option after all. There had been a rush to scale down or close psychiatric wards, which cost the NHS money to run, on the assumption that council social-services departments were dealing with those who had previously been hospitalized. The chief executive of the charity SANE, Marjorie Wallace, warned: "When these people are well, they can be cared for in the community, but they need skilled, experienced medical help and proper supervision, not to be left in some bedsit to deteriorate. When a crisis occurs, they should be admitted to hospital if necessary. This is not happening. The shortage of beds – particularly in the big cities – is at the heart of the problem."[35] Whatever the problems, there can be no argument with the claim Clarke made when the National Health Service and Community Care bill was published, that it was "the most important piece of legislation to affect the NHS since its foundation".[36]

In assessing what Clarke's main health reforms achieved, it is pertinent to establish two things they did not do. First, they did not "privatize" the health service, as the opposition claimed and the public feared they would do. NHS trusts have continued to treat NHS patients, for whom health care is still available free at the point of delivery. Clarke was not universally believed at the time when he repeatedly denied that he was privatizing the NHS, but he can legitimately say that he was telling the truth. On the other hand, the reforms have not allowed the government to spend less on health care. On the contrary, the health budget took off as never before. When departmental spending limits were being set in autumn 1989, Clarke boasted that "I have been spectacularly more successful than any of my predecessors" in obtaining extra funds for the NHS.[37] The NHS budget continued rising as the general election grew nearer.

One of the great growth areas has been the management of NHS trusts. In five years, from 1986–87 to 1991–92, the number of NHS managers multiplied from 510 to 12,420, and the cost of paying them rose from £25.7 million to £383.8 million. The highest paid of them all, according to a study by Incomes Data Services in December 1993, was Tim Matthews, chief executive of Guy's and St Thomas's Trust, in London, who was paid £96,000 a year plus up to £8,000 in performance-related pay – about twice the pay of the Minister of State for Health – with a £20,000 Saab thrown in. The number of administrators increased by 18,000 to 134,990 between 1989 and 1992. In that same period, the number of NHS midwives and nurses fell. The health service also did its bit to aid recovery in the motor industry, by increasing its bill for staff cars from £54 million to £70 million between 1992 and 1993. Late in 1993 a Cabinet minister, the right-wing Welsh Secretary John Redwood, publicly complained that the service was being taken over by "men in grey suits" using "strangulated management jargon".[38]

However, this is apparently not something which need cause alarm. It was what the government intended, if retrospective ministerial statements are taken at face value. In March 1994, the health minister Dr Brian Mawhinney claimed that the NHS was "clearly under-managed" before 1986.[39] So when Clarke complained, as he embarked on the reforms, of a "ramshackle bureaucracy", and that some health authorities were about to run out of money through "managerial incompetence",[40] that was just his way of saying that the NHS was "under-managed". Curiously, though, even NHS trusts can lose money too, despite the efforts of their well-paid managers driving company cars. In March 1994, 25 trusts out of 151, or one in six, were running at a loss.[41]

More worryingly, there was a general perception that the reforms had gone wrong – a view shared by the left, who thought the whole experiment should never have begun, and the right, who wanted it taken further until something resembling a genuine market in health care was operating. *The Economist*, in an editorial which was calling for the reforms to go further, warned that "corruption, malpractice, blunders and waste seem to be engulfing an institution which was once a source of national pride".[42] The government itself did not set out general criteria by which to judge the success or failure of the reforms and did not appear to want to encourage too much investigation. However, one detailed academic study was carried out by the King's Fund Institute, a charity that conducts research into health care, which broadly concluded that awarding GPs the power to control their own budgets had worked, in that patients who visited fund-holding practices had a noticeably shorter wait for X-rays, blood tests or other services which required a visit to hospital. In other words, hospitals responded more quickly to doctors who had money to spend. Even this improvement is vulnerable to political criticism because it opens up the vista of a "two-tier" service, but the report's authors thought that could be resolved eventually as most or all GPs become fund-holders. In other respects, the report found little or no evidence that the quality of health care or the efficiency with which it was delivered had improved.[43] The evidence of the first three years was that all the upheaval and expense of creating trust hospitals had been for nothing.

There is, however, one identifiable political gain for the government that introduced the reforms. They have undoubtedly changed the political culture of the NHS. One of the problems for a Conservative health minister was that at moments of crisis the entire NHS staff, managers and all, might unite against the government. "He stands alone", Norman Fowler complained in his memoirs. "Nor can he rely on the help of those who in any other industry or service you might expect to be on his side ... few employers have to contend with their management arm solemnly sitting down and condemning [them]."[44] However, with a new breed of NHS managers in place, who know that they owe their large salaries and perks to the Conservative government, that problem has been removed. If Clarke's reforms do nothing for hospital patients, they should do something for the Conservative Party.

Clarke would have liked to stay on as Health Secretary until after the first trust hospitals were established in April 1991. From the party's point of view, he was doing well and it would have made sense to leave him there. But, as usual, Mrs Thatcher's priorities overrode his. Moving Clarke out into another department was almost the last thing she did before her sudden and dramatic downfall.

CHAPTER ELEVEN

THE FALL OF THATCHER

Who brought down Margaret Thatcher? The baroness herself is in no doubt about it: it was her own Cabinet. "I could have resisted the opposition of opponents and potential rivals and even respected them for it; but what grieved me was the desertion of those I had always considered friends and allies and the weasel words whereby they had transmuted their betrayal into frank advice and concern for my fate", she claims.[1] Or, more graphically:

> The candid friend Ken Clarke, the candid minister Malcolm Rifkind, the candid loyal friends all with the same message. What hurt most of all was that this was treachery – while I had been away, signing a treaty for my country, for the end of the cold war! It was treachery with a smile on its face. Perhaps that was the worst thing of all.[2]

After her fall, Mrs Thatcher became increasingly obsessive, isolated and hurt. It was said that she might be, well, a couple of chapters short of a full set of memoirs. Anything she says about her own downfall, therefore, must be treated with suspicion. Clarke himself is adamant: "There was no treachery against her ... A Cabinet, that was prepared to support her, gave her wholly sensible advice: that she had been defeated, and must now withdraw."[3] His view, and that of most of the Tory establishment, is that her support decayed from the outside inwards: first, the general public turned against her, because she had been in power too long and had inflicted the poll tax on them, then backbench Conservative MPs deserted her, and finally her Cabinet ministers advised her, as advisers must, that her position was hopeless.

As a rule, senior Conservatives avoid giving an "ideological" explanation of political events, even when they are as fascinating as the fall of Margaret Thatcher. Like most of the main players in the last days of Thatcher, Clarke has spoken at length, on and off the record, about his interpretation of those events. He is reluctant to discuss the part played by Sir Geoffrey Howe, because Sir Geoffrey was his former mentor, but it is not impossible to fill in the gaps and see the events approximately as Clarke sees them. His account is not radically different from those given by numerous other ministers or ex-ministers, except that he is less sympathetic to Thatcher than some. What is missing from them all is a satisfactory underlying explanation as to why a figure as imposing and experienced as Mrs Thatcher should suddenly be ruthlessly expelled from office by her own supporters.

Clarke is one of numerous Conservatives who have expressed the opinion that she should have resigned in summer 1989, after she had completed ten years as prime minister. It emerged from her memoirs that the former Foreign Secretary, Lord Carrington, privately advised her to resign then. She suspected, no doubt rightly, that he was speaking for others as well as himself. According to Lord Whitelaw, not resigning in 1989 was "probably her greatest mistake",[4] but in her defence it must be said that if she had done as she was asked, she would not have been succeeded by John Major or anyone else of her choice. In May 1989, Sir Geoffrey Howe would have been her most obvious successor, unless the party decided to opt for someone younger, in which case Kenneth Clarke might have had an outside chance. It was not until the reshuffle of July 1989, in which John Major replaced Geoffrey Howe as Foreign Secretary, that she had her successor in place. She heartily intended to go on for at least two years after the next general election.

Here we see the germ of one possible explanation of why she was removed from office. Nigel Lawson, for instance, says that after eleven years "people had tired of her, and wanted a change".[5] A lot has been said since her fall about the supposed ruthlessness of the Conservative Party in dispatching its leaders when they have outlived their usefulness. It is so ruthless, apparently, that a prime minister who has strode the world stage and led them to victory in three general elections in a row can be sacked on the mere suspicion that she might not be able to pull it off a fourth time. If Mrs Thatcher had become an electoral liability to the party she had dominated for so long, there is no doubt that the biggest single reason was the introduction of the poll tax. The tax had been designed to be easy to understand. Whereas under the old rating system, few people really understood what a precept of such-and-such an amount to the pound really meant, a poll tax bill of, say, £300 per head meant exactly that in most cases. The architects of the poll tax had thought

this clarity would force councils to keep their bills low, overlooking the possibility that public anger might be directed at the government which invented
it. By the spring of 1990, Britain was beginning to look like a nation in revolt
again. Normally law-abiding people were threatening to refuse to pay their
bills. Thousands took to the streets in protest. One evening late in March,
London's West End became the scene of a pitched battle between rioters and
police, ending in 341 arrested and 132 hurt. Cars were overturned and torched,
windows smashed and shops looted. Then the residents of Mid-Staffordshire
had just discovered the size of their first poll-tax demands when they were
given an opportunity to vent their feelings in a by-election. The result was
sensational: a Conservative majority of 14,654 became a 9,449 majority for
Labour, one of the biggest electoral swings between the two main parties
since the war. An opinion poll around that time gave Labour the highest level
of support ever registered by a political party. On 2 April, Alan Clark noted
fretfully that MPs "are now talking openly of ditching the Lady to save their
skins".[6]

The final element in the story is the wholly unexpected behaviour of Sir
Geoffrey Howe, who resigned from the Cabinet at the beginning of November 1990, in protest against anti-European remarks that the prime minister
had made when answering questions on the recent EC summit in Madrid,
and then delivered an explosive resignation speech, which ended with the
words: "The time has come for others to consider their own response to the
tragic conflict of loyalties with which I have myself wrestled for perhaps too
long."[7] This amounted to an open invitation to Michael Heseltine, who had
been waiting on the back benches for nearly five years, to make his bid for
the leadership.

At a personal level, there was considerable sympathy for Howe on the
"wet" wing of the party. Numerous Cabinet ministers have described the
rudeness and contempt with which Mrs Thatcher addressed the deputy prime
minister in front of embarrassed colleagues. Clarke owed Howe a debt for
helping him in his early days as an MP and more recently for backing him up
during the ambulance dispute, and still considered him to be a prime minister
manqué. He too though that Sir Geoffrey had been provoked beyond endur-
ance. The occasional pat on the head, or a show of deferring to his judgement would have been enough to keep him in the Cabinet and perhaps to
save Mrs Thatcher's own position. But that does not mean that he thought

Howe was right to resign. Clarke, after all, had sat through the same statement without finding it necessary to quit the Cabinet. Other pro-Europeans in the Cabinet, apart from Howe, thought they had done rather well to tie Thatcher down to reading out an agreed text on the Madrid statement, although she read it through gritted teeth and betrayed her real feelings when she was ad-libbing afterwards. Say what you like about her, Thatcher swinging the handbag was good theatre and most of her ministers took gleeful pleasure in listening to her give vent to her archaic prejudices. And like other Cabinet ministers, Clarke expected Howe's resignation speech to be a dutiful piece of hypocrisy setting out what an honour it had been to serve in her government and how his continuing mission would be to carry on the good work from the back benches, and so on. Instead, to his surprise, Howe's going turned into an unforgettable parliamentary occasion. Mrs Thatcher was surprised too. "I was just amazed at the mixture of bile and treachery that poured out", she complained later.[8]

The "Margaret did this, then Geoffrey did that" school of history is very much in keeping with the image that the Conservative Party has of itself – as scarcely a political party at all, more an association of sensible folk who deal with problems in a common-sense sort of way, as and when they crop up. The poll tax is now agreed to have been a mistake that was put right, and so provides a handy explanation of why Mrs Thatcher had to go. But if we accept that the poll tax and Geoffrey Howe brought her down, it does seem rather odd that Howe did not even mention the subject in his explosive resignation speech.

The Thatcherites are more overtly ideological than other Tories, and more likely therefore to see the downfall of their heroine as having come about through politics rather than a chapter of accidents. They are in no doubt that she was ousted because the Cabinet was divided and that most Cabinet ministers, with Clarke leading the charge, betrayed her. If we extend the term "Cabinet ministers" to include a few big-league political players who had left the Cabinet in dramatic circumstances – Michael Heseltine, Nigel Lawson, Nicholas Ridley and Geoffrey Howe – this version of events fits the facts rather well.

There is no real evidence that people generally were "tired" of Margaret Thatcher. Most of the population had never warmed to or voted for her in the first place. However, to the end of her time in power and afterwards, she continued to fascinate even those who were repelled by her. The fact that by May 1990 she was the most unpopular prime minister since records began was important, but not decisive. The previous record was one she had set herself in 1981, but she had survived that crisis; her new record was soon broken by John Major, who survived. The council elections in May 1990 were not the unmitigated disaster they might have been. Whilst Labour did well around most of the country, it scored badly in central and west London, notably in the boroughs of Wandsworth and Westminster, which were frequently cited as flagships for Conservative local government. The party chairman, Kenneth Baker, adroitly dressed up this small amount of good news as if it were a national triumph. By summer 1990, Thatcher could claim to be over the worst, and if she had survived the crisis of November 1990, she would have had no qualms about calling a snap general election as the troops returned victoriously from the Gulf, and might have won it.

The legend that the Conservative Party ruthlessly disposes of leaders who have overstayed their time should be treated cautiously too. Since the war, the Conservatives have been led by six men. Sir Winston Churchill was eighty years old when he summoned the two most senior members of his Cabinet and told them: "I am going and Anthony will succeed me. We can discuss the details later." Sir Anthony Eden led Britain into the Suez fiasco, then retired ill to Bermuda. Harold Macmillan was also ill and in pain when he chose to be succeeded by Sir Alec Douglas-Home, who had almost no experience of the House of Commons, whose appointment had scandalized powerful figures like Iain Macleod and Enoch Powell, and who did not want to carry on anyway after losing a general election. It was only the ousting of Edward Heath in 1975 which could really be classed as ruthless, and that was after Heath had led the Conservatives to defeat in three general elections. Mrs Thatcher had lost only the 1989 European election, and by-elections in a few seats which the Tories could be confident of retaking at the next opportunity.

All in all, the idea that a clear-eyed Conservative Party saw that it could not win again under Mrs Thatcher's leadership and axed her for that reason looks very like a rationalization after the event. Even if some MPs were prompted to vote for Michael Heseltine because of the poll tax, an outright majority voted for Mrs Thatcher. The contest would not have taken place at all, neither would she have stood down after winning it, if the Cabinet had been solidly behind her.

The Cabinet was not deeply divided over the poll tax. It had provoked rebellions on the back benches, but they were relatively easily contained, whilst the Lords backed the government overwhelmingly. It was only when the legislation collided with the general public that it turned out to be the greatest single blunder Mrs Thatcher ever made. But she was not alone in making it. By her lights, this was a pretty good example of collective decision-making. Thatcher was not the one who demanded that local government finance be reformed by the year 1990. The call came after a riotous Scottish Tory conference in 1985. Under Scottish law, unlike English and Welsh law, property had to be revalued for the purposes of domestic rates once every five years. The 1985 revaluation produced rate increases of something like 20 per cent, almost wiping out Conservative support in parts of the country. George Younger, the Scottish Secretary, pleaded with the Cabinet not to put Scotland through the same ordeal again in 1990. The Conservative Political Centre published a pamphlet in 1985 by the Scottish MP Michael Forsyth, with the self-explanatory title: *The Case for a Poll Tax*.

The task of devising a new form of local taxation was taken up by two ministers in the Environment department, both of whom were seen as Heathmen rather than Thatcherites, but who both had ambitions to get on. It was William Waldegrave, an intellectual, who assembled the committee of experts which developed the idea of a flat-rate charge, and Kenneth Baker, the self-publicist, who sold it to an informal meeting of Cabinet ministers assembled one weekend at Chequers. The scheme then went into the Conservative manifesto and, remarkably, was barely challenged by the Labour Party until after the 1987 general election. It was examined for two-and-a-half years by a Cabinet sub-committee, on which sat, among others, Norman Fowler, Douglas Hurd and John Wakeham. Alan Clark, who attended one meeting, remembers seeing eleven other ministers there, who all appeared to be agreeing with the prime minister. The only dissenter was Nigel Lawson, who says in his memoirs that the only backing he got came from John MacGregor, his second in command at the Treasury. MacGregor once piped up in Lawson's absence and "had his head well and truly bitten off for his pains"[9] However, both Lawson and MacGregor kept their heads down when the proposal went to a full Cabinet meeting. There the only person who spoke against it was Peter Walker. When the legislation was published, Lawson refused to put his name to it, but John Major, as his new deputy, had no such qualms. He was one of the sponsors of the bill, and after he became prime minister continued defending the principle behind the tax even as he presided over its abolition. Another signatory was Kenneth Clarke.

By 1987, when the tax was clearly government policy, there was still a dispute between the past and present environment secretaries, Kenneth Baker and Nicholas Ridley respectively, over whether it should be phased in, co-existing alongside domestic rates for a few years, or brought in all at once. Ridley, and his new deputy, Michael Howard, wanted it on the statute books right away. Their hand was strengthened by delegates to that year's Conservative conference, particularly Gerry Malone, who later went on to be deputy chairman of the party. Malone, who had just lost his seat in Aberdeen, made an emotive call for an immediate end to domestic rates. After hearing him, Mrs Thatcher leant over to Ridley and whispered: "We shall have to look at this again, Nick."[10] As Clarke later said, with the candour that makes him one of the more attractive Conservative Cabinet ministers:

> It was a disastrous mistake, looking back, let's face it, and it went totally wrong. In the end where it went wrong was the total complication of collecting it. I certainly think that only Nigel Lawson can honestly claim truthfully to have been against it all the way through. Practically every other member of the Government had their hand dipped in the blood.[11]

This all gives the lie to the idea that if Mrs Thatcher had bowed out in May 1989 she and the country would have been spared the chaos that the Conservatives inflicted on local government finances. Scotland had already received its first poll tax bills, without setting off a reaction in the Cabinet. Nigel Lawson claims: "We were regularly informed by Malcolm Rifkind, who had inherited his enthusiasm for the tax from his predecessor George Younger, that in reality it was all working out pretty well."[12] The legislation introducing the tax to England and Wales had been through parliament, and the rebellions defeated. With Thatcher gone, the formidable trio of Lawson, Walker and Heseltine might have mounted some sort of action to prevent it being enacted, but the only alternative they could have offered in the time available was more years of domestic rates, which would certainly have provoked uproar at the next party conference. A post-Thatcher Cabinet is likely to have gone ahead with the new tax anyway, ameliorating it with large helpings of central government grant, and blaming the departed premier when it all went wrong. Similarly, they would have held her responsible when boom turned to recession in 1990, instead of heaping blame on the departed Nigel Lawson, as she and John Major did.

And without Thatcher, Britain would have immediately joined the Exchange Rate Mechanism of the European Monetary System. Europe was the issue that split the Conservative Cabinet. Like many English people who had lived through the war, Margaret Thatcher simply did not like Germans. In fact, her suspicions seemed to extend to anyone hailing from the western part of the continent of Europe. By her way of thinking, to quote Sir Geoffrey Howe's resignation speech, it was "a continent that is positively teeming with ill-intentioned people, scheming, in her words, to extinguish democracy."[13]

The late Nicholas Ridley, who was loyal to her to the end, recorded sitting beside Mrs Thatcher as she carried out the distasteful duty of addressing the European Parliament in Strasbourg, an institution she despised. "You could feel the waves of hostility emanating from her", he says. Ridley of course blamed the Europeans. "Her forthrightness and her tenacity were alien to Latin politicians ... Deep down they resented her because she was so utterly unmanoeuvrable." [14] However, it was the very fact that he agreed with her on this issue which forced him to resign in July 1990, after he had told the editor of the *Spectator*, Dominic Lawson, that a single European currency was "a German racket designed to take over the whole of Europe", and that the French are Germany's "poodles". He added: "You might just as well give in to Adolf Hitler."[15] Dominic was not the only member of the Lawson family who had heard anti-German sentiments like that uttered in high places. According to Nigel Lawson's memoirs, Ridley felt safe to speak as he did because "he had many times heard Margaret utter precisely the same sentiments in private – as, indeed, had I." Mrs Thatcher, he adds, "regarded the continental Europeans with distrust and, in private, with undisguised distaste and hostility."[16]

Of Mrs Thatcher's two most senior ministers, Howe was a Thatcherite only in domestic economic policy. He had been one of the draughtsmen of the 1972 European Communities Act and was almost as inspired by the European idea as Heath. Lawson, by contrast, had written an essay in his journalist days in praise of British nationalism. However, since 1985 he had been convinced that the pound needed a stable exchange rate. On Sunday, 25 June 1989, just as Mrs Thatcher was preparing to leave for another EC summit, her Foreign Secretary and Chancellor called at 10 Downing Street to deliver an extraordinary ultimatum: either she set some sort of realistic deadline for Britain's entry to the ERM, or they would both resign. The prime minister heard them out in icy silence. On the plane to Madrid, and at the hotel, she coldly refused even to speak to Sir Geoffrey Howe, closeting herself away with her loyal foreign-affairs adviser, Charles Powell. However, the summit produced a breakthrough, the so-called "Madrid Conditions" for British entry to the ERM, which were ignored in practice but at least conceded enough of a principle to keep Lawson and Howe in the Cabinet for a few months.

Four weeks later, Mrs Thatcher took her revenge by demoting Howe to the second-rank job of Leader of the House of Commons. Although he was shocked and humiliated, he did not resign. Instead Lawson did, the following November, having been exasperated by a *Financial Times* article in which Sir Alan Walters, who was on the point of returning as a part-time economic adviser in 10 Downing Street, dismissed the ERM as "half-baked".[17] Later the same month, there was the first direct challenge to Mrs Thatcher's leadership of the Tory Party. Since the challenger was Sir Anthony Meyer, a 69-year-old Tory pro-European who had never risen as high as a junior minister, she was in no danger of losing. She actually beat him by 314 votes to 33, with 24 abstentions. Nonetheless, it brought home to the growing number of enemies in her own party that she could be challenged, if someone could be found with enough nerve to cross the barbed wire.

Until the autumn of 1990, Mrs Thatcher could at least take comfort in one thing: there was no sign of a Liberal Democrat revival. The third party had been doing so badly that she devoted part of her conference to some jokes at its expense, likening it to the dead parrot from the classic Monty Python comedy sketch. The humour was well-scripted and went down well. Clarke was reported to have remarked afterwards that "She should do it more often: she can be very feminine."[18] But later the same month, the Conservatives experienced a nasty bite when the Liberal Democrats suddenly came back to life during the Eastbourne by-election, wiping out the 16,923 Tory majority.

Worse was in store at her last EC summit in Rome, at the end of October. For once, she was entitled to expect a friendly welcome, since she had just been prevailed upon by John Major and Douglas Hurd to take Great Britain, belatedly, into the ERM. Instead, she was caught in an ambush by the

Germans and French, who intended to use the occasion to speed up Europe's progress towards a single currency. On her return, Mrs Thatcher made a carefully worded statement to the House of Commons, meticulously drafted to avoid offence to any wing of the Conservative Party. But under questioning from MPs, she made a caustic reference to a pet scheme of John Major's, the "hard ecu", which Britain was promoting as a free-market alternative to that of a unified currency made in Brussels. Showing a quixotic unconcern for the problems faced by British officials who were supposed to be promoting the hard ecu abroad, the prime minister implied that she did not expect many people would ever want to use it as legal tender. The most striking image broadcast to the nation that night was of Mrs Thatcher, contemplating the prospect that the pound sterling might one day disappear in favour of a Euro-currency, exclaiming "No, no, no." For Sir Geoffrey Howe, it was too much. After the money markets had closed the following evening, it was announced that he too had quit.

This had immediate and unexpected consequences for Kenneth Clarke. At that time, the government was in trouble over its education reforms. The minister in charge was the inconspicuous John MacGregor, who seemed to be unable to convince either parliament or the teaching profession that the government's plans for student loans, city technology colleges and a wide-ranging national curriculum were workable, partly because he did not believe it himself. Presented suddenly with a vacancy, Mrs Thatcher seized the opportunity to push MacGregor upstairs into the post of Leader of the House. She then attempted to shore up her own position by asking Norman Tebbit to return to the government as Secretary of State for Education and Science, but he declined. At this point, on the morning of 2 November, she decided to send for Kenneth Clarke.

It was a slightly embarrassing offer. Only recently, when the job was held by his rival Kenneth Baker, Clarke had been indiscreetly running Education down as a soft option compared with the rigours of managing the NHS.[19] Now he tried to talk his way out of being moved by pointing out a political difficulty. Since 1982, Mrs Thatcher had been interested in an idea put to her by the right-wing Institute of Economic Affairs, that the state should issue parents with vouchers with which they could purchase an education for their children at the school of their choice. It was her devoted admirer, Keith Joseph, who persuaded her not to include the idea in the 1983 election manifesto, whereupon the IEA accused him of having been got at by his civil servants. It popped up again suddenly in the run-up to the 1986 council elections and, if Mrs Thatcher had had her way, it would have been included in the following year's election manifesto, and would, presumably, have been introduced with Kenneth Baker's 1988 education bill.

As usual, Mrs Thatcher persisted despite the opposition all around her. For all her dissatisfaction with John MacGregor, she seems to have thought he was a minister she could bully into line. By 1990, vouchers were available to school leavers, allowing them to "buy" places on training schemes. In what turned out to be her last speech to a Conservative Party conference, in October, Mrs Thatcher said: "It's the first voucher scheme we have introduced and I hope it won't be the last." When she sought to recall Tebbit to the colours, it was doubtless in the hope that he would back her up. However, she cannot have had much faith in Kenneth Clarke, given his previous opposition to tax breaks for private health insurance. He now told her that he was opposed to vouchers, and if he took the job it would have to be on that understanding. His first policy pronouncement, only nine days after his appointment, was that "I have never been in favour of vouchers. I don't think they play any part in the government's plans."[20] Three days later, the Labour leader Neil Kinnock invited the prime minister, at Question Time in the Commons, to "join me in agreeing with her new Secretary of State for Education and Science in his very firm opposition to the daft idea of education vouchers." Indeed, he invited her three times to say that she agreed with Kenneth Clarke, and three times she gave an evasive answer.[21] About two hours later, when Clarke himself was asked by his Labour shadow, Jack Straw, whether education vouchers would be in the next election manifesto, he replied: "Plainly they will not ... The idea of vouchers for schools is not on the government's agenda. It need not be and will not be on the agenda because we have found a better way."[22]

Behind the scenes, government officials did their best to play down this open disagreement between the prime minister and her new education minister. It was suggested that Mrs Thatcher's conference speech had been misunderstood, that she was not referring to vouchers for parents of school children, but to qualified students who would use them to buy their way into university or polytechnic, and that anyway Clarke had her "tacit approval"[23] before he stamped on the whole idea. This is all gloss. In her memoirs,

Mrs Thatcher complains that Clarke "publicly discounted my advocacy of education vouchers".[24]

Nonetheless, this overt split in the cabinet did not get the front-page treatment it deserved, because it was overwhelmed by greater events. On the day when the matter was raised in parliament – indeed, in the short interlude between Kinnock's exchange with Thatcher and Clarke's with Jack Straw – Sir Geoffrey Howe had made his resignation speech. Delivered to a packed Commons, it was one of those rare occasions in politics in which those who were anticipating drama got more than they expected. Years of pent-up humiliation were compressed into an attack of deadly ferocity, made all the more effective by the quiet tone of its delivery. His timing was also deadly. November is the dangerous month for Conservative leaders: the rules say that any challenge must be mounted within four weeks of the Queen's Speech, which is normally made at the end of October. It was 13 November. The destruction of Margaret Thatcher would be complete in less than nine days.

At every stage in this story, Europe had been the trigger. Even the fact that there was a credible contender waiting on the sidelines to challenge Thatcher was attributable to Europe: the Westland saga, which provoked Michael Heseltine's resignation, had been an argument over whether Europe needed the capacity to manufacture its own defence equipment. With the high command hopelessly split, the middle ranks were called upon to settle the issue. The 152 Tory MPs who voted for Michael Heseltine on the first round, and the 16 who abstained, obviously had their own reasons for doing so. Some were pro-Europeans; some may simply have thought that they had a better chance of a government job under a new prime minister; some may have been swayed by the comparison between the energy of the Heseltine campaign and the aloofness of Mrs Thatcher, who chose to be at an international conference in Paris when the votes were cast. It is said that the biggest single factor was the poll tax. Whatever the reason for the result of the first ballot, it was not the event which actually forced her resignation. She came bouncing back to London the following morning vowing to fight on, and brazened her way through a Commons statement on the Paris summit as if nothing had happened. A few hours later, she gave up. What defeated her was that eleven Cabinet ministers out of fifteen whom she consulted in her room behind the Speaker's chair advised her that her cause was lost.

Up to this point, Kenneth Clarke had not been directly involved, but from here he was a central player. How to describe Clarke's behaviour depends, as they say, on your point of view: on the day of Thatcher's resignation, her admirer Nicholas Ridley blamed Cabinet "treachery" for bringing her down; another admirer, Alan Clark, says that Kenneth Clarke was "loathsomely conspiring";[25] on the Tuesday after Thatcher's fall, as the Commons waited for her to take Prime Minister's Questions for the last time, a right-wing Tory MP named David Evans told him publicly that if he had been "loyal" the previous week, backbench MPs would have been able to retain the leader of their choice.[26] However, Kenneth Clarke claims to have acted throughout in the spirit of true friendship. Perhaps. What can be said is that if there was treachery in the Cabinet, he was a leading traitor; if there was plotting, he plotted; but if, on the other hand, there were only friends persuading the prime minister to face reality, he was persuasive. More than any other incumbent Cabinet minister, with the possible exception of Malcolm Rifkind, he behaved as if he wanted her out of office.

On Monday, the day before the vote, he was one of a trio of Cabinet ministers who met in John Wakeham's room at the House of Commons, the third being John Gummer. All three had sniffed the wind and anticipated that the next day's ballot would not be decisive. Thatcher's immediate circle of advisers thought otherwise; they were so sure of victory that they had no contingency plan to cover the possibility of her returning from Paris with her position still under threat. That was what the ministers discussed. All three believed that unless she won outright, she would be too damaged to stay in office. Obviously, if she had confounded their expectations the following day by routing Michael Heseltine, all three would have rallied behind her; but in a book published on the anniversary of her fall, entitled *A Conservative Coup*, the political commentator Alan Watkins regarded this meeting as significant enough to be called a "plot". That produced angry disclaimers from the politicians concerned, including a memorandum from Kenneth Clarke saying:

> The meeting between John Wakeham, John Gummer and me was not pre-arranged and did not involve anything that could be described as a "plot". It was a discussion between three supporters of Mrs Thatcher who were concerned about the possible result of the first ballot and who wished to ensure her return from Paris in a position to consider the next steps.[27]

Nonetheless, it was from this cabal and others like it that Cabinet ministers struck up the informal agreement which forced Mrs Thatcher's resignation.

Hearing that she had won by fifty-two votes, four short of the result she needed, simply hardened Clarke's determination that her premiership must end. His reaction in the circumstances was peculiar but not wholly out of character. At the very time when other Cabinet ministers ducked for cover, he popped up in every available television or radio studio to defend her. That evening, there was a meeting at the home of the former deputy chief whip Tristan Garel-Jones, in St Catherine's Place, Westminster, which has its place in folklore. There were ten ministers and one parliamentary private secretary present, five of them – Chris Patten, Norman Lamont, Malcolm Rifkind, Tony Newton, and William Waldegrave – from the Cabinet. They reached a consensus that Mrs Thatcher was heading for defeat in the second ballot, and it would be better if Douglas Hurd and John Major were released from their obligation to support her so that they could enter the contest. Clarke should have been among the guests, but no one had been able to contact him to invite him, because he was too busy dashing from one interview to another.

His purpose in creating this smokescreen, Clarke says, was to allow Mrs Thatcher to make a dignified return from Paris, surrounded by formal declarations of loyalty, so that she could be respectfully informed the next day that she had to go. On Wednesday, John MacGregor went round in his capacity as Leader of the House, seeking the opinions of Cabinet ministers. Clarke gave him a blunt reply. A second bout between Thatcher and Heseltine would split the party; he could no longer support her; and in his view Douglas Hurd and John Major should put their names forward, he said. He repeated the message when Thatcher's campaign manager, Peter Morrison, rang to ask for his support in the second ballot.

And that, he supposed, would be the end of the story. In the Conservative Party, there is a legendary group called the "men in grey suits" who turn up like the grim reaper at the moment when it is time for a prime minister to resign. No prime minister, it was commonly thought, could survive their visit. At lunchtime on Wednesday, a little group which included John MacGregor; the party chairman, Kenneth Baker; the Chief Whip, Tim Renton; and the chairman of the all-important backbench 1922 Committee, Cranley Onslow, lunched with Mrs Thatcher in 10 Downing Street and gave a passable impersonation of men in brown trousers. MacGregor, for example, had spoken to seventeen Cabinet ministers, twelve of whom had said she was heading for defeat, but did not tell her. The only significant development was that Thatcher reluctantly agreed to a suggestion that she should meet her senior ministers singly later in the day, ostensibly to ask for their support. As she left Downing Street, she declared to waiting journalists: "I fight on, I fight to win." As the lunch party broke up, John Wakeham privately suggested to Kenneth Baker that Kenneth Clarke could be Thatcher's campaign manager in the next round, when he already knew that Clarke did not want her to be a candidate.[28]

Presently, Mrs Thatcher was at the Commons despatch box, not quite for the last time, reporting back on the Paris summit. She behaved as she always had, without a trace of humility or self-doubt, without displaying the slightest inclination to pull out. According to one inside account, "Kenneth Clarke, rock hard in conviction that she ought to go, listened to the statement with his eyes firmly fixed on his boots, lest the TV cameras alight on him looking incredulous. He could not believe what he was hearing."[29] He caught Chris Patten's eye. They both retired behind the Speaker's chair, to discuss the appalling prospect that she really might fight on. Norman Lamont joined them briefly and agreed that she should go.

Later, Clarke and Patten shut themselves away with Malcolm Rifkind, in his room in the Cabinet corridor. We know this because who should put his head around the door but the ubiquitous Alan Clark, who had decided that the way to save Mrs Thatcher was to persuade Patten to stand against her, splitting the left vote. "Clarke wasn't friendly at all. If he had said anything to me, I'd have answered 'Fuck you', so just as well", he recorded.[30] Clark, of course, went away convinced that he had caught Thatcher's "three great ill-wishers" conspiring. Clarke was still there around 6 p.m., when the party chairman, Kenneth Baker, turned up. By now, Rifkind had moved on, but two whips, Tristan Garel-Jones and Alistair Goodland, and a Treasury minister, Richard Ryder, were present. All five were angry at Baker for encouraging Thatcher to fight another round. According to Baker: "Ken Clarke was even angrier, saying, 'If she decides to stand then I want a full meeting of the Cabinet tonight.'"[31]

At about 6.15 p.m., Kenneth Clarke went into Thatcher's study, the first of a string of Cabinet ministers who trooped in for one-to-one conversations with her. Thatcher describes the meeting thus:

His manner was robust in the brutalist style he has cultivated: the candid friend. He said that this method of changing prime ministers was farcical, and that he personally would be happy to support me for another five or ten years. Most of the Cabinet, however, thought that I should stand down. Otherwise not only would I lose, I would "lose big". If that were to happen, the party would go to Michael Heseltine and end up split.[32]

If Clarke really told her he would be "happy" to support her for another five or ten years, he was stretching the truth. At some point that afternoon, he had made up his mind that, whatever she decided, he was not going to serve in her Cabinet any longer. After he had spoken to her, according to Kenneth Baker, "Ken spent the rest of the evening in the House, busily contacting other Tory MPs and telling them that if Margaret stood again, 'I will resign as we are crashing on to great folly.' When he left the House late that night he was convinced that she was going to go on."[33] For a time, it was believed that he even told her so to her face. This is one of those rumours which cannot quite be attributed to Kenneth Clarke, but appear to have drifted from his direction. When asked during a Channel Four interview whether Mrs Thatcher had known of his intention to quit her government, he said: "Yes, I am sure she did."[34] She, on the other hand, is adamant: "Contrary to persistent rumours, Ken Clarke at no point threatened to resign."[35]

Although their versions of the conversation cannot be reconciled, the point is not particularly significant. At the time, Thatcher was under extreme stress, and there is evidence that throughout the day she was having hints dropped in her presence without hearing them properly. She was listening out for what she wanted to hear and blocking out unpleasant thoughts. Even if he pulled a punch, Clarke can take credit for being the first person to penetrate the wall of denial and bring home to her that she was finished. In all, she spoke to sixteen Cabinet ministers during the evening. Afterwards, she drafted the resignation statement that was released the following morning.

John Major's campaign for the leadership took off that same day. Douglas Hurd's suffered from a surfeit of unmotivated Cabinet ministers lending their names to his campaign without making a serious effort to secure his election. Hurd was too pro-European to pick up the right-wing vote. His other great disadvantage was being an Old Etonian up against a man who had come up the hard way. Clarke's support for him looked odd because most of the grammar-school element was in the Major camp. Asked why, he is reputed to have said that Hurd's people needed one peasant, if only to pour the drinks. There were actually more sensible reasons for supporting Hurd, since his politics and Clarke's were very similar. Also "young bishops vote for old popes." John Major was three years younger than Clarke, so with his election Clarke's chances of ever being prime minister diminished.

CHAPTER TWELVE

EDUCATION SECRETARY

All over Whitehall, ministers were experiencing a sense of being let out of school. The headmistress was gone, taking that fearsome handbag with her, and there was a new school captain who listened to the opinions of other prefects before expressing his own, if indeed he had one. "I wish there had been more discussions like this during the past few months. Perhaps she would have avoided some of the pitfalls", a relieved Kenneth Clarke is supposed to have said as he emerged from one amicable Cabinet meeting.[1] While the new prime minister visited the troops in the Gulf, fantasized about the pound becoming stronger than the Deutsche Mark, and fretted over the availability of motorway lavatories, other ministers went about their business undisturbed.

For the next eighteen months, therefore, we see Clarke in his true colours. Most of his brief term as Secretary of State for Education and Science was occupied with tidying up the legislation introduced by his predecessor but one. In that time, he talked tough, made an appearance of taking a professional interest in eyeball-to-eyeball confrontation, was radical on a couple of side issues of no great importance, while on the main issues he conciliated and gave ground. Generally, he left the education system in no worse a state than he found it, steering himself through what was extremely dangerous territory for a Conservative minister without harming his future. He had not wanted the job, and it was inconvenient to be so new to it at the time when John Major was putting together his first cabinet. Major, quite reasonably, took the view that there could not be two changes of Education Secretary in the same month; therefore Clarke had to stay put whilst Kenneth Baker, Norman Lamont, Chris Patten and Michael Heseltine were promoted. At best, he could claim to be seventh man in the new administration. All of those who were now ahead of him, except for the patrician Douglas Hurd, had been behind him in the mid 1980s.

When Clarke was trying to avoid being transferred to Education, he is reputed to have suggested to Mrs Thatcher that she appoint William Waldegrave instead. He certainly had the academic qualifications, but she refused to hear of it. "He is an Etonian!" she replied.[2] This was a strange objection from someone who was not wont to be so fussy about putting former public-school boys in control of the state education system. Clarke was the fifth education secretary appointed by her. Of the previous four, Kenneth Baker had spent part of his boyhood at grammar school, before being sent on to St Paul's, one of London's most demanding private schools, to ensure that he won a place at university. The others were Mark Carlisle, ex-Radley College, her favourite Sir Keith Joseph, an Old Harrovian, and John MacGregor, a scholarship entrant to Merchiston Castle, Edinburgh. She should also have known that Clarke was not a product of the state education system either.

Moreover, like almost every other Cabinet minister, Clarke had balked at the idea of putting his own children through the state system. The only Cabinet ministers who had done so were the Social Security Secretary Tony Newton, who, as MP for Braintree, was conveniently placed to enable his two daughters to go to Chelmsford High School, which is well known as one of the best state schools in Britain, and the Environment Secretary Chris Patten, whose daughters went to a state primary school. The Clarkes went through what Kenneth called the "classic agonies"[3] of liberally inclined middle-class parents before they took their children out of the state system at the age of eleven, sending their son to King Edward School, Birmingham, where the fees were £2,250 a year, and their daughter to Edgbaston High School, at £1,971 a year.[4] "We could have moved house to a part of the country that had particularly good state schools", he later explained. But that would have been like "buying state education through your mortgage".[5]

This sensitive question about where ministers' children went to school led indirectly to one of the most comical episodes of Clarke's tenure as Education Secretary. Interviewed in *Woman* magazine, he was asked whether his own decision to educate his children privately was not "the most damning condemnation of our system of education", to which he replied, with admirable directness:

I have never met anybody who did not wish to send their children to independent education if they could afford it. This is a very bad thing indeed, which has developed over the last 20 years. I'm absolutely typical of a parent who wouldn't have contemplated sending my children to independent schools originally.

I know some political opponents like to say they sent their children to state schools. But in most cases I regard that as either hypocrisy or sacrificing their children to promote their own political career.[6]

That first sentence swiftly became the most famous observation Clarke ever made about education. He was, of course, trying to make the point (elaborated in a third paragraph not reproduced here) that independent schools were attractive because of their better discipline and higher academic standards, and that the way to correct the unfair advantage enjoyed by children of the wealthy was to make the state system better. Clarke was aggrieved that the *Daily Mirror* should quote the first sentence of his reply but not the one which followed – though the second sentence was in its way the more damning, since it dated the beginning of the decline in British schools back to about 1971. In that year, Margaret Thatcher was Education Secretary and for fifteen of the ensuing twenty years there had been a Conservative government. The *Mirror* report was taken up in the Commons by Labour's education spokesman Jack Straw, who accused Clarke of making a "ludicrous" statement; whereupon the Secretary of State for Education and Science blew a gasket:

You are quoting the *Mirror* … only a buffoon would quote the *Mirror* … The *Daily Mirror*, read by morons, produces that particular sentence.[7]

A politician of Clarke's experience should have known better. Tabloids are more adept at insulting people than politicians are. He seemed to realize he had made a mistake, because later in the same debate he tried to retract, saying his remark had been "somewhat misguided". It was too late: the following morning's *Daily Mirror* produced a two-word headline in white on black across its entire page – YOU MORONS – accompanied by a reminder: "That's two fingers to 8,230,000 voters, Minister." One-eighth of those voters, incidentally, were thought by market analysts to be Tories. The newspaper invited reader participation: those who thought Kenneth Clarke was the moron were offered a telephone number to ring; and, by way of balance, another phone line was opened for those who thought he was a prat.[8] The poll produced an astonishing 59,000 callers, of whom 36,966 judged Clarke to be a prat, and 21,855 a moron – a majority of 15,111 for the prats, as it were.[9] The *Mirror* celebrated this result by printing his photograph on their front page upside down, which seemed to irritate him more than anything else about the entire episode. During an interview on *Newsnight* that night, he mentioned this grievance several times.

The real cause of his annoyance, without doubt, was that he had been pushed into a corner where he did not want to be. He was not an ideological champion of private education, any more than private health care. The right wing of the Conservative Party believed in education vouchers or in allowing parents to offset their school fees against tax, or both. Clarke opposed both ideas and, as we have seen, was prepared to take Mrs Thatcher on over vouchers, as he had over tax breaks for private health care. He did not believe in leaving education to the market any more than health and for the same reason, that the customer was not in a position to refuse to buy the service. "I don't believe you can produce a market because there is no bottom line. Tax relief for school fees and vouchers are right wing things," he said.[10]

Nonetheless, the quality that Mrs Thatcher singled out in Clarke as appropriate for an education minister was that he was an "energetic and persuasive bruiser, very useful in a brawl".[11] Her language is illustrative, in that it suggests that to Mrs Thatcher and her Cabinet the state education system was a battlefield where opponents had to be knocked into submission. This was one respect in which she departed from Conservative tradition. Whilst state education had become entangled in inevitable political controversies in the past, every previous Conservative administration since Bonar Law's had aimed to defuse the issue by compromise and retreat. There had been a classic example when Thatcher herself was Education Secretary, when the issue of the day was comprehensive education: the Conservatives were prepared to back local authorities like Buckinghamshire and Manchester which stood their ground against the spread of comprehensives, and to object, as the newly elected Kenneth Clarke did, to some of the administrative measures taken by Labour councils to enforce the abolition of the eleven-plus. Nonetheless, Mrs Thatcher approved more schemes to create comprehensive schools than any other Education Secretary, Conservative or Labour.

Since the First World War, there have been three truly momentous education acts, all sponsored by Conservative ministers. The first two – the Fisher

Act of 1918 and the Butler Act of 1944 – were consensus measures reflecting the perceived need to achieve social cohesion after a European war, and arrived at after meticulous consultation with all political parties represented in parliament, and with the Churches and other interested parties. The third was the 1988 Education Reform Act, steered through parliament by Kenneth Baker. This was introduced with minimal consultation: the "consultation papers" were issued in July 1987 – that is, at the start of the school holidays – and responses had to be in within two months, or before the schools returned, thus ensuring that parents were not influenced by their children's teachers in the "consultation" period. Nor was it a consensus measure; indeed, it appeared that antagonizing Labour local authorities and swathes of the teaching profession was part of its very purpose. In her address to the 1987 Conservative conference, Mrs Thatcher claimed that children in Britain's inner cities were having educational opportunities "all too often snatched from them by hard-left education authorities and extremist teachers".[12]

One might ask what these extremist teachers had ever done to offend the Conservatives. They certainly had not harmed the expensive education of any Cabinet minister's child. Bearing in mind that the offenders were specifically located in inner-city schools, their young charges were generally the children of Labour voters. Yet the voters persisted in returning "hard-left education authorities" to power irrespective of the havoc allegedly being wreaked on classroom teaching standards. The only way the Conservatives could prevent Londoners from supporting their "hard left" Inner London Education Authority, for instance, was by abolishing it. This suggests that the political strains and stresses which produced the Baker reforms were the product of something more than the worries of parents from the inner cities.

To understand the reforms, it is necessary to refer back again to the general political situation in 1988. First, there was the collapse of the two-party system. This had produced the return of a Conservative government which had vowed to be radical, and which had a big enough majority to get anything it wanted to through parliament. In that sense, the Baker education reforms happened for the same reason as the poll tax, the privatization of the water industry and Clarke's health reforms: because there was no political force big enough to stop them.

In a sense, Kenneth Baker was himself a political force too small to stop the reforms to which his name is linked. Although it is often called the Baker

Act, and the days when schools are closed because teachers are immersed in extra paperwork are known as Baker Days, his claim to its paternity is doubtful. It was an immensely detailed piece of legislation, and it is well known that Baker's grasp of detail was as weak as his aptitude for public presentation was strong. The policies were thrashed out in a Cabinet subcommittee dominated by Margaret Thatcher and her adviser Brian Griffiths, a former director of the Bank of England whom she had appointed head of the Number 10 Policy Group. "At the end of it," Nigel Lawson recalls, "Margaret would sum up and give Kenneth his marching orders. He would then return to the next meeting with a worked-out proposal which bore little resemblance to what everyone else recalled as having been agreed ... After receiving a metaphorical handbagging for his pains, he would then come back with something that corresponded more closely to her ideas."[13] Kenneth Clarke was brought into the process as the minister responsible for inner cities, and co-wrote the section of the 1987 Conservative manifesto which prefigured the 1988 legislation.

The legislation was conceived in a period when the government was boasting that it had reversed Britain's chronic political and economic decline. Yet there were areas of visible failure. Unemployment still ran into millions. Crime was still inexorably increasing, particularly among the young. There was vandalism, truancy and indiscipline in inner-city schools. Moreover, the teaching profession was becoming politicized. For the first time in decades, teachers were prepared to strike, which they first did in 1985 when the government refused to fund their pay award. Pay had become a grievance because, relative to other employees, teachers' living standards were slipping: in 1975, their salaries were 40 per cent above the white-collar average; by 1990, that figure was down to 5 per cent. There was also a spreading tendency in the profession to blame problems in the classroom on a government that was deliberately widening the gap between rich and poor and that had effectively introduced permanent mass unemployment as an instrument of economic policy. It was becoming difficult to instil a love of learning and a respect for authority in youngsters who had nothing to look forward to but a lifetime on the fringes of the economy. The teachers' problems were made worse by the squeezing of the state education budget. We have seen that in providing for their children, almost all Conservative ministers have stuck to the principle that money can buy high standards. The principle applied to the rest of the nation's children was, to quote Clarke, "When you are dealing with standards of health care, standards of education, you just can't buy them."[14]

Thatcher's longest-serving Education Secretary, Keith Joseph, was almost self-flagellating in his belated belief in public frugality; during five annual spending rounds when he was Education Secretary, he never went before the so-called "Star Chamber" – the Cabinet committee that used to arbitrate in public spending disputes – to appeal for more funds for education. In 1993, after a study which took two years and cost £1 million to carry out, the National Commission for Education disclosed that in the ten years to 1991, once allowance had been made for the large proportion of the education budget that is taken up by salaries, spending on state education had not increased at all in real terms; as a proportion of public expenditure and of gross domestic product, it had fallen.[15] This bears out the view formed by Ian Gilmour, a member of the 1979 Cabinet:

> The Thatcher government was unable to understand the concept of an intel-
> lectual investment, because it does not produce immediate cash returns. An
> under-educated society will in due course become socially unstable and eco-
> nomically inefficient, but Thatcherites were too blinkered to appreciate that
> simple point. For them, immediate economies and tax cuts were far more im-
> portant than the long-term future of the country.[16]

That is a view from the Tory left. From Downing Street, it was of course unthinkable that the government that had produced an economic and political miracle could be responsible for the decay in educational standards. There was a much more satisfactory explanation to be had: standards and unemployment were high at the same time that the main teachers' union and a number of Labour councils had shifted noticeably to the left: *ergo* left-wing teachers and left-wing councillors were to blame. Just as Europe was "teeming with ill-intentioned people" so, in Mrs Thatcher's eyes, inner-city schools became staffed not by professionals daily doing their best as pay and working conditions deteriorated, but by malicious elements intent on teaching their pupils "anti-racist mathematics, political slogans, that they had an inalienable right to be gay and that our society offered them no future".[17]

There were two main strands to the education bill, one of which imposed central control over what was taught in the classrooms, via the national curriculum, while the other was intended to release schools from the control of fanatical councillors, through the creation of grant-maintained schools, a process known colloquially as "opting out". The idea of a core curriculum common to all schools was not in itself controversial. It had support right across the political spectrum, although the proposals presented in Baker's bill did not. It was proposed that the curriculum would apply to all children from the ages of five to sixteen, who would be tested at the ages of seven, eleven, fourteen and sixteen. There were to be three "core" subjects – English, mathematics and "combined sciences" – and five more "foundation" subjects – technology, a modern language, history and/or geography, art/music/ drama/design, and physical education. There were another eleven "additional subjects", including religious education, which was compulsory under the 1944 Act.[18] All of this inevitably threw up controversy over what the "foundation" subjects ought to be, how they should be taught, to what extent it was realistic to test children as young as seven, whether the testing should be by teachers or outsiders, and how competitive the system was to be. It not only caused trouble between the government and the educators, but within the Cabinet too, with Mrs Thatcher accusing Kenneth Baker of conceding too much ground to civil servants and other professional advisers.

The central proposal in the bill, which took up 42 of its 136 clauses, was to give parents the right to remove their children's school from local-authority control and give it grant-maintained status. This could be done by a simple majority vote, although there was no equivalent provision for opted-out schools to return themselves to the bosom of their local council. Once out, the school would then be supervised and legally owned by its board of governors, who answered to the Department of Education. At the time, Baker was quite specific that this piece of legislation was designed to give parents an opportunity to free their children from the pernicious influence of left-wing Labour councils. In this it spectacularly failed, except in the London borough of Lambeth, where everything that was bad about Labour in local government seemed to be concentrated. Elsewhere, parents used the legislation to escape from Conservative councils. By 1993, there were eleven local education authorities within whose boundaries there were more secondary-school children in opted-out than in council-run schools. Lambeth was one. Another three were London boroughs which had been Labour controlled in the mid 1980s but were now Tory: Brent, Ealing and Hillingdon. The others were far removed from the strongholds of the Labour left, in the home counties and rural England.

However, freeing parents from left-wing councils was not the only purpose of the opting-out legislation, nor even necessarily its main purpose.
There is a parallel here with the health reforms in which Margaret Thatcher
had set out to make private health care more widely used in order to make
it less politically sensitive, but which encountered opposition from Kenneth
Clarke. In education, she hoped to create a large "middle stratum" out of
those who could not afford private-school fees, but who would be able to do
something other than simply send their children to the nearest comprehensive.
Variety and choice were the catchwords behind the policy. The children of
discerning parents capable of operating the system to their advantage would
concentrate in the schools with the best reputation locally. Other schools
would either close, thereby presumably setting the process of self-selection
off again, or they would become permanent sink schools for children with
no future. One means of achieving this, which Kenneth Clarke supported
when he took up office, was "open enrolment", which allowed popular
schools to increase their enrolment until they had reached the limit of their
physical capacity. Coupled with a revised system under which the funds received by a school were proportional to its intake, it meant that, in a phrase
popular with ministers at the time, money followed the pupils into the popular schools. Other schools would then become half empty and underfunded,
but the local authority would be unable to do anything about it.

Of all the problems thrown up by the 1988 Education Act, the one which
was exasperating teachers more than any other was the national curriculum
as it applied to children aged between fourteen and sixteen. By that age,
children are beginning to have an idea of what they will do in adult life; but
the National Curriculum Council, a government quango set up after the 1988
Act, proposed to give them no choice but to continue studying all ten subjects
until they were sixteen. Clarke simply gave way to the teachers. He conceded
that the government line was "inflexible and undesirable", and announced
that only English, maths and science would be compulsory to GCSE level.[19]

However, the arguments thrown up by the national curriculum were about
much more than numbers. The government had taken it upon itself, through
the National Curriculum Council, not merely to tell teachers what subjects to
teach but how to go about it. Their actions were fuelled by the suspicion
that trendy new teaching methods were putting too much emphasis on
self-expression and too little on the old-fashioned grind of accumulating

knowledge. What the Conservatives wanted was not quite the teaching method of Mr Gradgrind of *Hard Times*, with its emphasis on facts, facts and facts, but a system that would be more orderly and disciplined than the anarchy that they imagined had taken over in the classroom. Clarke wrote:

> I do not expect to persuade our teachers to return to rows of desks and the use of the blackboard, but there must be some purposeful education carried out in the happy chaos that has replaced them. Geography lessons should not all be conducted in sandpits, and every primary science lesson does not need pools of water.[20]

Politicians were, rightly, alarmed that every year schools were disgorging pupils who had not learnt how to spell, or even to read easily. Soon after Clarke took office, education inspectors reported that one pupil in five was not being taught to read properly. Clarke quickly disposed of the idea that this could be blamed on a government which had been forcing teachers to take larger classes in deteriorating buildings. He told the Commons Select Committee on Education:

> Today's schools are the best resourced we have ever had ... I won't take responsibility for things that are utterly beyond my control ... They are not my schools. They are the local authorities' schools ... As Secretary of State one of the things I have had to get accustomed to is that I do not own a school, I do not employ a teacher or appoint a head teacher.[21]

On another occasion, he said:

> The repair and maintenance of buildings is the responsibility of local government. Many of them neglect it and I understand why. There's always competition for funds, so the tendency is constantly to give priority to staff, teaching, whatever, and to put off your maintenance for a time ... local authorities run schools and they have more money to spend per pupil than ever before ... The public don't understand that. They don't see where the responsibility lies.[22]

Naturally, then, poor reading standards must be the responsibility of local authorities and teachers – not all, but those who had been experimenting with new teaching methods. "The Left continues to be concerned more with how children are taught than with what they are taught, and that attitude is a great challenge to our educational standards", Clarke told the Tory Reform Group, in a speech hailed by the *Daily Mail* as a "ferocious attack on the enemies of high standards in schools".[23]

One of the problems identified by the school inspectors was the polarized dispute between champions of "phonic" and "real book" teaching methods. Under the phonic method, children learn the sounds associated with individual letters and so build up words; the "real book" or "look and say" method teaches them to identify whole words and books to stimulate their interest. About one school in twenty was relying exclusively on "real books". This, it might be supposed, was a debate best left to those with enough direct experience to make an informed judgement. However, in waded Kenneth Clarke:

> Phonics appear to have a proved method of success. All the reports show that the method is used by the overwhelming majority of teachers who achieve success. Most of the new methods turn out to be no good at all compared with the traditional one. The real-books method seems to me rather cranky.[24]

There is another answer, commonly practised in state schools, which is to combine both methods. Mercifully, Clarke did not legislate to ban "real book" teaching.

History was another subject that greatly exercised politicians. There was a deep suspicion that children were not being taught dates, names of kings and queens and other character-forming facts, but rather were being taught to sympathize and identify with people who lived in the past as if they were characters in fiction. In her memoirs, Mrs Thatcher describes this as the hardest battle she had to fight over the entire national curriculum. She was quite clear in her mind that history was "an account of what happened in the past ... which means knowing dates".[25] The government's own History Working Group, however, produced findings which she regarded as "too skewed to social, religious, cultural and aesthetic matters" and, to make it worse, her minister, John MacGregor, defended them.

It fell to Clarke to answer one question: when did history end and current affairs begin? The position he inherited was that history was that which took place before the early 1960s. The teaching of more recent events, it was assumed, might be contaminated by political bias. Clarke decided to modify the definition of history as being from Roman times until "circa 20 years ago". It was also his decision that pupils who were opting out of history at the age of fourteen should have to study the Second World War. It was a concession; nonetheless it left state school pupils in a position where they were required to know about the Gunpowder Plot before they were eleven, but the current conflict in Ireland was not recognized as a subject to be studied during history lessons. Or, as Jack Straw put it, "pupils in state schools will not be able to learn about the origins of the Gulf war until 2011, while those in private schools will be allowed to learn about them tomorrow."[26] Clarke replied that no teacher was banned from telling classes about recent events, even if they were not on the curriculum. Truly, there was no subject so far removed from politics that it did not require Clarke to hold an opinion on it. He was so exasperated by the amount of complex detail in the curriculum that he sacked the National Curriculum Council chairman, Duncan Graham – "unfairly", in the opinion of Kenneth Baker, who had appointed him.[27] Graham had spent a lifetime in education. His successor, David Pascall, was a BP executive and former Downing Street adviser.

The first reports from national curriculum working parties to reach Clarke's desk, in January 1991, concerned the arts and music. The argument, which carried on for another year, was partly over whether music lessons, for example, should be principally given over to making music, or to listening and learning about its history. There were also disagreements about whether there should be less emphasis on European music, given the mixed intake in inner-city schools. In his draft orders published in January 1992, Clarke overrode the National Curriculum Council to put more emphasis on doing than knowing. He ruled that five- to fourteen-year-olds should spend two-thirds of their music lessons "performing and composing" and only one-third "listening and appraising". However, despite his well-known preference for jazz over Western classical music, he dismissed fears that few primary school teachers were qualified to introduce seven-year-olds to Mozart and Stravinsky. The Committee chairman, Sir John Manduell, principal of the Royal Northern College of Music, accused him of "flying in the face of professional opinion to a breathtaking degree".[28]

The chairman of the arts working party was Professor Colin Renfrew, Master of Jesus College, Cambridge, who had been the intellectual leader of the "Cambridge mafia" thirty years earlier. His old friendship with the Secretary of State did not prevent his report from being sent back too. Only a week earlier, Clarke had upset the working party by deciding that the arts would be optional for children over fourteen; now he wanted their conclusions simplified, with more emphasis on knowing the work of great Western artists. After a year Lord Renfrew, as he now was, complained that the changes introduced by Clarke and his advisers were "unworkable", adding: "I am trying to avoid saying that they do not know much about art, but they do not have a great deal of specialist knowledge."[29]

A month after rejecting the first report sent to him, Clarke was sent a 75-page document from a working party on physical education, which was to be compulsory for five- to fourteen-year-olds, and returned it with a stiff letter complaining that it would be too expensive to implement and was written in language "comprehensible only to the specialist". The committee chairman Ian Beer, headmaster of Harrow, could only reply that one of its members was the Wimbledon footballer John Fashanu, who "found it all perfectly comprehensible".[30]

On grant-maintained schools, there was little ground for compromise. Either schools opted out, or they did not: if they did not, the government had lost and local councils had won. Ideologically, Clarke had no problem with grant-maintained schools. He positively supported them, and verbally he gave the opting out process all the encouragement its backers could ask for. In his first speech to parliament in his new capacity, he vowed that he was "determined" to see more opting-out schools. Later he revealed that his "ideal" would be that every secondary school in the country would be grant-maintained.[31] Subsequently, he was booed at an education conference in Leeds when he rubbished claims that the government was in effect bribing schools to opt out, calling them "paranoid nonsense".[32]

Actually, there is solid statistical evidence to back up this "paranoid nonsense". It is undisputed that when a school opts out, its central grant more than covers the loss of financial support from the local council. In theory, the difference only covers the cost of the administrative burden which the school takes over from the local education authority. In fact, the calculation is made in a way which ensures that the grant-maintained school never loses but usually gains at the expense of local-authority schools. Indeed, it would be surprising if it was not so. Even as he insulted his opponents, Clarke must have known there was substance to their claims, as he implicitly conceded in an interview with the *Guardian* a few days later, in which he appeared chastened by the experience of being barracked:

We are concentrating on building up the grant maintained sector and when we get successful applicants they are currently enjoying the experience of having the Department of Education looking particularly at their capital requirements ... We are at the pioneer stage. I have no doubt these schools regard it as a bonus extra. If they have gained an advantage, they have gained it as a result of their courage.[33]

Predictably, these bonuses continued after the "pioneer" stage had been passed. By 1993, it was calculated that about £20 million worth of annual subsidy had effectively been transferred from local education authorities to grant-maintained schools, equivalent to about £300 per pupil per year.

However, verbal backing was about all that Clarke gave to the opting-out process. He did not pander to right-wing opinion by waiving the rule which imposed a five-year gap before an opted-out school could change its status, for example by setting entrance exams. "Bringing back the Eleven Plus and going back to grammar schools and going back to the '44 Act I think is ridiculous and totally impractical", he said.[34] Nor did he legislate to increase the rate at which grant-maintained schools were coming into being. It was the barest trickle. When Clarke took office, there were forty-four secondary schools under what was called "local management", and another fifty-four had applied for a change of status. John MacGregor had indicated in his speech to the Conservative Party conference that the right to opt out would shortly be extended to primary schools. There had reputedly been just one expression of interest. Six months later, the total number of secondary schools that had broken their ties with their local councils was seventy-one, with forty-four decisions pending and others in the process of organizing ballots. "The number of schools that are in favour of grant maintained status has almost doubled during the five months that I have been in the Department", said Clarke. "It is obvious that we are about to have a flood of applications."[35] But the flood had not begun when Clarke left the department. One inhibiting factor was that Labour had vowed to return all opted-out schools to the control of their local authority, but even after the election the departure rate was slow. The one-thousandth application to opt out reached the Department of Education in November 1993. By May 1994, the tally was 1,101 – or less than 5 per cent of state schools.

Long before then, there had been the first political scandal at a grant-maintained school, when a group of governors at Stratford School, in east

London, attempted to sack the head teacher. Each side in the long-running dispute accused the other of corruption, intimidation and insulting behaviour. When Clarke stepped in, it was to protect the teacher against the governors. He appointed two new governors, threatened to close the school down if the situation was not resolved, and subsequently sent letters to three governors telling them they were not suited to sit in judgement on the teacher, and threatening legal action if they defied him.[36] All in all, it was the sort of incident that the creation of grant-maintained schools was intended to prevent.

To the reforms bequeathed by his successor, Clarke added some of his own. In one sudden raid, he removed all colleges of further education and all sixth-form colleges from the control of local councils, transferring them to a new quango appointed by and responsible to him. School league tables originated from a piece of legislation which Clarke introduced to the Commons in November 1991. Their purpose was to expose first the councils and then the individual schools with bad academic records. The main criticism of the league tables is that they work in favour of schools that take in bright pupils, giving no recognition to those in deprived areas that manage to produce creditable examination results in extremely difficult circumstances. It was almost inevitable that inner-city schools, administered by Labour councils, would have a lower pass rate than schools in the Tory shires. Clarke accepted that the point was "relevant", but countered: "If one thinks of enough footnotes, qualifications, reasons and explanations, one can demonstrate that there is no difference between one school and another."[37] Once the first tables were published it was evident that, for all their faults, they were enormously popular with parents and were here to stay.

Clarke was also the minister who privatized the schools inspectorate, although he denied that it was a "privatization", in that schools were receiving something that was not there before. Published reports on individual schools by HM Inspectorate of Schools were rare. A school would be reported on perhaps once every forty years. Clarke claimed that it would be two hundred years before every primary school in the country had been inspected. Some councils, like Lancashire, carried out none at all; others did not publish them when they were carried out. Clarke legislated so that every state school would be inspected every three or four years, but not by local councils. Instead there would be private teams on a list approved by HM Inspectorate, and schools would be given the funds to hire the team of their choice. Clarke envisaged that there would be between three and five thousand inspectors producing six thousand reports a year. This legislation was humiliatingly defeated in the House of Lords less than a week before the 1992 general-election campaign began. The peers rejected the idea of schools choosing their own inspectors, saying that the Chief Inspector of Schools must make the selection and, moreover, that councils must retain the right to inspect their own schools. With an election so close, there was nothing Clarke could do but concede.[38]

Clarke had not wanted to be at the Department of Education. While he was there, he was dealing principally with reforms introduced by someone else. During most of that time, the prospect of a general election was never far away. His being there had prevented him from being promoted by John Major, and the chances were that he would move on as soon as the election was over. After fifteen months, the former education editor of *The Times*, David Tytler, who had been the first journalist to interview Clarke in his capacity as Education Secretary, concluded that "he is treating the job like a barrister – mugged up on the run and then as eloquent and challenging as possible, with a generous sprinkling of soundbites, very little of it under-pinned by knowledge or facts."[39] In April, it was over. The Conservatives had returned to power, unexpectedly, with a secure majority, and one of what are called the "great offices of state" beckoned Clarke.

CHAPTER THIRTEEN

HOME SECRETARY

More often than not, to be appointed Home Secretary is the kiss of death to a Conservative politician's career, as the minister is caught between an ever-increasing crime rate and the thirst for retribution within the party rank and file. On the face of it, Clarke's credentials were not promising. Despite having practised as a criminal lawyer, he had never shown much interest in the politics of law enforcement or the other issues for which a Home Secretary is responsible. He had a reputation for being a liberal, based on his permissive views on abortion and his lifelong opposition to hanging. Normally, that would be enough to guarantee a hostile reception at Conservative Party conference.

Unexpectedly, Clarke's singular achievement as Home Secretary was to offend the police so thoroughly that it became an outside possibility that most officers would vote Labour. The Opposition was understandably grateful for his gift. However, it should be said in Clarke's defence that in every government job he had held, he had been merciless towards what he saw as entrenched interest groups: after the way he had behaved towards ambulance drivers, doctors, school teachers, shipyard workers and the rest, it would have been grossly out of character for him to tread softly when it came to the police. Still, it was a shock for the officers on the receiving end, after years of being almost the only public-sector workers to be treated considerately by the Conservative government.

There are other reasons besides his reception from the police to think that Clarke was lucky to move jobs after only twelve months. If he had stayed longer, it is probable that liberal opinion would have become increasingly hostile to him without his gaining any new friends on the Tory right. Although he was on the liberal wing of his own party, he was confronted with desperately serious crime figures to which the government had no convincing answer other than harsher penalties for those who were caught. It is the official view of the Conservative Party, supported by Kenneth Clarke, that unemployment, inner-city deprivation and other related social problems are not contributory causes of crime, but that the breakdown of discipline in the home, the classroom and society at large are. It is not a great surprise, then, that Clarke's most significant law-and-order measure was to increase the power of the state to imprison children aged between twelve and sixteen.

More seriously for Clarke, he was implicated in the Matrix Churchill case, in which ministers behaved as if they preferred to have three innocent businessmen go to prison rather than allow the embarrassing truth about arms sales to Iraq to be made public. In this, Clarke acted in a way which he believed was correct in law, although it contributed to a state of affairs that was manifestly wrong. Nonetheless, he survived twelve difficult months in an impossible job, emerging as the strong man in a team headed by a weakened prime minister. That was testimony to his extraordinary resilience.

The variety of issues which go before a Home Secretary for decision is greater than for any other Cabinet minister other than the prime minister, and Clarke found himself having to deliberate on problems far removed from the core business of crime prevention. One of his first actions was to set up a Boundary Commission to redraw the map on which the next general election would be fought. There obviously had to be changes to a map which had last been revived before the 1983 election, because the size of the electorate in English seats now ranged from nearly 93,000 in John Major's Huntingdon seat to just over 42,000 in Chelsea; but it was a politically sensitive issue, because it was widely assumed that change would hugely benefit the Conservatives at Labour's expense. Despite the sensitivity, Clarke set up the Commission without conferring with other parties first, claiming that it must complete its findings by 1 December 1994 to be sure of being in time for the next election. In the event, as the Commission's recommendations unfolded, it became apparent that clever lobbying by the Labour Party had minimized the political effect of the boundary changes.

In complete contrast, the Home Secretary had difficulty keeping himself from being drawn into the disintegration of the marriage of the Prince and Princess of Wales. Any public illusions about their relationship were destroyed by the sensational publication of private telephone conversations, first between the Princess and a close friend, and later between the Prince and a woman who was evidently his lover. The question of how these calls came to be tape-recorded and leaked has never been satisfactorily answered. The notion that amateurs who make a hobby of intercepting telephone calls could accidentally tune in to any member of the royal family is simply not believable; the odds against it happening to two royals at about the same time are incalculable. There was a *prima facie* case for believing that someone with the sophisticated equipment and inside knowledge available to the security services might have been involved. Certainly, as the shadow home secretary Tony Blair pointed out in the Commons, the transcripts were either forgeries or were genuine, and whichever was the case, a criminal offence had been committed.

Despite his lifelong habit of walking straight towards political trouble, this time Clarke and his Home Office ministers were like the three monkeys who saw, heard and spoke no evil. Faced with a barrage of questions from journalists, who were in no doubt that the transcripts were genuine, Clarke dismissed them with what he intended to be a flippant remark: "Well, it appears someone's been bugging the Royal Family." Unfortunately for him, that statement, from a Home Secretary, was written up as sensational confirmation that foul play had taken place, most notably in the *Daily Mirror*, whose royal correspondent James Whitaker had a new book out on the subject. The next day in the Commons, Clarke had to do some rather desperate back-pedalling, insisting that he had no idea whether the royals had been bugged or not. "No serious person has come up with any evidence from which one could begin to investigate the rather daft allegation that MI5 is bugging the royal family,"[1] he said. It was all, he suggested, a stunt to sell "nasty books". On the other hand, no one has then or since come up with any other plausible explanation as to how their telephone conversations were made public, a question on which Clarke showed a remarkable lack of curiosity.

Clarke also had to explain away the peculiarly helpful attitude taken by the Home Office press office during the US presidential election, when journalists inquired whether Bill Clinton had applied for British citizenship as a student at Oxford University in the late 1960s, to avoid the draft. The Conservative Party had long-standing ties with the Republicans, so the hint that British civil servants might have been involved in trying to undermine the Democrat candidate was embarrassing, particularly in view of the fact that by then he had won. Clarke insisted that the press officers had acted "on their own volition" and that he had ordered that politically sensitive requests for information were to come to him in future.[2]

In combating terrorism, there is no sign that his instincts were libertarian. Almost the first decision Clarke took as Home Secretary was to give the security services precedence over the police in tracking down IRA units and other terrorists on the mainland. He had met the Commissioner of the Metropolitan Police and the Association of Chief Police Officers before the decision was announced. They were not pleased, but Clarke did not present them with any choice. Looked at from the point of view of protecting civil liberties, MI5 is one step further away than Scotland Yard from public accountability. However, Clarke stressed that he was not giving MI5 officers the power to make arrests; if caught, IRA bombers would go through the normal judicial procedure. The decisive argument was that administratively it made no sense for an IRA assassination in Lichfield to be investigated by one force, a bomb attack in London by another, while a third was gathering intelligence in Northern Ireland. For that reason, the move provoked less of a political reaction than the annual ritual of the renewal of the Prevention of Terrorism Act.

The PTA was introduced by a Labour Home Secretary, Roy Jenkins, in the wake of the Guildford, Woolwich and Birmingham pub bombings in 1974. At the time, he described it as "draconian"; and the Labour Party subsequently had second thoughts about the powers it conferred to hold suspected terrorists for seven days without charge, or deport them from the mainland without presenting any evidence, concluding that the Act was unnecessarily repressive and an assault on civil liberties. Consequently, the Labour Party began to vote against the Act. The annual renewal of the PTA is now the one occasion in the parliamentary calendar on which cross-party cooperation over Northern Ireland routinely breaks down.

This show has been going on for so long that it is now possible to compare the performances of different Home Secretaries, rather as one might compare the ways Shakespearian actors approach a familiar role. Kenneth Clarke never quite achieved the Olympian more-in-sorrow-than-in-anger tone of Douglas Hurd; but, on the other hand, he was subtler and less offensively partisan than his successor, Michael Howard. Appearing in the 1993 performance of the Prevention of Terrorism Act debate opposite Labour's Tony Blair, Clarke conceded: "He is as opposed to terrorism as I am, and does not intend to give help or encouragement to terrorists in this country, but he is in danger of doing so by accident."[3]

This exchange can be seen in a new light since the revelation that the government was having secret dealings with the IRA, despite John Major's famous statement that "it would churn my stomach" to talk to people who "murder indiscriminately". Part of the truth about these meetings is established, part is still disputed, but it appears that contact had begun by the time Clarke was lecturing the opposition on the danger of giving encouragement to terrorism, although he may not have known about it then. When he found out – if Sinn Fein's information is accurate – his first reaction was alarm at the way public opinion would react. According to Sinn Fein's version of events, he was present at a ministerial meeting on 17 May 1993, with John Major, Douglas Hurd, the Northern Ireland Secretary Patrick Mayhew, and advisers, to discuss an offer from the IRA of a two-week ceasefire. According to Martin McGuinness of Sinn Fein, "Clarke's advice was that the opening of public negotiations with us was 'too risky with the government under siege'."[4] If that is what he said, he can be criticized on two grounds: first, that he seemed to have been concerned only about the survival of the government, when the more important question was whether there was an opportunity for peace in Northern Ireland; second; he was being too cautious. On the whole, public opinion accepted the government's duplicity rather calmly, apparently taking the view that anything which could bring the violence to an end was worth a try.

Clarke was restrained in his use of the Prevention of Terrorism Act, adding just two Irish citizens to the list of eighty-one already banned from the mainland, and signing seventeen orders extending the detention of suspects, although ten of those were in fact held without charge for only four days. It was not many years since the British judicial system had been compelled to own up to a glaring miscarriage of justice in the case of the Guildford Four, who were imprisoned for fourteen years for bomb attacks they did not commit. The single most disturbing aspect of the story is how they were prevailed upon to confess soon after they had been arrested and held under the provisions of the PTA. Clarke conceded that they had been mistreated, but claimed that the PTA "was not the cause of the miscarriage of justice".[5]

Since 1988, the courts and successive Home Secretaries have been confronted with a series of sensational claims of miscarriage of justice. In each, the pattern was similar: horrific murder had been committed, public opinion demanded that somebody be caught quickly, and very soon someone had confessed under interrogation, with the result that defendants received life sentences with little prospect that they would ever be released. Later, the confessions began to look irregular and suspicion spread that the police had picked up the wrong people. The cases that had attracted most attention involved those who had been convicted of IRA atrocities in the mid 1970s. On the day before Clarke received a barracking from the Police Federation, the trial of three retired Surrey detectives accused of fabricating evidence against the Guildford Four had just ended with their acquittal.

Clarke's predecessor but one, Douglas Hurd, had told Merseyside police to reopen the case of the sordid murder of a 13-year-old boy named Carl Bridgewater, in September 1978. He was out on a delivery round when he was killed with a sawn-off shotgun at a farm in Stourbridge, in the West Midlands. It appeared that he had disturbed a burglary. A man named Patrick Molloy allegedly confessed to police that he had been upstairs during a burglary at the farm, and had heard a shot fired. He did not give evidence at the subsequent trial in Stafford Crown Court in 1979, but his confession was apparently sufficient to convict Vincent Hickey and James Robinson, who were jailed for life with a recommendation that they serve at least twenty-five years, and Michael Hickey, Vincent's seventeen-year-old cousin, who was detained at Her Majesty's pleasure. Molloy, who was sentenced to twelve years, later withdrew his confession, claiming it was beaten out of him. He died in prison. The others have never ceased to maintain their innocence. Their case has been examined in five television documentaries and a book by Paul Foot, which suggested that the probable killer was a man who committed a similar crime nearby. Language experts have thrown doubt on Molloy's confession. In 1988, their appeal was turned down. Then it emerged that the detective who took Molloy's confession was fined thirteen days' pay in 1987 for fabricating a confession. The men's hopes of release were abruptly crushed in February 1993, when Clarke refused them leave to take their case back to an appeal court. He said: "Nothing has emerged from my review to cast doubt on the safety of these convictions." The men's solicitor, Jim Nichol, suggested that Clarke had made this decision because "morale is at an all-time low in the police, so that sort of decision was inevitable."[6]

Another case, dating from much earlier, was that of Derek Bentley, who was hanged after his accomplice in a warehouse raid had shot and killed a policemen. Bentley, who was nineteen, had been captured before the shot was fired, but was alleged to have shouted "Let him have it, Chris!" The killer, Christopher Craig, escaped the death penalty because he was a juvenile. Bentley is reported to have had the mental age of an eleven-year-old, and at the time there were pleas for a reprieve, backed by a recommendation from Home Office officials, which the Home Secretary of the time, Sir David Maxwell Fyfe, ignored. Bentley's sister, Iris, had battled for years to try to clear her brother's name, and by 1993 there was considerable doubt that he ever shouted the fatal words "Let him have it", which anyway could be interpreted as a plea to Craig to hand over his gun. This case also went to Clarke, who astonished the reporters assembled to hear his decision by telling them that he was satisfied that the jury had made the right decision:

> Because the law provides that, when two or more persons are engaged in a criminal activity with an intention to use force if necessary to resist ... both are responsible for the consequences of whatever use of force actually occurs.[7]

He also had to consider whether to extradite two British women, Susan Hagan and Sally Croft, former members of a religious cult set up by the Bhagwan Shree Rajneesh in Antelope, Oregon, who were wanted on a charge of conspiring to murder state attorney Charles Turner in 1985. It would have been very unusual for Britain to refuse an extradition request from the USA, particularly on a charge this serious; but the women, who were both in their early forties, attracted some public sympathy because they were obviously no threat to the law in Britain, and faced jail sentences of up to twenty years if convicted. They claimed that the evidence against them, provided by former cult members as part of a plea bargain, was unreliable and that local hostility to the cult made it impossible for them to receive a fair trial in Oregon. Nonetheless, in April 1993 Clarke ordered their extradition.

His decision in the case of the two women was upheld by the Divisional Court in 1994, but the other two cases threatened to return to haunt Clarke after he had left the Home Office. It emerged that one of the country's leading forensic psychologists, Eric Shepherd, had examined the confession that convicted the four men in the Bridgewater case and had concluded that it was fabricated, and Clarke apparently knew that when he declared the convictions were safe. Dr Shepherd said he found the former Home Secretary's decision "incomprehensible", and warned, "This whole run of statements and the confession are wholly unreliable."[8] Not long afterwards, three High Court judges criticized Clarke's decision not to grant a conditional post-humous pardon to Derek Bentley, and called upon his successor, Michael Howard, to consider doing so. Their judgement was that Bentley should have been reprieved, even if he was guilty. Clarke defended himself saying: "I followed the precedent that a royal pardon was only given where innocence was established."[9] It may be that, in both cases, Clarke was applying his legal training to reach the decision that he thought was correct in law. However, if he was swayed by fears that police morale had been undermined too much to risk demoralizing the force any further, that problem was partly of his making.

The warnings of impending conflict between Clarke and the police came early on, phrased in the coded language of politicians. In his first newspaper interview since his appointment, the new Home Secretary said: "They must expect me to be helping them to command the public confidence across the full spectrum of law abiding citizens."[10] On the same day, Clarke claimed he was "startled" by the press reports of "some of the things I am supposed to be doing" and the criticism he had attracted from Police Federation officials because of them.[11] A week later, he gave a speech to the Police Federation annual conference which was so full of tributes to the force that he was warmly applauded as he left, and it was only later that the implications appeared to sink in. Sergeant Mike Bennett, chairman of the Metropolitan Police Federation complained: "We've been kippered and he was on his way back to London before we realized. It was a speech delivered with an iron fist in a velvet glove."[12] Two months later, an anonymous senior officer at Scotland Yard was reported as saying:

> The people in this building, they thought they were in bed with Mrs T, and the romance would last forever. When we were hanging Arthur Scargill out to dry, or getting the new technology into Wapping, running the ambulance service or looking after thousands of prisoners on remand, nobody asked us then about value for money.[13]

There were three things Clarke did which were not calculated to win him friends within the police force. The first was to make MI5 the lead organization in the fight against terrorism, in preference to Scotland Yard; then, he launched an inquiry headed by Patrick Sheehy, chairman of B.A.T. Industries, into police pay and conditions; and finally, he proposed a drastic reorganization of the management of the police forces. The reorganization threw up an embarrassing series of political disasters for the government, including defeat in the House of Lords; but fortunately for Clarke, he had moved on, handing the poisoned chalice to his old rival from Cambridge, Michael Howard. Nevertheless, these events were mild compared to the reaction the government might have faced if it had tried to implement the Sheehy report.

The Sheehy commission spent a year drawing up its report, visiting half the police forces in Britain and devoting three months to hearing oral evidence, and eventually published its findings in July 1993. It proposed to put all ranks on short-term contracts rather than "jobs for life", to cut starting salaries by £2,000 a year, to introduce performance-related pay based on a points system, scrap casual overtime, restrict housing allowances, sickness benefits and pensions, and introduce a new mechanism for summary dismissal. "Some officers do a better job than others; the good performers and the poor performers know who they are; and so do their supervisors", the chairman claimed.[14] To the police, it opened the vista of insecurity and lower pay in a job already made uniquely dangerous by the increasing propensity of criminals to resort to violence.

Opposition began with the Police Federation, who organized a rally in Wembley Stadium which produced an extraordinary turnout of around 21,000 police, at which Labour's shadow home secretary Tony Blair was loudly cheered.[15] Clarke was heckled at the Federation's annual conference in May, where the chairman, Alan Eastwood, warned: "I have truly never known a time when the service, at every level, has been so demoralised."[16] Sergeant Mike Bennett, who seems not to have been a fan of Clarke's, called him "an arrogant, rude social snob, an autocrat who would struggle in the modern business world ... at home in the boardroom but all at sea on the shop floor", comments which were gleefully reproduced on the front page of the following day's *Daily Mirror*.[17]

Subsequently, police authorities, senior ranks and then chief constables also came out in opposition to parts of the report. Michael Howard waited until October 1993 to test the reaction, then dropped the more controversial of Sheehy's proposals. He went ahead with the abolition of three managerial ranks of chief inspector, chief superintendent and deputy chief constable, and announced a system of performance-related pay rather less complex than Sheehy had proposed. Whether Clarke would have gone ahead with fixed-term contracts and performance-related pay for police constables is a matter of conjecture, but the report was his initiative and it is reasonable to assume he would have been more committed to its outcome than his successor was. One interesting observation is that despite all his years as a health minister responsible for educating the people about the evils of smoking, he appears to have found more of a kindred spirit in the head of a giant tobacco firm than in all the police officers in Great Britain.

He had a good working relationship with another member of the Sheehy committee, Eric Caines, who had been Director of Regional Organization at the DHSS when Clarke was a junior health minister, returning as NHS Director of Personnel when Clarke was Secretary of State. His views on public-sector pay and conditions were as forthright as Clarke's. He believed police and nurses should be on short-term contracts with performance-related pay. Late in 1993, he was appointed Professor of Health Service Management at Nottingham University on the recommendation of the university's vice-chancellor, a fellow member of the Sheehy committee. His application was supported by a reference from Kenneth Clarke. He had no previous academic experience, but was the only applicant interviewed.[18]

The case for reorganizing the police was that they were costing £6 billion a year, an increase in real terms of 50 per cent since 1979, whilst public confidence in them had been undermined by exposure of police corruption and fabricated confessions, and by a considerable drop in the proportion of crimes solved. The number of crimes solved per officer per year had gone up, so had the number of officers, but neither of these improvements had kept pace with the relentless rise in crime. The police appeared to be costing more and accomplishing less. Clarke's solution was true to form. Where once he had created trust hospitals and grant-maintained schools, both of which had removed themselves from the control of locally elected representatives, now he seemed to be aiming for trust police forces, run more like businesses without interference from elected councillors. Some of his proposals were uncontroversial: he announced in March 1993 that Home Office control over police recruitment was to be abolished, in place of which Chief Constables were to be given more control over their budgets, within limits set by the government, and that there was to be a police authority for London. He also proposed that there be fewer police forces, cutting their number from forty-three to twenty-five. Of itself, that created problems about local democratic accountability: the larger an area covered by a police authority, the larger and more unwieldy it needed to be to represent all the local authorities within its area.

However, local accountability was not an issue in which Clarke displayed any interest whatsoever. According to newspaper reports evidently based on a Cabinet leak, he planned to abolish outright the system of dual funding, under which the police are paid for jointly by central and local government, and hand to the Home Secretary the power to set police budgets without any local consultation. This ran into heavy Cabinet opposition, led by William Waldegrave, Douglas Hurd, David Hunt and Ian Lang. Michael Howard, who as Environment Secretary might have been expected to welcome anything which reduced the powers and budgets of local councils, also opposed him, and was reportedly appalled by the "hole in corner" manner in which important constitutional questions were being resolved in secret.[19] By the time the proposals were announced publicly, in March, they had been rewritten to allow local councillors to occupy half the seats on police authorities, the other half being taken up by magistrates and other local people nominated by the Home Secretary who would be looking for people with "relevant management experience".[20] The obvious implication is that there would be a high proportion of local business leaders. Moreover, the chairman of the authority would also be appointed, not elected, Clarke said.

It was on this point that Clarke's successor, Michael Howard, was forced into a humiliating climbdown when his Police and Magistrates' Court bill was before the House of Lords. Howard had already brought Britain's judges out in opposition to him by proposing to end a defendant's "right to silence", which the Lord Chief Justice, Sir Peter Taylor, said "would seriously trouble me and other judges". Even here, the hand of Howard's predecessor could be detected: Clarke had told the Commons in March 1993 that "the time has come to look again at the so-called right to silence."[21] The idea of a Home Secretary hand-picking chairmen of police authorities provoked an eruption among Tory grandees in the House of Lords, led by the venerated William Whitelaw. Howard had no choice but to climb down. He had played the law-and-order card for all it was worth, setting the tone of the previous autumn's Conservative Party conference with a right-wing speech promising twenty-seven new crime-busting initiatives and exalting the effects of prison; conse-quently he paid the political penalty when it all went wrong. However, if Clarke had been at the Home Office for another eight months, he would have been the one who ran up against the judiciary, in a political battle he would probably have lost.

For several years, the main parties had tried to avoid making immigration a party-political issue, with varying success. It threatened to become an issue in the early 1990s because of a sudden increase in the number of applications for political asylum, which had run at about 5,000 a year in the mid 1980s, but which in 1991 had suddenly hit 45,000. Clarke's predecessor Kenneth Baker had proposed to deal with this by taking the fingerprints of all appli-cants, and their children if they had any, to see whether they had applied before and whether they were also claiming social security. This and other measures had been agreed by the Cabinet, where Baker had forceful backing from David Mellor, Michael Heseltine and Peter Lilley, but had not reached the statute book because of the general election. It therefore fell to Clarke to get it through parliament, which he did during 1993, although during the previous year the flow of applicants for asylum had dropped almost as suddenly as it had risen, falling to 24,500.

However, a new problem had arisen from the war in what had formerly been Yugoslavia, whose citizens were arriving in Britain at a rate of 4,000 a month at the end of 1992. In November, Clarke abruptly changed the rules, so that any former Yugoslav, other than those bearing passports issued by the new governments of Croatia and Slovenia, would need visas before they were admitted. Within days, that had produced an embarrassing situation in which almost 200 Bosnian refugees who had been taken by the British char-ity ALERT to the Austrian border were applying to the British Embassy in Vienna for visas. Clarke refused all but 14, claiming that the other 180 were "indistinguishable" from two million other Yugoslavs who might want to escape, and blaming ALERT for ignoring his warnings about the need for visas.[22]

On the wider issue of political asylum, Kenneth Baker's attempt to legis-late had been delayed by the chorus of criticism it attracted from almost everybody directly concerned. Clarke yielded to the Law Society, the Bar Council and Church leaders by conceding an automatic right of appeal for refugees refused asylum, but beyond that gave little away, even adding a

measure which took away the right of appeal from prospective visitors denied a visa and immigrants whose grounds for appeal were "manifestly un-
founded". He defended his corner on the standard grounds that it was bad
for race relations, and bad for people who were genuinely fleeing from
political persecution in their home countries, if others were allowed to remain because they had made bogus applications for political asylum which
had taken so long for the authorities to process than they had put down
roots in Britain before their cases were decided. "If we are too generous," he
said, "it is the population of our inner cities, our urban poor and our home-
less who will be the main sufferers."[23] He backed this up with sweeping claims
that nineteen out of twenty claims were "bogus", and that "most applications
are from people who have travelled on international airlines and arrive ...
calmly and in comfortable circumstances; many have been in this country for
some time before suddenly realising they face persecution at home." When
Tony Blair suggested to him that he was being "callous", Clarke flew into the
attack, accusing Labour of being "naive and emotional" and of retreating
into a "Mickey Mouse make-believe world in which everybody who applies
for asylum in the UK is a traumatised victim who arrives trembling on our
shores."

This was colourful language for someone who had always prided himself
on being an enemy of racism. It is possible that Clarke was genuinely shocked
by any suggestion that he would connive in the deportation of political
refugees. Alternatively, he may have been fired up by some of the xenophobic
enthusiasm of some Tory MPs – like Tony Marlow, for example, who summed
up the argument by saying that "we are concerned with the wishes and desires
of the people of this country, whereas the Opposition are concerned about
foreigners."[24] Moreover, these foreigners had no votes.

What had once been a straightforward issue about domestic race relations
had been complicated by Britain's uneasy relations with the EC. The Treaty
of Rome specifies that "the internal market shall be an area without internal
frontiers in which the free movement of goods, persons, services and capital
is ensured..." British ministers had accepted that European citizens could
not be prevented from entering Britain; but they were now being told that
the same applied to anyone who had entered any EC country legally. One
effect was that if a Frenchwoman married a Madagascan, he had a right to
join her in Great Britain, but if a British woman married a Pakistani, he still

had to fight his way through British immigration control. For all his enthusiasm for Europe, Clarke certainly had no intention of ironing out this anomaly by bringing British immigration law into line with Europe's. He told the Commons: "Our race relations laws are the most comprehensive in Europe ... they are undoubtedly the best in Europe ... British immigration law, I dare say, is superior in almost all respects to that on the continent."[25]

Given the superiority of British race relations, an interesting question arose as to why the number of blacks in British prisons was proportionally higher than whites, and why a disproportionately large number of black suspects denied the charges laid against them by the police and demanded trial by jury. Questioned on the statistics by the black MP Diane Abbott, Clarke declared himself mystified. "I can think of no clear explanation ... They demonstrate a higher level of contact between ethnic minority people and the legal system."[26]

Meanwhile, there were problems about the contacts which some persistent juvenile offenders were having with the legal system. The law discouraged any penalty more serious than a reprimand for a child under the age of sixteen caught committing a petty offence, and in more than 90 per cent of cases it was accepted that this was adequate; but the police complained that a small number of hardened young villains were making a disproportionate contribution to the crime figures, by offending over and over again and laughing off their reprimands. In March 1993, Clarke announced that he proposed to put a stop to this by giving magistrates the power to make a "secure training order" against children aged twelve to fifteen who committed three or more imprisonable offences and had broken the terms of a supervision order. The order would last up to two years, half of which would be spent in specially constructed detention centres away from the children's home towns.

When this proposal was eventually enshrined in legislation, after Clarke had left the Home Office, it emerged that the government really was thinking of very small numbers of offenders. In all, just five centres big enough for forty children each were being envisaged. One would be for young girls. Even so, it seemed to set government policy into reverse. For all their right-wing, punitive instincts, the previous two Home Secretaries had been trying to reduce the prison population, particularly the number of under-age offenders behind bars. After the appalling case of a fifteen-year-old boy who committed suicide in Swansea jail in 1990, the government had set itself a deadline of 1995 for ending the practice of remanding young prisoners to adult jails, an undertaking which Clarke repeated within days of taking office.[27] A riot and siege at Strangeways prison, Manchester, in April 1990, which lasted twenty-three days, had brought home the problem of prison overcrowding. There had been 1,647 prisoners in Strangeways when the riot began. Clarke promised that when it reopened, having been virtually rebuilt, there would be no more than 500.

Inevitably, faced with a problem in a public service, the Conservative government called in the private sector. There was already one new prison, at Wolds, being run by a private company when Clarke became Home Secretary. In July 1992, he signed an order for a second, Blakenhurst, to be built and managed by a private firm, and the following year signed another order enabling the government to contract out existing prisons. Strangeways was to be one of the first. Clarke also converted the prison service into a "Next Steps" agency, which means that ministers were no longer answerable for its day-to-day management. Like trust hospitals, agencies can pay their senior executives salaries higher than the highest paid civil servants. He used that freedom to go outside the prison service to recruit a new director-general of prisons. The job went to Derek Lewis, chairman of the satellite television company UK Gold, and former chief executive of Granada, which paid him a £579,550 "golden goodbye". His starting salary was £125,000, with bonuses that potentially took it up to £167,000.[28] The previous director-general of prisons was paid £63,000, close to what Clarke was paid as Home Secretary.

Reducing the prison population had been one of the aims behind Kenneth Baker's 1991 Criminal Justice Act, which was running into heavy criticism by the time Clarke succeeded to the post. One objection to it was that it prevented magistrates from taking a defendant's previous convictions into account in passing sentence. Consequently, first offenders were being as heavily punished as those who returned to the courts time and time again. However, there was a much greater outcry about another innovation from the same act, the "unit fines" system which tied magistrates to a mechanical formula based on the type of offence and on the defendant's disposable income. This had produced some absurd results, usually when defendants had failed to fill in the form detailing their income and consequently received the maximum fine. Thus, one youth was fined £1,200 for throwing a crisp packet out of his car window. The penalty was reduced to £48 on appeal.

Having said on several occasions that time was needed for the implications of unit fines to be considered further, Clarke moved suddenly as public opinion built up against the system. In May 1993, just as an uncontroversial bill dealing with money laundering was completing its journey through the parliamentary process, he suddenly announced that he was amending it in order to repeal the offending sections of the 1991 act. The decision had general support, but the manner in which it was announced enraged the normally mild former SDP leader Bob Maclennan, who accused Clarke of "utter gall, effrontery, lack of sense" and of acting in a "monstrous" manner. This unexpected outburst gave rise to one of Clarke's most memorable parliamentary insults, when he suggested that Maclennan "go away, lie down in a dark room, keep taking the tablets and think carefully about whether the Liberal Democrats have any opinion one way or the other..."[29]

It was this capacity to move suddenly into the attack from weak ground that had been the making of Kenneth Clarke. But as his period at the Home Office drew to an end, even the *Sun* was demanding more matter in his art. Their columnist Richard Littlejohn was allocated almost a whole page to lay into the "arrogance born of ignorance" of the Home Secretary:

> Clarke has stepped into Norman Tebbit's size 10 bovver boots. But there is a fundamental difference between them. Tebbit believed in something. Clarke appears to believe in absolutely nothing at all, except maybe Kenneth Clarke ... Chancellor? Prime Minister? There's even a question mark over his performance as Home Secretary. With Britain riddled with record and increasingly savage crime, Clarke shrugs off the figures and concentrates his efforts on confronting the police...[30]

It was not just a matter of crime statistics. There had been two things that the Conservatives were reputed to be better at than any other party: supporting the police and running the economy. Now they had run into trouble in both quarters, and the government was unpopular as never before.

CHAPTER FOURTEEN

THE TAXMAN

It is an axiom that Conservatives believe in keeping taxes down by keeping government expenditure under control. "That is what distinguishes the Conservatives from all other parties", Clarke claims. "That is the big divide in British politics."[1] By the latter part of the 1980s, the Thatcher government had achieved the double feat of economic growth and low rates of income tax. The achievement was "irreversible", according to what Clarke said in 1987, because the government had broken the bad old habit of borrowing money in lean times to evade difficult political decisions.[2]

It is now clear that this Thatcherite rectitude about spending public money ended with the fall of Thatcher. The new administration devoted its first eighteen months to preparing for a general election that it was in severe danger of losing, and increased spending on all the main government departments, including health, education and social security. There is no doubt that it did so: the facts are in figures published by the government, and were explicitly confirmed by Michael Portillo, the minister in control of public spending.[3] Anyway, there was a good reason for increasing government spending, other than the purely selfish wish to win popularity before an election: in 1990, Britain had entered a recession, and from the 1930s until 1979 it was the accepted view that the surest way to revive a flagging economy was for the government to pump money into it.

Had the Conservatives fought and won the 1992 election on the grounds that they now believed in Keynesian economics again, and were borrowing money that would have to be repaid later, no one could have begrudged them victory or complained about the tax increases that followed. However, notoriously, they did not. They fought their entire campaign around the central message that a Labour government would increase taxes by an average of £1,000 a year, whereas "keeping control of public spending will enable us to cut taxes while bringing the government's budget back towards balance."[4] Although Clarke did not invent that highly specious figure for Labour's proposed tax increases, which was primarily the work of the Treasury ministers Norman Lamont and David Mellor, he had no compunction about repeating and improving on it long after the election. A few days before his own first Budget, he accused John Smith of having intended to add £2,050 a year to the tax burden of an annual salary of £25,000.[5]

If Norman Lamont did not already know the true state of the economy when this line was being peddled to voters, he certainly knew soon afterwards, and constructed his next budget around the need to reduce the government's debt. Of all the measures he took, the one which sank most immediately into the public consciousness and caused the greatest resentment was the introduction of VAT on gas and electricity bills. This was widely assumed to have been the main cause of a disastrous by-election defeat in Newbury in April, which produced the biggest swing against the Conservatives for twenty-one years. That result caused a build-up of feeling within the party which John Major could not afford to ignore. Within a month, he had sacked Norman Lamont, and Kenneth Clarke had taken over as Chancellor of the Exchequer.

For a time, Clarke was like a child blessed by fortune. Inflation, which was at 1.3 per cent per annum when he took office, hovered there for a month then fell in July to 1.2 per cent, the lowest figure for thirty years. The "underlying" rate, which excludes mortgages, also fell, though not by so much. Unemployment continued to tumble. In May, it went down for the fourth consecutive month, knocking 80,000 off the previous December's total. In June, the "adjusted" total fell by another 7,600 to 2,909,200. The trade balance was also moving in Britain's favour at the same time that the pound was gaining on the money markets, to the extent that the Chancellor was under pressure to lower interest rates, which were already at their lowest level since 1977. It is little wonder that the aggrieved Lamont, on the first occasion that he asked the prime minister a question from the back benches, prefaced it with a sarcastic comment: "This month, like the last, has seen a remarkable catalogue of good economic indicators ... I congratulate the new Chancellor on the rapid success of his policies."[6]

However good the "indicators" were, the voters were not impressed. The Newbury defeat was capped by an even worse result in Christchurch in July, when a Tory majority of 23,015 vanished as the Liberal Democrats took the seat by a startling margin of 16,427, in the biggest by-election swing ever recorded against any government since 1945. This setback was also attributed to the impending imposition of VAT on fuel. Like any other one-off explanation for a by-election upset, this assumption has to be treated with some caution: the announcement had not yet come into effect, so no one had yet seen an increase in their fuel bills. Clarke visited Christchurch to promise "not to let the pensioners down" and that "there is no question of pensioners being unable to turn on their heating."[7] The fall in interest rates had had a much more direct impact on Christchurch's population, which included an unusually large proportion of retired people living off their savings. Nonetheless, VAT on fuel was certainly a contributory cause. As Clarke's first budget approached, the main point of interest was whether he would scrap VAT on fuel, or put up extra money to alleviate its impact. But, in fact, this was only a sideshow. His real problem was that the good economic news had been purchased by allowing the government to accumulate a mountain of debt, which was forecast to exceed £50 billion, much bigger in real terms than the one which had confronted Sir Geoffrey Howe prior to his celebrated budget of 1981.

The short-term political problem which this created for Clarke was that the Tory right feared he would revert to type as the party's "Mr Public Services" and, when forced to choose between raising taxes or cutting public spending, he would tax. He was frantically lobbied over the intervening months by groups of MPs, who claimed some success in winning him over to cuts in public spending, and yet came away thinking he wanted to raise taxes further than they would like. What they did not know was that Clarke had decided to do more than just keep public borrowing under control; he was drawing up a timetable for eliminating it altogether. Perhaps he consciously imitated the man he thought should have been prime minister, and planned a Budget that was meant to induce shock on first hearing and inspire admiration later. What he produced, oddly, was a delayed shock. He was the toast of the Conservative Party on the evening of Budget Day. Three months later, the party was asking itself what went wrong.

For those interested in the details of Westminster procedure, Kenneth Clarke's Budget speech on 30 November 1993 made history in that it was the first to be delivered in the autumn, and the first to tell the people not only how they were to be taxed but also how the government proposed to disperse

their money, a procedural change for which Clarke was indebted to his predecessor, Norman Lamont. Spending plans had hitherto been dealt with separately, in what was called the Autumn Statement: Clarke rattled through that
and his new tax measures in just an hour and a quarter. It was because of this
procedural change that there were two Budgets in 1993.

To the average wage earner, the Budget's main significance was that it
combined the most severe tax increases for a generation – so steep that taxes
were projected to absorb a significantly higher proportion of the nation's
output than they had under the last Labour government – with almost equally
severe limits on public spending. To reduce the government's overheads, the
unemployed and people who were off work through illness were required to
accept cuts in their meagre incomes. Local authorities were made to increase
council-tax bills by 7 per cent simply to offset their loss of government
support. Public-sector employees were told that their pay would be frozen
for the third successive year. Yet Kenneth Clarke delivered all this bad news
with such good humour, concealing the austerity measures behind such careful political camouflage, that he sat down to deafening cheers from Conservative MPs, and triggered a surge in share prices. There were none of the
long, gloomy faces that were seen on the Tory side after Sir Geoffrey Howe's
performance in 1981. Instead, that weekend's *Spitting Image* included a sketch
in which the Cabinet cruelly told John Major to go and sit in the corridor
outside so that Ken could take his chair. The short-term political success of
the Budget cannot be denied; it was not until early in 1994 that the Conservatives began to pay for it. It will not be known until about the year 2000
whether it achieved its stated objectives of "lasting recovery and rising living
standards" and of sorting out public borrowing "once and for all" by eliminating government debt altogether "by the end of the decade."[8]

To deal with the last of these subjects first, government finances were in
a worse mess when Clarke inherited responsibility for them than at any time
since 1974–76, when the Heath and Wilson governments were grappling with
the impact of the oil crisis. The public sector borrowing requirement had
reached £50 billion, or almost 9 per cent of gross domestic product. For a
decade, it had never been above 4 per cent of GDP; prior to that, in 1981,
Geoffrey Howe had constructed the Budget which set unemployment soaring
above three million from a fear that the PSBR might go as high as £14 billion,
or about £30 billion at 1993 prices. However, Norman Lamont's spring

Budget had attempted to meet the problem with £6.73 billion worth of tax increases, which, it was forecast, would reduced the 1997–98 PSBR to £30 billion.

Against all expectations, Clarke decided to go further, by cutting the deficit to £38 billion in 1994–95, six billion below the target set by Lamont, to £12 billion in 1997–98, and just £2 billion by 1998–99. These targets pleased the money markets: by Wednesday evening, the FTSE share index had risen to a new high, adding £16 billion to investors' funds in a single day. Sterling gained in value compared with the German mark by half a pfennig on Budget day, despite the fact that British interest rates had been cut a week earlier to their lowest level for sixteen years. Clarke managed this without including in the Budget any single item of news so obviously and intelligibly bad that it would dominate the next day's headline. The public normally judges Budgets by what they do to the basic tax rates and the prices of everyday items like petrol, drink, cigarettes, or domestic fuel. No Conservative Chancellor was likely to increase the basic rates of income tax, which Clarke duly left unchanged at 20p, 25p and 40p in the pound. Most of the pre-Budget speculation in autumn 1993 had been about VAT. Enough hints had been dropped to ensure that commentators knew better than to expect that Clarke would reverse Norman Lamont's decision to impose VAT on household electricity and gas bills; it was even hinted that he might go further, by introducing the whole 17.5 per cent increase at once. The move that the newspaper industry most feared and half expected was that other zero-rated items, like newspapers, would be subjected to VAT.

Instead, what happened was that Clarke announced a more generous package than was expected to help low-income families meet the cost of higher fuel bills. It would cost the government £416 million in 1994–95, and more than three times that figure two years later. More than 40 per cent of the money Lamont had proposed to raise through VAT on fuel had been returned to the nation's pensioners. Clarke was hard on smokers and drivers, putting cigarettes up by 11p for a packet of twenty and petrol up 13.6p a gallon, with further increases in car tax and insurance premiums; but he was exceptionally lenient on drinkers, making no increase in the duty on beer or spirits and putting only 2p on a bottle of wine. He announced that spending on health and social security would increase. Then, towards the end of his address, he led his audience on with an expert tease. He had announced tax increases of

£1.75 billion for the coming year, but the PSBR was to fall by £5.5 billion, a gap of £3.75 billion. How was this gap to be bridged?

> Most commentators realised that one of my options must be to extend the VAT base. The main candidates are food, children's clothes, transport, sewerage and newspapers. A powerful case for each of them can be made, and no amount of lobbying need put us off, but before looking at that...

And off he went at an apparent tangent, talking about ceilings on departmental spending totals, and reduced interest payable on government debt, which meant that estimates for government spending given in Lamont's March Budget could be revised downwards.

> As a result of that achievement – and only because of that – I can now confirm that I have no need this year to propose any changes to the VAT base.[9]

The following morning's *Financial Times* said that Clarke had "donned the mantle of a fiscal magician by conjuring away previous gloomy projections of large budget deficits"; while the front page of *Today* was dominated by a cartoon of Clarke as the comedian Tommy Cooper, making £3 billion worth of public debt vanish "just like that". The worst public debt problem in a decade and a half was to be cleared up in five years, without a single headline-grabbing spending cut or tax increase. It did not take long, however, for the analysts to see also that the two 1993 Budgets had produced between them "the biggest tax increases in modern history",[10] combined in Clarke's case with "the most Draconian assault on the growth of public spending" since 1979, harsher even than Sir Geoffrey Howe's.[11]

Clarke's "achievement" in closing the £3 billion in his accounts was relatively easily explained. All Budget calculations include a large sum for contingencies, to protect individual departments from having to make severe and unexpected cuts midway through the financial year. Thus, despite Geoffrey Howe's austerity, Britain was able to meet the unexpected cost of the Falklands War. What Clarke had done was halve the £7 billion contingency reserve and then, instead of spreading the remaining £3.5 billion among government departments, had made them lower their totals by that amount. The biggest single loser from this exercise was local government, whose grant was to be £860 million lower than previously planned. The defence budget was cut by £260 million, which was less than expected; housing by £250 million, leaving officials at the Housing Corporation "rather shell shocked"[12] as they contemplated how they would cope after their government support had fallen by nearly a third in two years; and transport by £210 million. Lord Palumbo, Chairman of the Arts Council, warned that it was "a black day for the arts", as his council's grant was cut by £3.2 million.

Although the social-security budget was to be increased, two groups were exceptionally hard hit. Invalidity benefit, paid to those unable to work, was to disappear from April 1995, to be replaced by a new "incapacity benefit" and strict rules to define who was entitled to it. Incapacity was to be measured under a points system: 25 points for anyone who "cannot walk at all", or is "unable to handle a book so as to read it"; 9.5 points for a claimant who "cannot pick up and carry a 5lb bag of potatoes in either hand separately"; but just 3 points for a claimant who "can walk 400 yards without stopping".[13] The effect of putting the sick through this obstacle course, the House of Lords was informed on the day after the Budget, would be to strike off about 250,000 people who were already claiming disability benefit and disallow about 70,000 new claims every year. Moreover, incapacity benefit, unlike invalidity benefit, would be taxed.

For the jobless, who numbered 2,855,100 in the most recent official total, Clarke had a special announcement. No longer would they be "unemployed", receiving either the dole or income support. They became "job seekers", with a "job seeker's allowance". There were just two catches. One was that the "contributory element", which previously had been the difference between unemployment benefit and income support, would be payable for only six months, instead of a year. The second was that there would be "a much closer link between the receipt of benefit and the claimant's demonstrated willingness to look for work".[14] This passage produced a stronger reaction than any other in the reply to the Budget speech from the Labour leader John Smith:

> My stomach turned when I heard about ... the continued and vicious assault upon the welfare state. At a time of high unemployment, to cut the time for unemployment benefit from one year to six months is ... odious, odious in the extreme.[15]

Clarke's tax increases came in a form which meant that the average taxpayer would not be able to judge their effect at a glance. Moreover, as Norman

Lamont had done in March, Clarke phased in the introduction of his tax measures, so that the combined effects of the two Budgets would be felt in tranches. The most significant move was another reduction in mortgage tax relief, which had already been attacked by Lamont in the spring. He announced that its value would be reduced in April 1994 from 25 per cent to 20 per cent of the cost of a £30,000 loan; Clarke announced a further 5 per cent fall a year later. That was greeted with mixed relief by mortgage lenders, who had feared that this anachronistic subsidy for home owners might be abolished outright. Married couple's tax relief was also scheduled to fall to 15 per cent at the same time.

In contrast to Nigel Lawson, who tried to maintain a record of abolishing at least one tax with every Budget, Clarke introduced two entirely new ones: a 3 per cent levy on home, holiday and car insurance policies, and a new £5–£10 tax on air flights. That was one respect in which Clarke broke with the tradition established by Conservative Chancellors since 1979. Another was that he actually increased taxes for the very rich. During the run-up to the Budget, the shadow chancellor Gordon Brown had fronted a very effective campaign about the tax loopholes available to the extremely well paid, encapsulated in an unusually entertaining party-political broadcast featuring Hugh Laurie and Stephen Fry. It was contrary to orthodox Conservative thinking even to admit that the rich were still indulging in tax evasion. They were supposed to have lost interest in elaborate tax dodges after the government halved the top rate of income tax. The previous year's Conservative general-election manifesto had proclaimed:

> Higher taxes do not always bring in more money. In practice, they can bring in less. The Conservative government has more than halved the top rate of tax. Yet top rate taxpayers today provide a bigger share of our tax revenues than they did before.[16]

This canard appeared in an unsigned editorial in the *Sunday Times*, backed by columns of statistics, in the same month as the budget.[17] As a bald fact devoid of context, it is true: the top 1 per cent of taxpayers – that is, those quarter of a million individuals with a gross annual income of around £70,000 or more – contributed 17 per cent of all tax revenue in 1993–94, compared with 11 per cent in 1978–79.[18] However, during those fifteen years, there had been a dramatic widening of the gap between the highest and lowest incomes. In the last year of the Labour government, the top 1 per cent had a combined income of £5 billion, on which they paid an average of 46p in the pound in tax. Fifteen years later, they were paying an average of 32p in the pound, but on incomes which had increased sixfold to a total of £32 billion. Average incomes meanwhile had risen less than fourfold.[19] So the rich were paying proportionally more tax because they earned vastly bigger incomes from which to pay it.

One reason why it was suddenly important once again to come to the defence of the very rich was a suspicion gaining currency on the right that Clarke was back to his old Heathite tricks of trying to construct a pay policy. The evidence against him was twofold: his treatment of the government's own employees, and his plea for pay restraint in the boardroom. Public-sector workers had been subjected to a 1.5 per cent limit on pay increases across the board in 1992, which was billed at the time as a one-off to hasten Britain's recovery from recession. As early as July 1993, Clarke was dropping hints that something of the sort would be repeated that year. In September, he persuaded the Cabinet to keep up the squeeze on public-sector pay, and on the day after the Budget he announced what amounted to a freeze on public-sector pay. Any increase would have to be paid for through greater efficiency. "People's approach to pay is going to have to be conditioned by the fact that you are talking about very low figures for inflation compared with the experience of the past 20 years", he said. "The annual pay rise isn't going to be at the kind of levels that we all got used to."[20]

Meanwhile, there had been big increases in the salaries of some of Britain's highest paid directors, which did not make the government's self-appointed task of holding down their own employees' pay any easier. In March 1994, Clarke told *Today* newspaper:

I don't think any politician or government has the power to intervene and stop people being paid by their companies. But I do think that with the rates of taxation having been reduced, people should think twice before allowing their boards to award them excessively high salaries.

I share the general public attitude to the one or two spectacularly high salaries and pay-offs reported. They are unnecessary.[21]

It would be a big leap from exhorting company bosses to restrain themselves to legislating; but the mere fact that the Chancellor felt he was entitled to comment on pay increases implied that he did not believe in the unfettered operation of the free market. One of the business executives whose pay had been well publicized was his former boss, Lord Young, now the £430,000-a-year chairman of Cable and Wireless, a company he had helped to privatize. Lord Young's reaction to the Chancellor's remarks was: "We should reward success but penalise failure. There have been far too many cases of people walking away with money for failure. I am not overpaid or rewarded. I get paid a lot of money, but not in comparison with international levels."[22]

Clarke is adamant that he gave up believing that a government could control incomes by statute as long ago as 1980, so the right have nothing to fear from him in this respect.[23] But he is obviously aware that, as taxes are increased, stories of lavish boardroom salaries or outrageous tax avoidance become that much more politically sensitive. Up until the Budget, Clarke had poured buckets of ridicule over Gordon Brown's claims as to how much could be clawed back by closing tax loopholes. Earlier in the month, he had told the Commons: "When we investigate the matter closely, to discover whether closing the so-called loopholes would raise any revenue, it becomes obvious that that would be about as much use as brass washers."[24] Now he cheerfully admitted that "the tax avoidance industry is always ingenious",[25] before announcing that he proposed to increase the tax yield by £2 billion over two years – that is, £4,000 a year for each taxpayer in the £70,000-plus bracket – by abolishing seven lucrative dodges. For instance, it was not widely known that, until Clarke's Budget, it was possible to claim tax relief on payments made to blackmailers and other extortionists.[26] He also put an end to the practice of avoiding national insurance and postponing income tax by paying senior executives in "gold bars, coffee beans, cowrie shells or other exotic payments in kind".[27]

There was another statistic to be extracted from the Budget that had a political significance that almost went unnoticed at the time. Clarke had worked it out so that government debts would be reduced to only 2.75 per cent of GDP in 1996–97. There is a section in the Maastricht Treaty which urges all the states in the European Union to reduce government debt to 3 per cent of GDP or less by that year as a necessary step towards the creation of a single European currency. This was, of course, an incredibly sensitive question within the Conservative Party. There are Tory MPs who would sooner bring down their own government than have the British pound disappear, subsumed into a European currency. Despite his reassuring talk about the ERM being dead, Clarke has never abandoned the idea that European governments can control their exchange rates, or that the single market will eventually be served by a single currency. Even after Black Wednesday, he told the Commons: "I am surprised that I keep being asked about economic and monetary union. I made my first speech in the House of Commons in favour of it in 1971 or 1972 [1971, in fact] and have not changed my views."[28] If he intended to clear the way for monetary union he had taken the right steps, and with such subtlety that the first commentator to notice was Christopher Huhne, writing in the *Independent on Sunday* five days later. However, when he was questioned, Clarke pleaded innocence:

> I did not do it deliberately. I did not start by saying that we have to hit the Maastricht criteria and, therefore, that is going to be the judgement of the PSBR. I started from the principle that we had to take decisive action now to get public finances under control ... It is a happy coincidence, although given I was in favour of Maastricht, and given the budget opinions I was in favour of as well, it is not surprising that the two roughly coincide.[29]

Another example of how good luck was Kenneth Clarke's constant companion in 1993, perhaps, was the fact that he had been spared a decision on whether or not Britain should be renegotiating its way back into the Exchange Rate Mechanism, from which it had been forcibly ejected the previous year. Before Clarke could be drawn into this political minefield, the ERM effectively collapsed when the French franc ran into the same problem that had beset sterling, and the Bundesbank was as unwilling as ever to risk inflation by lowering German interest rates.

At his first meeting of EC finance ministers in Luxembourg, on 7 June, Clarke pronounced that: "Conditions in Germany are so far out of line at the moment that the conditions are not there for anyone to talk about rejoining the ERM."[30] No one in Britain felt able to disagree. Eight weeks later, Clarke rushed to Brussels on a Sunday to be present at the death of the ERM. The previous week, the Bundesbank had once again refused to make an appreciable reduction in German interest rates, the franc had fallen almost to its lowest permissible level, and the recession-hit French government simply could not keep up the struggle to save their currency. After a twelve-hour emergency session, the finance ministers agreed in the early hours of Monday morning, 2 August, to reform the ERM more or less out of existence. The technical position was that the ERM's two trading bands of 2.25 per cent and 6 per cent were replaced by a single band of 15 per cent. This implied that if sterling, for simplicity's sake, were to rejoin the ERM at its 1987 level of three Deutsche Marks then it could rise to DM3.45 or fall as low as DM2.55 before the Chancellor would be required to do anything about it. In reality, it meant that the attempt to manage exchange rates within the EC had been postponed indefinitely, because of the strains imposed by the cost of reunifying Germany

It also gave the British a precious opportunity to gloat. Clarke emerged from the long meeting in good humour, to announce that "others have discovered the fault lines in the ERM which the British have been pointing out." Despite having been kept up well into the night, he was awake early the following morning in order to be able to tell listeners to Radio 4's *Today* programme that, far from being a stormy, crisis-ridden summit, "some of it was extremely boring". And he claimed: "My contribution was to ensure that talks didn't break down."[31] This was a change from Britain's usual role as the EC's chief troublemaker. The ERM in its old form may never be seen again. At any rate, that is Clarke's prediction.[32] But the case for a single European currency is not automatically discredited by the failure of one attempt to achieve it by an indirect route. Accidentally, or on purpose, Clarke had helped line Britain up to take part in monetary union, should it begin on time.

In a more general departure from the Thatcher era, the overall effect of Clarke's tax reforms was more "progressive" than "regressive", in that they tended to load the bigger increases onto the higher paid. There were exceptions. Tobacco taxes, for instance, are notoriously hard on the poor, although they provoke very little reaction from the left. The squeezing of unemployment and invalidity benefits would also inevitably be felt most among the poorest. The Institute of Fiscal Studies calculated that the poorest 10 per cent would suffer more from the combined Clarke and Lamont Budgets than those in the second decile, which included large numbers of pensioners who would benefit from Clarke's measures to limit the impact of VAT on fuel. After that, people were harder hit the further up the income scale they were, until about three-quarters of the way up the ladder, when the effects tailed off. Reducing mortgage tax relief, for example, only impacted on home owners, but people with mortgages of more than £30,000 were proportionally less affected. Similarly, fuel tax only affected car owners, but the richer the car owner, the less he was hurt by it. Even so, the top 10 per cent were reckoned to have been harder hit than the poorest 30 per cent.[33]

In raising taxes at all, and moreover in concentrating the pain on the middle-class, middle-income property owners who are the backbone of Conservative support, it might be supposed that Clarke had again broken with the tradition set since 1979. Far from it. Over fifteen years the Conservatives had increased the burden on most taxpayers, partly of course to pay for the reductions bestowed on the very wealthy. By 1993–94, the average taxpayer was parting with approximately 21p in the pound in income and national insurance, compared with less than 20p in the last year of the Labour government, a 1.5p increase. As we have already seen, those at the very top had had their liability cut by 12p in the pound. Those in the bottom half of the income scale, with annual incomes below about £12,000 a year, had had their tax burden increased under Margaret Thatcher, but decreased in the run-up to the 1992 election, putting them back where they started, with a direct taxation liability of just un. a 13p in the pound. (They were, of course, made worse off by the Tory principle of increasing indirect taxation, like VAT; and none of these figures takes into account what had happened to those who were too poor to pay any tax, whose standard of living had gone relentlessly downwards.) The losers were those in roughly the £12–26,000 income bracket, that is, in the top half of the income scale, but below the top 10 per cent, for whom income tax and national insurance had risen from 19.5p to 21.5p on average in fifteen years.

However, increased taxes had been combined with rising incomes, which meant that everyone outside the bottom 10 per cent was better off in real terms: it was just that the rich were proportionally much better off than everyone else. Until the Lamont/Clarke Budgets, overall tax had at least not increased any faster than national output. Taxes, including national insurance and council tax, consumed 34.5 per cent of gross domestic product in 1993–94, compared with 34.75 per cent in 1978–79. On that figure, the Conservatives could still just lay claim to being the party of low taxation; but the official documents accompanying Clarke's Budget announcement revealed that tax was due to start overtaking output, and would rise to 38.5 per cent of GDP in 1998–99.[34] After twenty years of Conservative government, the proportion of the nation's output consumed by taxation would have risen by more than a tenth. "What would the proverbial Rip Van Winkle make of it?" asked the *Financial Times* columnist, Samuel Brittan; his own answer was that "Mr Van Winkle might assume that a Labour government had come into power around 1979–80, determined to lever the tax burden upwards."[35]

CHAPTER FIFTEEN

THE UNREAD TREATY AND THE "DREADFUL HOLE"

John Major's world fell apart on 16 September 1992. Until Black Wednesday, he had been doing so well. Through the Gulf War, the difficult negotiations with other EC leaders at Maastricht, and the general election he had looked an unlikely hero, the antithesis of Margaret Thatcher; and perhaps for that reason the country took to him, making him the most popular prime minister since Harold Wilson. It seemed that nothing could go wrong. Major even confided to executives of the *Sunday Times* that sterling might be on the point of replacing the Deutsche Mark as the strongest currency in Europe. His was a comfortable, crisis-free government, a government of "the pals", as the right-wing journalist Frank Johnson nicknamed it. The main "pals" were the trio who had been Treasury ministers when Major was Chancellor of the Exchequer and had organized his leadership campaign: Norman Lamont, the chief whip Richard Ryder, and the "Minister for Fun", David Mellor.

Then, in one dramatic day, the centrepiece of the government's economic policy collapsed. Having spent billions trying to prop up the value of sterling, and having raised the bank rate from 10 per cent to 15 per cent in a single day, Norman Lamont was forced to concede defeat and pull Britain out of the European Exchange Rate Mechanism, so that sterling could tumble until it had found its market value. From then on, governing ceased to be a Sunday outing for John Major and his pals. As the government staggered from crisis to crisis, the Conservative press, with the exception of the *Daily Express*, turned on the prime minister with unheard-of ferocity.

In this sort of crisis, Clarke came into his own. His television and radio appearances multiplied, as they had during the Westland affair and during the fall of Thatcher. Although he had signally failed to win the war against crime, the Home Secretary was branching out to defend the government on the economy or whatever else was the issue of the moment. "Even if the crisis is a very bad one, there is no doubt that there is a certain excitement about it", he said later.[1] By May 1993, when he moved from the Home Office to be Chancellor of the Exchequer, it was a truth universally acknowledged that Kenneth Clarke was the next prime minister of Great Britain.

That position is a test of a politician's temperament. The list of ex-future prime ministers is long and distinguished, as Kenneth Clarke has pointed out often enough; as far back as 1986, he said: "There is a club for all the people who have been described like that – Roy Mason, Eric Varley, Francis Pym, Roy Jenkins and all those people. Yes, I am in that crowded company."[2] The pretender must face the constant, critical scrutiny of colleagues, commentators and opponents, and cope with the sheer fickleness of politics, by which whoever is in fashion one year must go into eclipse the next. The strain can be felt by anyone else in the immediate orbit, including wives, children, advisers and close friends.

Kenneth and Gillian Clarke had been happily married for almost thirty years. Their children had grown up and taken jobs away from politics and out of the public eye. Their personal finances had been sorted out. They had moved out of Birmingham after the 1987 election, to a house in West Bridgford, in Clarke's constituency. Then suddenly, as Clarke emerged as the strong man in a weakened Cabinet, his wife was subjected to intense and often unfriendly press interest, which cannot have been very pleasant but seems to have done no lasting harm. In the way that politicians can be turned into stereotyped figures, so was she; all of a sudden, she was the antithesis of Joan Collins, the woman in her fifties who was not obsessed with trying to look young. In other circles, that would count as normal behaviour, but for someone with a famous husband it was thought to be odd.

The feminist writer Beatrix Campbell interviewed Gillian Clarke in 1986, as part of a study of women in the Conservative Party, and found her to be "a strong believer in Tory family ideology",[3] but different from the run-of-the-mill Tory in her commitment to equality legislation and the Third World. Having worked as a volunteer for Oxfam for over two decades, she thought overseas aid should be used for development, not for increasing British exports. That was a view far removed from Mrs Thatcher's, as demonstrated in the unfolding story of Malaysia's Pergau Dam, which consumed a large part of Britain's overseas aid budget as a pay-off for an arms deal. Those who know Gillian Clarke say that she is a strong-willed and intelligent woman. In 1988, she won the National Patchwork Championships with embroidered wall hangings entitled "The Labours of the Months", twelve panels based on medieval manuscripts. She looks like the sort of person someone younger would feel they could turn to for advice. It was her looks, rather than her character, which received the attention of feature writers in the national press after Clarke became Chancellor of the Exchequer. *The Times* observed that she was unlikely to be photographed in a glossy magazine, because "her fingernails are too steeped in garden soil and her fashion sense is more grunge-granny, with stripy layers, mismatched pussycat bows and felt hats."[4] After she had been photographed outside 11 Downing Street on Budget Day, Lynda Lee Potter of the *Daily Mail* opened fire:

> There are those who say how commendable and refreshing that she continues to be her own woman, refuses to diet and sticks to her folksy hairstyle, giving the unfortunate impression that she's old enough to be her husband's mother. My own feeling is that on the biggest day of the Chancellor's life, she could have tried harder.[5]

Attacks like these tell us something about the women who make them. And they are invariably women journalists who are let loose to ridicule the way a woman dresses; that is to say, they are professionals who have sacrificed their domestic lives to spend long hours at work, where they must dress to impress. They are commenting on someone who could have been just like them. With her Cambridge First, Gillian Clarke could have gone straight into a well-paid job; but she chose to be a homemaker, bringing up her children full-time, and chose not to spend a fortune on face-lifts and cosmetics. "It is possible that in 20 years' time no women of even moderate means will appear looking like Gillian Clarke", wrote a *Guardian* columnist. "Today's young women have got the message that looking old is not an option."[6] It is not for women in competitive professions, at any rate. Clarke seemed to be mildly irritated when he was asked on *Desert Island Discs* about his wife's appearance. He said: "One or two of my friends have got wives who were models, so they tend to juxtapose pictures of my friends' wives walking down catwalks modelling alongside Gillian out on a country walk – all slightly silly." No sooner had this remark gone out on the airwaves than commentators were observing that there was only one prominent Conservative married to a model, namely Clarke's old rival Michael Howard. He had to take the first opportunity to deny that he had been referring to Sandra Howard.

The publicity also spilled over a little into the lives of the Clarkes' children. Their son Kenneth had become a banker, and so far has been a complete disappointment to gossip writers. Their daughter Sue had last attracted attention when she was starting work as a nurse and her father was Health Secretary. She is still a nurse, and married, and has given newspapers nothing more to write about since a brief phase as a teenage "punk". Clarke's brother, Michael, gave one interview which made the national newspapers. His sister Pat, a farmer's wife in East Sussex, stayed away from journalists. It is, on the whole, a private family apparently capable of coping with the stress of exposure without inviting more of it.

Another person drawn reluctantly into the public eye by Clarke's success was his political adviser, Tessa Keswick. In the Whitehall setup, political advisers are neither fish nor fowl. They work at a desk in a ministry as if they were civil servants, and are paid by the state, and like civil servants, they avoid making public statements or drawing attention to themselves – unless they go on to be politicians in their own right as Michael Portillo did. But they are not bound by the rules that prevent civil servants from taking sides in party politics and are usually appointed from outside the service. Keswick had been a councillor in Kensington in the early 1980s, and ran as a Conservative candidate in the 1987 general election, in a Scottish seat which she was never likely to win. Her relationship with Clarke is obviously close. She joined him at the health department in January 1989, in place of Jonathan Hill who went on to be John Major's political adviser, and stayed with him as he moved on from one government department to another. By 1994, she had reached a position where accusing fingers were pointed at her, holding her responsible for what were perceived to be Kenneth Clarke's mistakes.[7]

Keswick is said to be to the right of Kenneth Clarke. She is more instinctively Conservative and less fascinated by the game of politics than he is. She has what was known in pre-Thatcherite times as good breeding, having come from one of the illustrious families in Scotland, of the sort whose private tragedies fascinate readers of the *Daily Telegraph*. Her father is Lord Lovat, 24th Chief of the Clan Fraser of Lovat; one of her uncles is the Earl of Eldon. Most of the Lovats are not politically active, but there has been one outstanding exception in recent history. Another of Tessa Keswick's uncles is Sir Fitzroy Maclean, a former Tory MP and former SAS officer who was parachuted into Yugoslavia during the war to advise Churchill on the relative strengths of the competing partisan forces. His advice was to back Tito. She has been married since 1985 to Henry Keswick, the oldest of three brothers who are all prominent in the City. In the 1994 *Sunday Times* survey of Britain's rich, Henry and Simon Keswick were placed nineteenth, immediately behind the Guinness family, with a joint fortune reputed to have leapt in one year from £260 million to £550 million because of a boom in the Hong Kong stock market.[8] Their brother John Keswick is also getting along modestly well as chairman of Hambros Bank. The Keswick connection shows that too much can be made of Clarke's humble grandparents and his blokeish image. He is quite at ease in the company of people born into the ruling class.

Clarke stood up well to his year as prime-minister-in-waiting. Friends in the Amesbury Group noticed that he was, if at all possible, bouncier and more cheerful even than his normal self, and yet he managed to keep his personal relationship with the incumbent prime minister in reasonably good order. In the early part of 1994, he suddenly went out of fashion, and all attention switched to Michael Heseltine who had arisen for the second time from what seemed to be a political grave. The immediate trigger was the Scott inquiry into the supply of arms to Iraq, at which Heseltine acquitted himself with style; but the underlying reason for the fall in Clarke's standing was the same as that which had lifted him into the post of Chancellor of the Exchequer in the first place. It was the continuing crisis in the economy.

As well as making John Major look ridiculous, Britain's sudden ejection from the ERM stirred up the right wing of the Conservative Party, bringing to the surface all the anti-European sludge which had lain low since the fall of Thatcher. It now became an article of faith on the party's right wing that the economy had been in recession until 16 September, but had recovered on that day and had been growing ever since. A pro-European like Clarke could say over and over again that "the argument that the recovery started because we left the ERM is simply mythology",[9] but he was arguing with people who were not to be persuaded. A large section of the Conservative Party had not accommodated itself to the idea that Britain was to lose its independence in a union of European states. The failure of the ERM had convinced them that they were not only being patriotic but were guarding the nation's economic interests too, and the fact that the government now had a small majority gave them unprecedented power to make trouble.

It is a matter of opinion whether the treaty which John Major had negotiated with other EC heads of government at Maastricht in December 1991, with opt-out clauses by which Britain avoided committing itself to implementing new employees' rights or the timetable for achieving a common European currency, was important enough to split the Conservative Party and threaten the future of the government. It was certainly not as important as the treaty signed by Edward Heath twenty years earlier, which took Britain into the Common Market, and expert opinion generally seems to rate its significance below that of the Single European Act, which Margaret Thatcher signed in 1985–86 with no audible political repercussions. During the dispute which erupted over Maastricht in autumn 1992, there emerged a number of zealots, best described as Maastricht bores, who could cite large sections of the Treaty from memory in defence of their belief that it was a threat to the monarchy and the sovereignty of the British parliament. Margaret Thatcher was not the least of them. The Maastricht rebels ran their own office, produced their own literature, had their own sources of funds, and organized their own informal whipping system, and were generally the most organized splinter to defy the Conservative whips in living memory. Their leaders in the Commons were inconspicuous figures who had either never had a government job, even under Mrs Thatcher, or had not held on to the one they had. But Norman Tebbit would make frequent trips over to the House of Lords, whence he had retired after the general election, to be their cheerleader, and they were known to enjoy the covert sympathy of a trio of Cabinet ministers, Michael Howard, Peter Lilley and Michael Portillo.

Kenneth Clarke was not a Maastricht bore. Indeed, the one thing most people remember him saying about the Treaty was that he had never read it. This emerged when he appeared on the Sky television programme *Target*, with Norman Tebbit and the Labour MP, Austin Mitchell. He told Tebbit: "Nobody out there has read it – I have never read it. You should not waste your time unless you are particularly interested in the diplomatic minutiae."[10] He also hypothesized that John Major might not have read it either. Given the size of Sky television's audience this might have passed unnoticed, except that it was during the Conservative Party conference. On the same day, Lord

Tebbit waved a copy of the Treaty before the delegates, who were cheering him on, and exclaimed: "One of your ministers admitted on television he had not read it." Tebbit and Clarke then encountered one another at the party that the novelist Jeffrey Archer gives each year at conference, and engaged in what other guests described as an incandescent argument which carried on for some ten minutes, with Lord Tebbit giving rather better than he got, until the chief whip, Richard Ryder, took Clarke's elbow and steered him away.[11]

Whether or not he ever got round to reading it, Clarke was one hundred per cent in favour of ratifying it, with Britain's opt-out clauses attached. However, despite what he called his "silly spat" with Norman Tebbit, he was not the main target of right-wing resentment at this time. They had, after all, known all along where Clarke stood. The person who had really offended them was John Major, who had been the right's candidate in the leadership election two years earlier, but had belatedly turned out to be in the same tradition as other Treasury ministers: Thatcherite in his attitude to public spending, but pro-European. In October, as the first important vote on the Maastricht Treaty approached, John Major's press secretary told lobby journalists at a private briefing that if the government was defeated, John Major would resign. Even though it was not repeated in public, it was an extraordinary threat, and yet it had no effect on the leading anti-Europeans, who dismissed it as bluff. Naturally, they were equally unmoved by a simultaneous warning from Clarke that if the government was defeated even once it would be "seriously weakened".[12]

The text of Clarke's Commons speech during the Maastricht debate suggests that he may not be quite the same sort of Euro-enthusiast that he once was. At the time when he was involved in getting Britain into the Common Market, his position was quite simply that this country should have signed the Treaty of Rome in the first place, in 1959.[13] Anti-marketeers in the Conservative and Labour parties, including Nick Budgen, believed that he was an outright federalist. Budgen, who has known Clarke well for a very long time, believes he still is; others concede that he might not be, including Lord Tebbit who, during that famous confrontation at Lord Archer's party, reportedly said: "I entirely accept that neither you nor the Prime Minister are European federalists."[14] Certainly, "federalist" is not an epithet that Clarke wants to have stuck to his lapel because, he says, "the word is now loaded with meaning of a symbolic kind."[15] During the Maastricht debate, he declared:

> I am against the formation of a state of Europe ... We are all Gaullists now ... The idea of the founding fathers who created the original treaty of Rome was that ... in the end, one effectively has the institutions of a state with a common court, a Council of Ministers, an embryonic government and so on. In practice, that has not worked out.[16]

In Clarke's view, Maastricht's "most positive achievement"[17] was the so-called "pillared approach" which is supposed to point the way in which all future negotiations between EC governments will be conducted. The Maastricht Treaty created a European Union built on three "pillars", of which the Economic Community, or EC, was only one. The second pillar was a common foreign and security policy; the third was an agreement on justice and home affairs. It was the third pillar which particularly concerned Clarke, as Home Secretary. He rather daringly turned up to take part when it was debated line by line on the floor of the Commons, the first Cabinet minister to participate in the long-running argument over the details of the Treaty.

To a defender of the Treaty, like Clarke, these pillars protect the sovereignty of the nations that make up the union because, by defining the powers of the new European states, they also limit them. The British government knows that it is obliged by this treaty to comply with European laws on immigration, for instance, but that British soldiers are not required to wear European uniforms or fight the same wars as other European soldiers; therefore Britain is still a self-governing state. This argument, of course, did not wash with the anti-Maastricht faction. They noted that one of the first clauses in the Treaty declared "the union will be served by a single institutional framework", which seemed to contradict the idea that the three pillars are distinct and separate. They also observed that the Treaty created an entirely new person, the European citizen. One backbencher challenged Clarke to deny that the Queen would now become a citizen of the union of Europe. The Queen has never been a citizen before: in Britain, citizens are her subjects. Clarke was compelled to admit that it was probably true; but he was not greatly impressed. "I do not see why the Queen should be any more fearful of that prospect than anybody else is likely to be", he said.[18]

Another fear dredged up by Maastricht's opponents, which surfaced during the Danish referendum and may have been part of the reason why the Danes voted to reject it, was that the Treaty's reference to "the eventual framing of a common defence policy" implied that there would one day be a European standing army to which Britons could be conscripted. Again, Clarke was unimpressed. He said that it was a "fanciful notion" which "may have worked with a few gullible Danes", but did not impress him; whereupon he was accused by the Tory right of insulting Denmark.

As a Cabinet minister, Clarke had no choice but to defend the government's policy, opt-outs and all, or keep silent. There were a small number of Conservative MPs, including Edward Heath and Hugh Dykes, who agreed with the Labour Party that Britain should have signed up to the entire treaty, including the social chapter and the timetable for a single European currency. It is an intriguing possibility that, on the quiet, Clarke agreed with them more than was politic. He certainly seemed to be hinting at that in January, when he described Dykes as a person "with whom I have always shared very similar views on Europe".[19]

His Commons performances during the Maastricht saga were remarkable for the fulsome praise he heaped on his Labour "shadow", Tony Blair, who was making a good job of defending the Treaty against the Tory right and Labour left. This sort of praise was actually not helpful to Blair's position in the Labour Party, and at one point he half-jokingly said it would be easier for him if the Home Secretary reverted to his normal practice of knocking the opposition. Instead, Clarke came back to the next debating session to praise Blair again, and committed an enormous slip of the tongue. He said that Blair's "views on the European Community are indistinguishable from my own". Instantly, of course, Clarke recalled that he was supposed to be siding with the government in a dispute with Labour over the opt-out clauses and hastily corrected himself, saying:

> He has an unfortunate mental block on the social chapter ... whereas we declined to be drawn into that ... on economic and monetary union, Labour's position is that we should have assented, whereas the government decided to opt out of the immediate provisions of EMU and to reserve questions such as a single currency for a later date.[20]

With these mild words, Clarke put himself back in line with government policy.

The week after Black Wednesday, Major had to accept the resignation of one of the "pals". Stories about David Mellor's private life had been running like a soap opera over most of the previous two months. At first, Major sternly refused to allow them to influence the make-up of his Cabinet, but when the Commons met in emergency session in September, and Mellor's affairs were still making news, he was pushed by the Tory backbench 1922 Committee into accepting Mellor's resignation. That begged the question of whether he should have sacked him sooner. On television that evening, Kenneth Clarke defended the prime minister, saying "I know what I would think of the judgement of a Prime Minister who stabbed a friend in the back when he is in those sort of difficulties."[21] However, Mellor's departure only reinforced the impression that Major was a weak leader. The pattern would repeat itself: a minister was suddenly attracting bad publicity, the prime minister was four-square behind him; the problem grew, the prime minister capitulated and the minister departed.

The most important victim of this process was the Chancellor of the Exchequer Norman Lamont. After Black Wednesday, bad luck seemed to dog Lamont wherever he went. A series of stories surfaced around his private life, none of them particularly serious, but they combined to turn him into a figure of fun. He could probably have survived that, but after the debacle of Black Wednesday, his word no longer carried weight in financial circles. Even when he made an attempt to be humorous, by answering a question during a by-election in Newbury with the words "je ne regrette rien", he offended voters who thought there was *beaucoup* that he ought to regret. It was on the Sunday after the Newbury result that Clarke came out with one of his most memorable remarks, when he admitted that the government was in a "dreadful hole".

Even the "Cambridge mafia" deserted Norman Lamont. It was Norman Fowler, the new chairman of the party, who told Major finally that Lamont would have to go. On 26 May, the day after Lamont was sacked, Kenneth Clarke took his job, Michael Howard succeeded Clarke at the Home Office, and the job which Lamont had been offered as a consolation but had turned down, that of Environment Secretary, was taken by John Gummer. Lamont's departure left Major all the more exposed. Even when he set off on a trade visit to Tokyo four months later, vowing not to answer questions about his leadership or the open attacks on him by a handful of right-wing Tories, he was provoked into changing tack and appealing from halfway across the world for an end to "stupid internecine squabbling".[22] Clarke at once tried to help, with a few words that were intended to kill speculation that there would be a contest for the party leadership when the Commons returned in the autumn. He told a radio interviewer:

> Kenneth Clarke, Michael Portillo and Michael Howard and others who get canvassed by people trying to beat the Prime Minister over the head all share the Prime Minister's view of what the priorities are at the moment. Great attempts are being made in some sections to arouse interest in a leadership challenge. But I know of no person of real political judgement who would contemplate such a thing.[23]

This was seized upon by the *Daily Mail* as an admission that at least three ministers had been approached by MPs plotting the fall of the prime minister. In the same interview, Clarke admitted that the government was "still in a dreadful hole".

John Major's luck seemed finally to take a turn for the better at the party conference in autumn 1993. There were ominous signs of a right-wing revival, in the ecstatic ovation as Mrs Thatcher entered the hall, or the populist speeches from Michael Howard and Peter Lilley, who played to their audiences in the one case by promising to be tough on crime, and on the other by insulting Europeans; but Clarke seemed to go out of his way to avoid upstaging the prime minister, by giving a subdued and rather dull speech which included the line "Any enemy of John Major is an enemy of mine. Any enemy of John Major is no friend of the Conservative Party." Mrs Thatcher, who was on the platform listening, is reported to have told friends at a private lunch that it had "fallen flat". One of those present said: "It was a weak speech and she was delighted."[24] The right, who had seemed ready to support Clarke in the summer simply because he was not John Major, were beginning to lose faith in him, after he had dropped a series of hints that he was not going to take their advice that there should be no tax increases in his Budget. Meanwhile, John Major appeared to carry the day with his new campaign slogan, "Back to Basics". The initial success of Clarke's Budget also seemed to work in Major's favour, by giving the impression that the crisis in public finances was resolved and the government could look forward to recovery.

But afterwards "Back to Basics" took on a meaning rather different from that which Major and his advisers had intended. Briefly, it appeared to turn into a single-issue campaign against welfare payments for single mothers, after the Welsh Secretary John Redwood revived an old right-wing complaint that the benefits system encouraged girls to get pregnant. It was then taken up by the Social Security Secretary, Peter Lilley, who called for a civil-service briefing. The long background paper drawn up by officials from his department and the Cabinet Office was leaked to the Labour Party, and turned out to be of little use to the right. It said there was "no evidence" that women became pregnant simply to get themselves on the council waiting list, and "little clear evidence" that the higher benefits paid to lone mothers encouraged women to bring up children on their own. Most were unaware of how the system operated when they became pregnant.[25]

The following week, Clarke issued a veiled attack on the right, by saying in a television interview that "Back to Basics" had been "rather misunderstood and rather hijacked", and ridiculing the idea that women became pregnant "after consulting their welfare rights officer". He added: "I think the vast majority of single mothers wish to be self-sufficient and reliant, but if for some reason they cannot be so, it is the duty of the government to provide for vulnerable people of all kinds and make sure that no one has less than the basic standard of living."[26]

"Back to Basics" spectacularly misfired in the New Year, when half a dozen Conservative MPs ran into personal trouble of one kind or another, which suggested that they were not good at observing basic rules about personal morality. Stories of sexual peccadilloes entertained the nation, but they were not as serious in their implications for the health of the body politic as the intricate scandal of the Matrix Churchill trial.

This story is worth a book on its own, and will probably spawn several. Suffice it to say here that during the Iran–Iraq war, Britain claimed to be imposing an embargo on arms sales to either side, in line with the policy of the United Nations. Iraq's attempt to occupy Kuwait in 1990 provoked questions about how its army came to be well equipped. In no time, evidence began to emerge that part of Saddam Hussein's war machine had been made in Britain. One of the engineering firms which had been knowingly supplying Iraq with parts that had a military purpose was Matrix Churchill, in Coventry, three of whose executives went on trial for illegally breaking the arms embargo. After their arrest, the firm went into liquidation and its 600 employees lost their jobs. The trial collapsed when the former arms minister, Alan Clark, admitted in court that ministers had known about the sales at the time. Another blow to the prosecution was the judge's decision to release to the defence a number of sensitive documents which ministers had wanted withheld. Whatever was said in public, Saddam Hussein's vile regime was privately seen as a useful bulwark against Iran, and arms sales were good for the economy.

The shock was not just in the discovery that Britain had been supplying arms to one of the most violently repressive regimes in the world while claiming not to be. Closer to home was the prospect that the government had intended to sit by and allow three businessmen to go to jail rather than allow its real policy on arms sales to become public knowledge. One of the defendants, Matrix Churchill's managing director Paul Henderson, had even been working for the government in secret, by supplying MI6 with information about Iraq. All this could have been proved before the men were even brought to trial had the government not been anxious to keep embarrassing details of its Middle East policy secret. A number of ministers had signed public interest immunity (PII) certificates to prevent the relevant documents from being released. One of those ministers was Kenneth Clarke.

He had signed two PII certificates, which were both overruled by the judge. They were similar to certificates signed by the previous Home Secretary, Kenneth Baker, but different from others signed by ministers in the Foreign Office, the Defence Department and the Department of Trade. The other PII certificates covered internal communications between civil servants and/ or junior ministers and were intended to protect the secrecy of the government's own policy-making process. One of the certificates that Clarke signed would have limited the oral evidence given in the witness stand by the officer who was Paul Henderson's case officer in MI6. Under the terms of the certificate, the officer, codenamed John Balsom, would have been allowed to give evidence provided that his true identity was protected and he did not discuss MI6 operations. In the event, he gave evidence from behind a screen. The other certificate attempted to deny defence access to certain intelligence papers, on the grounds that disclosure would harm the national interest. The judge overruled it, but upheld a secondary claim, so that the papers were released with large sections blacked out.

These were not the only PII certificates Clarke signed during his period as Home Secretary. He also tried to deny defence lawyers acting for a New

Zealand helicopter pilot named Paul Bennett, who claimed to have worked for the CIA, access to telexes between the Metropolitan Police and South African police and file notes kept by the Crown Prosecution Service. Bennett was arrested at Heathrow in February 1991 and charged with obtaining £175,000 by deception, and spent two-and-a-half years in prison on remand before he was granted bail. When the Crown eventually handed over voluntarily the documents that his defence lawyers had applied to see, they demonstrated that the South African police had arrested Bennett and put him on a flight to New Zealand which conveniently stopped over in Heathrow, enabling Special Branch to pick him up in transit. As a result, the High Court quashed the case against him.[27] Clarke claimed in a statement that his PII had been justified, because it was undesirable that criminals operating across frontiers should know about the process of cooperation between police forces. "The fact that the prosecution and the court later decided that the interests of justice in this particular case overrode the PII claim does not change my view", he said.[28]

In the Bennett case, Clarke had acted at the behest of police who had bent rules in order to catch a man they suspected of fraud. The Matrix Churchill case reached to the heart of government, and was the subject of an inquiry headed, coincidentally, by the same Justice Scott who had been Vice-Chancellor of the Duchy of Lancaster when Clarke was its Chancellor. Clarke gave his evidence to the inquiry on 21 February 1994, claiming that he had acted in what he believed was the national interest by attempting to protect the confidentiality of the security services. He said, moreover, that "nothing that was relevant to Mr Henderson's case was cut out by my certificate. No one has ever claimed that Mr Henderson was prejudiced by my certificate." That claim was contested by Henderson himself, who told journalists that his trial would have been prejudiced if the judge had upheld Clarke's certificates.[29]

Clarke seemed very sure that he would be vindicated. He needed to be. Five days before the hearing, he had appeared on *Question Time* on BBC television with Labour's John Prescott, who painted him into a corner by asking him whether he would resign if he was criticized in Justice Scott's report, to which he said "Of course I will."[30] But his manner was almost bashful compared with the performance of Michael Heseltine, who not only echoed Clarke's promise to resign if he was found at fault, but arrived at the hearings like a show-business star, with Anne Heseltine at his side, to reveal that he had balked at signing PII certificates at all, doing so only after he was advised by the Attorney General, Sir Nicholas Lyell, that in law he had no choice.

For more than a year, it had been assumed that Heseltine was an extinguished volcano, working off his last few months in government. Politically, he had been deeply damaged by his tactless handling of the pit closures in autumn 1992, which provoked such a reaction that the government was forced into a temporary retreat. The following summer, Heseltine had a heart attack while he was on vacation in Italy, which seemed to put an effective end to his career. But in the early part of 1994, he was not only looking fit and well, but was taking trouble to seek out and cultivate obscure backbench Tory MPs, who could only assume that they owed this honour to a revival of Heseltine's ambitions. On the morning after his appearance at the Scott inquiry, the *Daily Mail* headline ran: "Mr Clean Back in the Running".[31] From then until Easter, Heseltine's stock rose inexorably, and Clarke's fell, until it seemed that the Chancellor's one hope was that John Major would hang on in office for a while to give Heseltine's undeclared campaign time to go wrong.

Nonetheless, just in case anyone thought he was standing aside for Heseltine's benefit, Clarke gave an interview to the *Independent*, in which he declared that "I would like to be a contender, but at a time of John Major's choosing, not mine."[32] On the day that the interview appeared, Clarke made an unfortunate slip of the tongue, when he was heard to say on national radio that John Major would be prime minister "to the autumn".[33] A few days later, Major complained that Clarke was "suffering from an engaging outburst of frankness and candour."[34] Although he insisted that he would remain in office, Major's standing had fallen to a point at which the implacable Tony Marlow stood up in the Commons and called on him to resign. It was the first time for thirty years that a prime minister had been attacked in that way by someone on his own side.

The rivalry between Heseltine and Clarke is said to have been part of the cause of the extraordinary fiasco in March, when Britain decided to play brinkmanship with Europe over the obscure question of qualified majority voting. Most of the population had not been aware that a form of block voting had applied to many of the most important decisions taken in Europe, under which the three largest countries, Germany, France and the UK, have ten votes each, Spain has eight, and the eight smaller EC countries have thirty-eight between them. These votes were not allocated in direct proportion to size, but were weighted slightly in favour of the smaller countries. However, a decision could be blocked if 30 per cent of the votes, or twenty-three votes out of seventy-six, are cast against. In March 1994, the EC was on the point of being enlarged to include Austria, Finland, Norway and Sweden, who were to be allocated fourteen votes, bringing the grand total to ninety. It was then assumed that twenty-seven votes, 30 per cent of the new total, would be needed to block a decision. For reasons that are hard to fathom, John Major decided to make opposition to this figure of twenty-seven a point of principle, and wound his party up to expect Britain to fight in the last ditch to preserve the smaller total of twenty-three. Then he capitulated, because he had no choice; Britain simply could not muster any allies in Europe other than Spain. His performance only served to send Tory MPs away on their Easter break more convinced than ever that they needed a new leader. Why Major ever started a fight on such weak ground is a mystery; although one contributory cause appears to be that neither Clarke nor Heseltine wanted to make enemies on the right by talking him out of it.

It had reached a point by Easter where received opinion in Westminster was that Major could not continue to the end of the year, although whether the mythical ruthlessness of the party would express itself was another matter. Also, just as it had been a racing certainty in 1993 that Clarke would be his successor, all the smart money had now switched to Heseltine by Easter. Heseltine's advantages were that he wanted the job more desperately than Clarke, and therefore was expected to make more concessions on Europe to the right wing than Clarke plausibly could. Clarke is a more sociable and emollient man than Heseltine, and has acknowledged that "party management is a key part of the process of government".[35] But his record as a pro-European is too long and too consistent for the right to have any illusions about him on this score. Heseltine's saving grace, from the right's point of view, is that he has no beliefs to stand in the way of his ambition. Heseltine was a political adventurer, in the old sense of the word. He took great risks and was addicted to grand gestures. Clarke was a reassuring character, an optimist who knew how to cheer the party up, the sort of leader they might turn to when they were down but still hopeful. By the spring of 1994, there was very little for the party to be optimistic about, and no solid evidence that even a change of leader would revive their fortunes. The cause of their spreading desperation was that, months after the event, the impact of Kenneth Clarke's first Budget was being felt.

The turning point, perhaps, was a headline in *The Times* in January, a full six weeks after the Budget, with the sensational message: "Tax: How you were better off under Denis Healey."[36] When all the tax changes, including VAT increases, were taken into account, even wealthy families were being more heavily taxed than in 1978–79, according to figures calculated for *The Times* by KPMG. As for the "average" family, there was no need even to bring in VAT: they were paying more income tax and national insurance than in the last year of the Labour government. This was the message from the Murdoch media empire, which had done so much for so long to keep the Conservatives in power. It was reinforced by a full-page editorial in the following morning's *Sun*, headed "What fools we all were to believe this lot."[37]

It was actually not Kenneth Clarke's fault, any more than it was the fault of other senior Cabinet ministers, that the Conservatives' promise to cut taxes had been so spectacularly broken. It was not Clarke who had allowed the deficit to build up; he was the man sent in to do the repair work. Besides, anyone who had listened carefully to what Clarke has said over the years should have known better than to believe manifesto promises. On this subject, he has been his usual insouciant self. "No man ever reads a party manifesto and believes every word of it – or if he does, he is some sort of automaton employed in Central Office or Transport House", he said in 1977.[38] After being tackled by the shadow chancellor Gordon Brown in summer 1993, he waved the problem away:

> His attack on our broken promises and all the rest of it were half-sentences taken from shredded speeches that somebody delivered on a wet night in Dudley.[39]

Moreover, to quote some half-sentences from shredded Clarke speeches and interviews, it emerges that the Conservatives never made a promise which they could now be accused of breaking:

> We did not pledge ourselves to retain the existing base of VAT. We are a party instinctively of low taxation. It is nonsense to interpret that as meaning that every Budget merely moves every tax down...[40]
> ...the manifesto contains no word about VAT or national insurance contributions...[41]

It is descending to the most puerile politics to claim that the Conservative

Party has ever said that in no Budget, at no time, will we ever increase any taxation.[42]

In a nutshell, if people voted Conservative expecting that their taxes would immediately go down, more fool them. Like John Major, Kenneth Clarke repeatedly insisted that the government was tackling an unforeseen and unforeseeable problem, that government debt had been forced up by prolonged recession. "Borrowing was bound to rise in the recession. It was the duty of the government to spend more on the welfare net to stop families falling through."[43] If the Conservative party had been more confident, it would have loved the sheer cheek of it all.

Until now it had been assumed that Michael Portillo, darling of the right, was too young to enter a leadership contest on his own account. Then, late in April, anonymous Portillo supporters briefed the *Sunday Telegraph* that their man had the backing of one hundred Tory MPs and was capable of pushing Kenneth Clarke into third place.[44] That can be taken as a wild exaggeration. Nonetheless, it opened up the prospect of a leadership election becoming a genuine clash of ideas rather than a beauty contest between two seasoned opportunists from the same political school. The point was underlined a week later, when Portillo gave a television interview in which he warned that political or monetary union in Europe would mean "giving up the government of this country".[45] Over the same weekend, Gillian Shephard, one of a dwindling number of Cabinet ministers determined to back John Major until the last, complained of the sense of "despair" caused by a "crazy" situation in which supporters of two Cabinet ministers – namely Heseltine and Portillo – were disloyally canvassing for support behind the prime minister's back.[46] Two days later, on 3 May, Portillo received a well-publicized telephone call from 10 Downing Street warning him to keep his public statements in line with party policy. This ought not to have been difficult, because Conservative policy on a single European currency was so ambivalent that it amounted to little more than prevarication, but Portillo's supporters thought it unfair that he should be rebuked a week after Clarke had been allowed to get away with telling a Tory backbench committee that they could accept that a single currency was inevitable.[47]

In the long term, there can be no compromise on this issue. Eventually, other European states will merge their currencies, however inconvenient that might be for the British Conservatives. Britain will then have to participate, or stay out. Many years ago, Clarke remarked in a telling aside that it was only Britain's first-past-the-post electoral system that held the Conservative Party together. Replace it with proportional representation, he said, and it would be "inconceivable" that he would be in the same party as someone like Ronald Bell, the former MP for Beaconsfield who was then the party's most prominent anti-marketeer.[48] Bell died in 1982, but with the passing of the years the rift within the Conservative Party over Europe has become more marked and more urgent, whilst for other reasons, electoral reform is more likely now than it ever was in the 1970s. Before his political career is through, Clarke may find that the prediction he made in 1977 has come true, and that he and the Tory right really have come to a final parting of the ways.

It is usually assumed that this will count against Clarke, should he be a candidate in a leadership election. Every Tory MP who opposed the Maastricht Treaty will vote against him. But the anti-European right is not as strong as it appears. It has support in the constituency parties, among the activists who go knocking on doors at election time for the Tory Party, but not in the City or in the boardrooms of companies that do business in Europe. If, as seems likely, a leadership contest becomes an ideological battle over Europe, victory will go to the pro-European candidate.

A MORI poll of MPs carried out during the winter of 1993–94 showed that Clarke had not only retained his place as the parliamentary performer most highly rated by his own side, but had increased his lead over both John Major and Michael Heseltine.[49] He has always been a politician's politician, more highly rated in Westminster than with the public at large. The option of playing the part of the outsider, the friend of the public who just happens to be resident in 10 Downing Street, which both Margaret Thatcher and John Major did so well, is closed to Kenneth Clarke. He is one of a handful of ministers who have held government office without interruption for fifteen years, and the only one who also held office in the early 1970s. He is a good-time politician. He enjoys life. He has done well by the capitalist system and the Conservative Party and, whatever anyone else's views, he thinks they both work splendidly. Such leaders can be a comfort to their party in times of trouble, and for the Conservative Party there is trouble ahead.

NOTES

1. BOYHOOD

1. He was described as the son of "a former miner", "mineworker" or "coal miner", for example, in the *Nottingham Evening Post*, 3 September 1985; *Daily Mail*, 13 April 1992; *Independent*, 20 September 1992; *Observer*, 30 May 1993; and by Sue Lawley on *Desert Island Discs*, BBC Radio 4, 20 February 1994.
2. The phrase is taken from Margaret Thatcher's speech to the Conservative Party Conference at Blackpool, October 1985.
3. *Today*, 3 March 1994.
4. *Desert Island Discs.*
5. *Nottingham Evening Post*, 19 September 1988.
6. Interview, Kenneth Clarke.
7. *Desert Island Discs.*
8. *Sunday Express*, 30 May 1993; *Sun*, 31 May 1993.
9. *Nottingham Evening Post*, 19 September 1988.
10. Hansard, 18 November 1971, col. 228.
11. *Today*, 9 May 1991.
12. For example, when he was challenged in the House of Commons by the Labour MP Jack Straw over whether he knew anything about state schools, he replied: "I attended one for my education, unlike the Honourable Gentleman who attended a minor public school." Hansard, 29 April 1991, col. 48. Straw was a scholarship boy.
13. Interview, Kenneth Clarke.
14. Interview with Kenneth Harris, *Nottingham Evening Post*, 12 March 1986.
15. *Financial Times*, 4 May 1991.
16. *Evening Standard*, 28 May 1993.
17. *Nottingham Evening Post*, 12 March 1986.
18. *Financial Times*, 4 May 1991.
19. Hansard, 22 January 1981, cols. 542–6.
20. Simon Hoggart, "The Tax Man", *Observer Magazine*, 28 November 1993.

21. Interview with David Freeman of Jazz FM, *Mail on Sunday*, 1 August 1993.
22. Interview, Jim Lester.
23. *Guardian*, 10 October 1994.
24. *Observer Magazine*, 28 November 1993.
25. Ibid.
26. *Nottingham Evening Post*, 12 March 1986.
27. Interview, Kenneth Clarke.

2. THE ORIGIN OF THE CAMBRIDGE MAFIA

1. Interview, Kenneth Clarke.
2. *Varsity*, 6 May 1961.
3. *Varsity*, 26 November 1960.
4. *Varsity*, 20 May 1961.
5. David Owen, *Time to Declare* (Michael Joseph, London 1991) p. 44.
6. Interview, Nick Budgen.
7. Hansard, 11 February 1986, col. 806.
8. *Varsity*, 3 March 1962.
9. *Varsity*, 2 February 1963.
10. John Dunn was interviewed for one of the first newspaper articles on the rise of the "Cambridge mafia", by Andrew Rawnsley (*Guardian*, 10 October 1988). On the "mafia" members as prototypes for modern politicians, see Peter Riddell, *Honest Opportunism – The Rise of the Career Politician* (Hamish Hamilton, London 1993) pp. 62–4.
11. *Varsity*, 3 February 1962.
12. Norman Fowler, *Ministers Decide – A Memoir of the Thatcher Years* (Chapmans, London 1991) p. 27.
13. *Varsity*, 25 February 1961.
14. *Varsity*, 11 November 1961.
15. *Varsity*, 25 November 1961.
16. Interview, Kenneth Clarke.
17. *Varsity*, 18 November 1961.
18. *Varsity*, 2 December 1961.
19. *Varsity*, 18 November 1961.
20. Interview, Kenneth Clarke.
21. *Varsity*, 25 February 1961.
22. *Varsity*, 3 June 1961.
23. *Varsity*, 20 January 1962.
24. *Varsity*, 2 December 1961.

25. *Varsity*, 27 January 1962.

26. *Varsity*, 28 April 1962.

27. Interview, Kenneth Clarke.

28. *Varsity*, 10 March 1962.

29. *Varsity*, 9 February 1963.

30. *Varsity*, 9 March 1963.

31. *Varsity*, 27 January 1961.

32. *Varsity*, 18 May 1963.

33. *Varsity*, 25 May 1963.

34. Fowler, *Ministers Decide*, p. 34.

35. *Varsity*, 11 March 1961.

36. *Varsity*, 21 October 1961.

37. *Varsity*, 18 November 1961.

38. *Varsity*, 26 May 1962.

39. *Varsity*, 24 November 1962.

40. Interview, Kenneth Clarke.

41. *The Times*, 7 March 1963; *Varsity*, 9 March 1963.

42. *Desert Island Discs*, BBC Radio 4, 20 February 1994.

43. Hansard, 22 May 1986, col. 574.

44. John Lenton, Nicholas Budgen and Kenneth Clarke, *Immigration, Race and Politics* (Bow Group Publications, London, March 1966).

45. Kenneth Clarke, Michael Worley, Ann Worley and David Anderton, *Regional Government* (Bow Group Publications, London, October 1968); *Nottingham Evening Post*, 19 September 1988.

46. Interview, Kenneth Clarke.

47. *Nottingham Recorder*, 3 October 1985.

48. *Guardian Journal*, 20 April 1964.

49. Interview, Kenneth Clarke.

50. Hansard, 2 November 1971, cols. 12–13.

51. *Guardian Journal*, 3 December 1966.

52. *Nottingham Evening Post*, 27 January 1969.

3. APPEAL TO
THE PRIME MINISTER

1. Norman Tebbit, *Upwardly Mobile*, (Weidenfeld & Nicolson, London 1988) p. 94.

2. Margaret Thatcher, *The Downing Street Years* (HarperCollins, London 1993) p. 7.

3. Interview, Kenneth Clarke.

4. *Nottingham Evening Post*, 17 July 1970.

5. Hansard, 8 July 1970, cols. 681, 693–4.

6. Ibid., col. 681.

7. Ibid., col. 693.

8. Hansard, 18 November 1971, col. 729.

9. Hansard, 2 November 1971, cols. 12–13.

10. *Nottingham Evening Post*, 3 November 1971.

11. *Sunday Express*, 23 April 1972.

12. Hansard, 8 March 1971, col. 129.

13. Ibid., cols. 126–7.

14. *Nottingham Evening Post*, 6 October 1972.

15. Interview, Kenneth Clarke.

16. Judy Hillman and Peter Clarke, *Geoffrey Howe – A Quiet Revolutionary* (Weidenfeld & Nicolson, London 1988) p. 104.

17. *Nottingham Evening Post*, 7 December 1970.

18. Interview, Kenneth Clarke.

19. Hansard, February 1972, col. 1201.

20. *Nottingham Evening Post*, 11 February 1972; *Guardian Journal*, 11 February 1972.

21. Interview, Nick Budgen.

22. Interview, Kenneth Clarke.

23. *Nottingham Evening Post*, 19 May 1971.

24. Hansard, 27 May 1971, col. 607.

25. *Nottingham Evening Post*, 28 October 1977.

26. Hansard, 22 July 1971, cols. 1777–80.

27. Hansard, 15 November 1978, cols. 474–5.

28. Hansard, 22 July 1971, col. 1779.

29. Hansard, 15 November 1978, col. 472.

30. Hansard, 22 July 1971, col. 1780.

31. Hansard, 2 November 1971, col. 13.

32. Hansard, 19 March 1974, cols. 959, 962.

33. Hansard, 16 February 1978, cols. 725, 729–30.

34. Hansard, 24 November 1977, col. 1865.

35. Hansard, 12 December 1977, col. 144.

36. Hansard, 24 November 1977, col. 1865.

37. Interview, Nick Budgen.

38. Hansard, 29 March 1972, cols. 591–6.

39. Francis Pym, *The Politics of Consent* (Hamish Hamilton, London 1984) p. 193.

40. Interview, Kenneth Clarke.

41. Interview, Lord Pym.

42. *Nottingham Evening Post*, 22 November 1973.

43. Jonathan Aitken, *Evening Standard*, 7 June 1971, quoted in John Campbell, *Edward Heath: A Biography* (Jonathan Cape, London 1993) p. 383.

44. Interview, Kenneth Clarke.

45. *Nottingham Evening Post*, 3 January 1974.

4. IN OPPOSITION

1. Interview, Kenneth Clarke.
2. Interview, Kenneth Clarke.
3. *Nottingham Evening Post*, 14 May 1975.
4. *Daily Telegraph*, 12 February 1973.
5. Keith Joseph, *Reversing the Trend: A Critical Reappraisal of Conservative Economic and Social Policies* (Barry Rose, 1975) p. 4.
6. Hansard, 10 April 1974, col. 484.
7. Ibid., cols. 533–4.
8. *Nottingham Evening Post* 30 January 1975.
9. Hansard, 29 January 1975, col. 450.
10. Norman Fowler, *Ministers Decide – A Memoir of the Thatcher Years* (Chapmans, London 1991) p. 73.
11. Hansard, 28 June 1976, col. 157.
12. Hansard, 13 July 1976, col. 440.
13. Hansard, 28 June 1976, col. 159.
14. Margaret Thatcher, *The Downing Street Years* (HarperCollins, London 1993) p. 631.
15. Hansard, 18 March 1975, cols. 1558, 1575.
16. Fowler, *Ministers Decide*, p. 74.
17. Hansard, 29 January 1975, col. 536.
18. John Campbell, *Edward Heath – A Biography* (Cape, London 1993) p. 667.
19. Interview, Kenneth Clarke.
20. Hansard, 18 December 1975, cols. 1800–1801.
21. Ibid., col. 1805.
22. *Nottingham Evening Post*, 19 January 1976.
23. Hansard, 20 October 1975, col. 153.
24. Hansard, 18 December 1975, col. 1808.
25. *Nottingham Evening Post*, 21 October 1975.
26. Fowler, *Ministers Decide*, p. 82.
27. Hansard, 27 February 1976, col. 820.
28. *Nottingham Evening Post*, 22 March 1976.
29. Hansard, 18 June 1976, col. 1030.
30. Ibid., cols. 1042, 1052.
31. Hansard, 16 July 1976, col. 1163.
32. Interview, Kenneth Clarke.
33. Hansard, 11 July 1974, cols. 1590–91, 1668–9.
34. Hansard, 27 January 1976, col. 351.
35. Nicholas Ridley, *My Style of Government* (Hutchinson, London 1991) p. 6.
36. Hansard, 24 July 1975, col. 850.

37. Hansard, 31 March 1977, col. 689.
38. Hansard, 22 May 1978, col. 1274.
39. Thatcher, *The Downing Street Years*, p. 14.
40. Interview, Kenneth Clarke.
41. Hansard, 27 June 1977, cols. 173–4.
42. Hansard, 11 May 1978, cols. 1551, 1589.
43. Speech to the Commonwealth Heads of Government Meeting, Melbourne, 30 September 1980; Thatcher, *The Downing Street Years*, p. 167.
44. Hansard, 23 February 1977, col. 1443.
45. Ibid., col. 1444.
46. Ibid., col. 1450.

5. MINISTER FOR ROADS

1. Interview, Jim Lester.
2. Interview, Kenneth Clarke.
3. Margaret Thatcher, *The Downing Street Years* (HarperCollins, London 1993) p. 26.
4. Norman Fowler, *Ministers Decide – A Memoir of the Thatcher Years* (Chapmans, London 1991) p. 110.
5. Interview, Kenneth Clarke.
6. Ibid.
7. Interview, Jim Lester.
8. Nigel Lawson, *The View from No. 11 – Memoirs of a Tory Radical* (Bantam, London 1992) p. 686.
9. *Daily Telegraph*, 9 September 1993.
10. Alan Walters, *Britain's Economic Renaissance* (Oxford University Press, New York and Oxford 1986) p. 79.
11. *Desert Island Discs*, BBC Radio 4, 20 February 1994.
12. Ian Gilmour, *Dancing with Dogma – Britain under Thatcherism* (Simon & Schuster, Hemel Hempstead 1992) p. 33.
13. Hansard, 24 June 1979, col. 1359.
14. Hansard, 14 April 1981, col. 288.
15. Hansard, 4 February 1981, col. 382.
16. Hansard, 9 May 1980, col. 804.
17. Ibid., col. 803.
18. Hansard, 25 March 1981, cols. 1021, 1050.
19. Andrew Roth, *Parliamentary Profiles 1987–91*, Vol. II, E–K (London 1989) p. 714.

20. John Carvel, *Citizen Ken* (Chatto & Windus/The Hogarth Press, London 1984) p. 148.
21. Hansard, 18 December 1981, col. 583.
22. Hansard, 24 February 1981, col. 938.
23. *The House Magazine*, 27 October 1980.
24. Gilmour, *Dancing with Dogma*, pp. 294–5.
25. *Nottingham Evening Post*, 8 November 1979.
26. *The Times*, 22 May 1986.
27. Fowler, *Ministers Decide*, p. 169.

6. HEALTH MINISTER, 1982–85

1. Judy Hillman and Peter Clarke, *Geoffrey Howe: A Quiet Revolutionary* (Weidenfeld & Nicolson, London 1988) p. 149.
2. Nigel Lawson, *The View from No. 11 – Memoirs of a Tory Radical* (Bantam, London 1992) p. 304.
3. Hugo Young, *One of Us – A Biography of Margaret Thatcher* (Pan, London 1990) pp. 300–301.
4. Hansard, 8 November 1982, col. 394.
5. Norman Fowler, *Ministers Decide – A Memoir of the Thatcher Years* (Chapmans, London 1991) p. 184.
6. Margaret Thatcher, *The Downing Street Years* (HarperCollins, London 1993) p. 277.
7. *Daily Telegraph*, 11 October 1984.
8. Hansard, 10 June 1982, col. 444.
9. *Guardian*, 13 March 1984.
10. *Nottingham Evening Post*, 3 July 1982.
11. *Daily Mail*, 17 July 1982.
12. *Nottingham Evening Post*, 19 July 1982.
13. *Nottingham Evening Post*, 3 July 1982.
14. *Guardian*, 20 August 1982.
15. *Guardian*, 24 August 1982.
16. Fowler, *Ministers Decide*, p. 174.
17. *Nottingham Evening Post*, 10 September 1982.
18. *Nottingham Evening Post*, 17 September 1982.
19. Hansard, 20 October 1982, cols. 447–9.
20. Hansard, 27 October 1983, col. 509.
21. Hansard, 27 June 1983, col. 428.
22. Hansard, 26 April 1984, col. 976.
23. Hansard, 2 July 1985, col. 210.
24. Hansard, 5 July 1984, col. 548.

25. Hansard, 25 March 1983, cols. 1240, 1192.
26. Hansard, 5 July 1984, col. 551.
27. Hansard, 7 February 1983, col. 725.
28. Hansard, 30 March 1982, col. 217.
29. Hansard, 25 March 1985, col. 160.
30. *Daily Telegraph*, 23 April 1985.
31. *West Midlands Regional Health Authority: Regionally Managed Services Organisation*, Committee of Public Accounts Fifty-seventh Report, House of Commons, 1993.
32. *The Times*, 16 November 1984.
33. Hansard, 8 November 1984, col. 239.
34. Alan Watkins, *A Slight Case of Libel – Meacher v. Trelford and Others* (Duckworth, London 1990) Ch. 14.
35. Hansard, 14 January 1985, col. 82.
36. Hansard, 26 February 1985, cols. 227, 222, 237.
37. Hansard, 20 December 1983, col. 358.
38. Hansard, 20 December 1983, col. 362.
39. *Mail on Sunday*, 1 April 1984.
40. Hansard, 2 May 1984, col. 459.
41. Hansard, 7 February 1985, col. 1229.
42. *Daily Telegraph*, 6 May 1985.
43. Peter Chippindale and Chris Horrie, *Stick It Up Your Punter! – The Rise and Fall of the Sun* (Mandarin, 1990) p. 140.
44. *Sunday Express*, 12 February 1984.
45. *The Times*, 7 May 1984.
46. Alan Clark, *Diaries*, (Weidenfeld & Nicolson, London 1993) p. 109.
47. Thatcher, *The Downing Street Years*, p. 418.

7. THE PAYMASTER GENERAL

1. This account of Clarke's appointment is drawn from Lord Young, *The Enterprise Years – A Businessman in the Cabinet* (Headline, London 1991) pp. 159–60.
2. *Daily Telegraph*, 3 November 1985.
3. *Guardian*, 3 November 1985.
4. Alan Clark, *Diaries* (Weidenfeld & Nicolson, London 1993) pp. 101, 363, 273, 397.
5. Young, *The Enterprise Years*, pp. 160, 164.
6. The originator of this phrase, according to Andrew Roth, was Andrew Rawnsley, writing in the *Guardian* (Andrew Roth, *Parliamentary Profiles 1987–91*, Vol. I, A–D (London 1988) p. 233). Subsequently Kenneth Clarke picked it up and used it to describe himself (*Financial Times*, 14 November 1987).

7. Interview, Jim Lester.
8. *Nottingham Recorder*, 3 October 1985.
9. *Nottingham Evening Post*, 10 October 1985.
10. Hansard, 11 February 1986, col. 804.
11. Hansard, 14 May 1986, col. 769.
12. *Guardian*, 4 March 1986; Patrick Wintour, "An Exotic View of Wapping", *Guardian*, 12 February 1987; William Shawcross, *Murdoch – Ringmaster of the Information Circus* (Pan, London 1993) pp. 334–57 *passim*.
13. *Guardian*, 13 February 1986; *Nottingham Evening Post*, 13 February 1986.
14. Hansard, 6 July 1987, col. 19.
15. Ibid., col. 22.
16. *Sunday Express*, 10 August 1986.
17. *The Times*, 2 September 1986.
18. *Daily Telegraph*, 30 August 1986.
19. Clark, *Diaries*, pp. 9–10.
20. Hansard, 3 June 1986, col. 784.
21. Hansard, 12 February 1987, col. 485.
22. Young, *The Enterprise Years*, p. 163.
23. Hansard, 20 March 1986, col. 429.
24. Nigel Lawson, *The View From No. 11 – Memoirs of a Tory Radical* (Bantam, London 1992) p. 434.
25. Young, *The Enterprise Years*, p. 173.
26. Hansard, 20 March 1986, col. 432.
27. *Daily Express*, 15 August 1986.
28. Hansard, 28 October 1986, col. 178.
29. Lawson, *The View From No. 11*, p. 679.
30. Clark, *Diaries*, p. 133.
31. *Nottingham Evening Post*, 12 March 1986.
32. Hansard, 6 February 1986, col. 450.
33. Ibid., col. 448.
34. Ibid., col. 455.
35. *Daily Mail*, 23 June 1986.
36. *Independent*, 24 October 1986.
37. *Nottingham Evening Post*, 23 June 1986.

8. CHANCELLOR OF THE DUCHY

1. *Desert Island Discs*, BBC Radio 4, 20 February 1994.
2. Lord Young, *The Enterprise Years – A Businessman in the Cabinet* (Headline, London 1991) p. 224.

3. *Daily Mail*, 30 May 1987.
4. Hansard, 12 February 1987, col. 489.
5. Hansard, 9 March 1987, cols. 88–90.
6. *Daily Mail*, 25 April 1987.
7. *The Times*, 23 March 1987.
8. Speech to 1987 Conference of Welsh Conservatives, quoted in Hansard, 9 June 1993, col. 359.
9. *Guardian*, 19 February 1987.
10. Hansard, 6 April 1987, col. 32.
11. *Sunday Express*, 15 March 1987.
12. *Financial Times*, 8 April 1987.
13. *Daily Mail*, 30 April 1986.
14. *Evening Standard*, 14 July 1987.
15. Young, *The Enterprise Years*, p. 251.
16. Alan Clark, *Diaries* (Weidenfeld & Nicolson, London 1993) pp. 162–3.
17. Young, *The Enterprise Years*, p. 255.
18. Nigel Lawson, *The View From No. 11 – Memoirs of a Tory Radical* (Bantam, London 1992) p. 291.
19. Hansard, 21 January 1988, col. 1219.
20. *The Times* 24 October 1987.
21. *Guardian*, 8 March 1988.
22. Hansard, 7 March 1988, col. 33.
23. Hansard, 22 May 1986, col. 543.
24. Hansard, 8 February 1994, col. 151.
25. Hansard, 4 May 1988, col. 939.
26. Hansard, 29 March 1988, col. 889.
27. Hansard, 8 June 1988, col. 859–61.
28. *The Times*, 6 June, 1986; *Guardian*, 6 June 1988.
29. Andrew Roth, *Parliamentary Profiles 1987–1991*, Vol. 3, L–R (London 1990) p. 1175.
30. *Financial Times*, 1 February 1985. For an analysis of British policy on space technology, see Martin Spence, "Lost in Space", *Capital & Class*, no. 52, 1994.
31. *The Times*, 14 October 1987.
32. Hansard, 28 October 1987, col. 293.
33. *The Times*, 4 November 1987.
34. *Financial Times*, 12 November 1987.
35. Hansard, 12 November 1987, col. 572.
36. *Financial Times*, 11 November 1987.
37. Young, *The Enterprise Years*, p. 327.
38. Hansard, 29 June 1987, col. 343.
39. Interview, Kenneth Clarke.
40. Hansard, 13 January 1988, col. 278.

41. Young, *The Enterprise Years*, p. 328.
42. Hansard, 23 February 1988, col. 170.
43. *Guardian*, 25 June 1988.
44. Hansard, 12 February 1986, col. 1003.
45. Hansard, 27 July 1989, col. 1293.
46. Hansard, 29 March 1994, cols. 902, 907–8.
47. Hansard, 21 July 1988, col. 1394.
48. Interview, Kenneth Clarke.
49. Interview, Nick Budgen.

9. HEALTH SECRETARY

1. Margaret Thatcher, *The Downing Street Years* (HarperCollins, London 1993) p. 614.
2. *Nottingham Evening Post*, 20 July 1987.
3. *Sun*, 28 July 1988.
4. *Today*, 28 July 1988.
5. *Nottingham Evening Post*, 29 July 1988, and 19 September 1988.
6. *Nottingham Evening Post*, 27 September 1988.
7. *Daily Telegraph*, 9 November 1993.
8. David Owen, *Time to Declare* (Michael Joseph, London 1991) p. 229.
9. Hansard, 16 January 1976, cols. 858–9.
10. Ibid., cols. 855–6.
11. *Today*, 10 May 1990.
12. *Daily Telegraph*, 9 March 1993.
13. Edwina Currie, *Life Lines – Politics and Health 1986–88* (Sidgwick & Jackson, London 1989) p. 47 and *passim*.
14. *Guardian*, 14 January 1989, 17 May 1989.
15. *Nottingham Evening Post*, 23 September 1988.
16. *Daily Mail*, 20 August 1988.
17. Currie, *Life Lines*, pp. 135–6.
18. *Evening Standard*, 31 March 1988; Currie, *Life Lines*, pp. 135–6.
19. *Daily Mirror*, September 1988.
20. *Nottingham Evening Post*, 8 June 1988.
21. Independent Television News, 3 December 1988.
22. Kenneth Baker, *The Turbulent Years – My Life in Politics* (Faber and Faber, London 1993) p. 276.
23. Hansard, 14 January 1971, col. 366.
24. Hansard, 5 December 1988, col. 20.
25. Ibid.

26. Hansard, 1 November 1988, col. 860.
27. Penny Junor, *The Major Enigma* (Michael Joseph, London 1993) pp. 145–6.
28. Hansard, 1 November 1988, col. 865.
29. *Independent on Sunday*, 25 February 1990.
30. Ibid.
31. *Guardian*, 19 December 1989.
32. Hansard, 9 November 1989, col. 1197.
33. Ibid., col. 1200.
34. *Daily Telegraph*, 23 January 1990.
35. Hansard, 9 November 1989, col. 1158.
36. *Sun*, 2 December 1989.
37. *Sunday Correspondent*, 7 January 1990
38. *Nottingham Evening Post*, 3 January 1990; *Daily Telegraph*, 4 January 1990.
39. *The Times*, 3 January 1990.
40. *Financial Times*, 4 January 1990.
41. *News of the World*, 7 January 1990.
42. *Daily Telegraph*, 4 January 1990.
43. *Guardian*, 6 January 1990.
44. *Financial Times*, 6 January 1990.
45. *The World This Weekend*, BBC Radio 4, 7 January 1990.
46. Junor, *The Major Enigma*, p. 187.

10. THE N.H.S. REFORMS

1. To journalists, 18 May 1991.
2. Speech to Conservative Party Conference, Blackpool, 11 October 1991.
3. *Daily Mail*, 7 October 1991.
4. Interview, *Today*, BBC Radio 4, 28 January 1989.
5. From my own note taken at a fringe meeting organized by the *Sunday Telegraph*, Blackpool, 8 October 1993.
6. Interview, *Nottingham Evening Post*, 19 August 1988.
7. Andrew Roth, *Parliamentary Profiles 1987–91*, Vol. IV, S–Z (London 1990) p. 1577.
8. Nicholas Ridley, *My Style of Government* (Hutchinson, London 1991) p. 40.
9. Margaret Thatcher, *The Downing Street Years*, (HarperCollins, London 1993) pp. 757–8.
10. Andrew Roth, *Parliamentary Profiles 1987–91*, Vol. III, L–R (London 1990) p. 1073.
11. Nigel Lawson, *The View From No 11 – Memoirs of a Tory Radical* (Bantam, London 1992) p. 617.
12. Hansard, 25 July 1989, col. 915.
13. Hansard, 31 January 1989, col. 190.

14. Alan Clark, *Diaries* (Weidenfeld & Nicolson, London 1993) p. 276.
15. Clark, *Diaries*, p. 197.
16. David Hencke, *Guardian*, 30 January 1989.
17. Speech at Blackpool fringe meeting, 8 October 1993.
18. Hansard, 24 January 1989, col. 859.
19. A.C. Enthoven, *Reflections on the Management of the National Health Service*, Occasional Paper 5, Nuffield Provincial Hospitals Trust (London 1985).
20. Thatcher, *The Downing Street Years*, p. 607.
21. *Guardian*, 10 March 1989.
22. *Daily Telegraph*, 11 March 1989.
23. *Observer*, 19 March 1989.
24. Hansard, 25 April 1989, col. 788.
25. Hansard, 23 May 1989, col. 790.
26. Hansard, 2 May 1989, col. 37.
27. Hansard, 5 May 1989, col. 37.
28. Hansard, 1 May 1990, col. 889.
29. Hansard, 27 June 1990, col. 347.
30. *The Times*, 4 April 1989.
31. Hansard, 12 July 1989, cols. 975, 977.
32. For an assessment of the Griffiths Report, the White Paper and its effects see Elaine Murphy, *After the Asylums – Community Care for People with Mental Illness* (Faber & Faber, London 1991).
33. Hansard, 18 July 1989, cols. 900, 1000, 1024–6.
34. *Report of the Inquiry into the Care and Treatment of Christopher Clunis* (HMSO, London 1994).
35. *Daily Telegraph*, 25 February 1994.
36. Hansard, 27 November 1989, col. 450.
37. *Independent*, 25 September 1989.
38. *Daily Telegraph*, 17 November and 18 November 1993.
39. *Daily Telegraph*, 1 March 1994.
40. Interview on *The World This Weekend*, BBC Radio 4, 4 September 1988.
41. Hansard, 15 March 1994, written answers col. 562.
42. *The Economist*, 19 February 1994.
43. Ray Robinson and Julian Le Grand, eds., *Evaluating the NHS Reforms*, King's Fund Institute (1994).
44. Norman Fowler, *Ministers Decide – A Memoir of the Thatcher Years* (Chapmans, London 1991) p. 177.

11. THE FALL OF THATCHER

1. Margaret Thatcher, *The Downing Street Years* (HarperCollins, London 1993) p. 855.

2. Margaret Thatcher, interview in *Thatcher: The Downing Street Years*, BBC 1, 10 November 1993.

3. Kenneth Clarke, interview in *Thatcher: The Downing Street Years*, BBC 1, 10 November 1993.

4. Lord Whitelaw, interview in *Thatcher: The Downing Street Years*, BBC 1, 10 November 1993.

5. Nigel Lawson, *The View from No. 11 – Memoirs of a Tory Radical* (Bantam, London 1992) p. 1002.

6. Alan Clark, *Diaries* (Weidenfeld & Nicolson, London 1993) p. 290.

7. Hansard, 13 November 1990, col. 465.

8. Thatcher, interview in *Thatcher: The Downing Street Years*.

9. Lawson, *The View from No. 11*, p. 562.

10. Nicholas Ridley, *My Style of Government* (Hutchinson, London 1991) p. 125.

11. Interview in *Maggie's Ministers*, BBC 2, 11 September 1993.

12. Lawson, *The View from No. 11*, pp. 582–3.

13. Hansard, 13 November 1990, col. 463.

14. Ridley, *My Style of Government*, p. 160.

15. *Spectator*, 13 July 1990.

16. Lawson, *The View from No. 11*, p. 900.

17. *Financial Times*, 18 October 1989.

18. *Guardian*, 13 October 1990.

19. *Independent on Sunday*, 25 February 1990.

20. *Daily Telegraph*, 12 November, 1991.

21. Hansard, 13 November 1990, cols. 444–5.

22. Ibid., col. 471.

23. *The Times*, 14 November 1991.

24. Thatcher, *The Downing Street Years*, p. 614.

25. Clark, *Diaries*, p. 365.

26. Hansard, 27 November 1990, col. 735.

27. Alan Watkins, *A Conservative Coup*, (2nd edn, Duckworth, London 1992) p. xvi.

28. Kenneth Baker, *The Turbulent Years – My Life in Politics* (Faber & Faber, London 1993) p. 402.

29. Bruce Anderson, *John Major* (Headline, London 1992) p. 249.

30. Clark, *Diaries*, pp. 363, 365.

31. Baker, *The Turbulent Years*, pp. 404–5.

32. Thatcher, *The Downing Street Years*, p. 852.

33. Baker, *The Turbulent Years*, p. 406.

34. Channel Four News, 1 July 1991.
35. Thatcher, *The Downing Street Years*, p. 852.

12. EDUCATION SECRETARY

1. Kenneth Baker, *The Turbulent Years – My Life in Politics* (Faber & Faber, London 1993) p. 427.
2. Joe Rogaly, "Chalk and Talk", *Financial Times*, 19 December 1991.
3. Interview in the *Independent*, 2 May 1991.
4. Andrew Roth, *Parliamentary Profiles 1987–91*, Vol. I, A–D (London 1988) p. 235.
5. *Independent*, 2 May 1991.
6. *Woman*, April 1991.
7. Hansard, 29 April 1991, cols. 49–50.
8. *Daily Mirror*, 30 April 1991.
9. *Daily Mirror*, 1 May 1991.
10. *Financial Times*, 17 June 1991.
11. Margaret Thatcher, *The Downing Street Years* (HarperCollins, London 1993) p. 835.
12. *Guardian*, 10 October 1987.
13. Nigel Lawson, *The View from No. 11 – Memoirs of a Tory Radical* (Bantam, London 1992) p. 610.
14. *Guardian*, 19 February 1991.
15. *Learning to Succeed: A Radical Look at Education Today*, Report of the National Commission on Education (1993).
16. Ian Gilmour, *Dancing with Dogma – Britain under Thatcherism* (Simon & Schuster, Hemel Hempstead 1992) pp. 214–15.
17. *Guardian*, 10 October 1987.
18. Brian Simon, *Bending the Rules – The Baker "Reform" of Education* (Lawrence & Wishart, London 1988).
19. *Daily Telegraph*, 5 January 1991.
20. Kenneth Clarke, "Shakespeare without the Ache", *The Guardian*, 26 April 1991.
21. *Independent*, 7 March 1991.
22. *Woman*, April 1991.
23. *Daily Mail*, 13 June 1991.
24. *Guardian*, 7 March 1991.
25. Thatcher, *The Downing Street Years*, p. 595.
26. *Guardian*, 26 March 1991.
27. Baker, *The Turbulent Years*, p. 198.
28. *Guardian*, 15 January 1992.
29. Ibid.

30. *Daily Telegraph*, 20 February 1991.
31. *Sunday Telegraph*, 24 March 1991.
32. *Guardian*, 15 February 1991.
33. *Guardian*, 19 February 1991.
34. *Sunday Telegraph*, 24 March 1991.
35. Hansard, 23 April 1991, col. 894.
36. *Guardian*, 19 February, 20 February and 6 March 1992.
37. Hansard, 19 November 1991, cols. 152, 153.
38. *Financial Times*, 6 March 1992.
39. *Guardian*, 4 February 1992.

13. HOME SECRETARY

1. Hansard, 13 May 1993, cols. 940, 948–50.
2. *Guardian*, 8 December 1992.
3. Hansard, 10 March 1993, cols. 956, 959.
4. *Guardian*, 3 December 1993.
5. Hansard, 8 May 1992, col. 305.
6. *Guardian*, 4 February 1993.
7. *Guardian*, 2 October 1992.
8. Independent Television News, 28 May 1993.
9. *Daily Telegraph*, 8 July 1993.
10. *Daily Telegraph*, 14 May 1992.
11. Hansard, 14 May 1992, col. 739.
12. *Daily Telegraph*, 21 May 1992.
13. *Observer*, 5 July 1992.
14. Patrick Sheehy, "Case of the Hostile Cops", *Guardian*, 26 July 1993.
15. *Daily Telegraph*, 22 July 1993.
16. *Guardian*, 20 May 1993.
17. *Daily Mirror*, 19 May 1993.
18. *Observer*, 10 October 1993.
19. *Observer*, 10 January 1993; *Financial Times*, 15 January 1993; *Daily Telegraph*, 16 January 1993.
20. Hansard, 23 March 1993, col. 766.
21. Hansard, 11 March 1993, col. 1093.
22. Hansard, 17 November 1992, col. 141.
23. Hansard, 2 November 1992, col. 22.
24. Hansard, 11 January 1993, cols. 642–44, 692.
25. Hansard, 9 June 1992, cols. 171, 165.
26. Ibid., col. 172.

27. Hansard, 14 May 1992, col. 738.
28. *Guardian*, 22 December 1992.
29. Hansard, 13 May 1993, col. 943.
30. *Sun*, 4 February 1993.

14. THE TAXMAN

1. Speech to businessmen, Conservative Central Office press release, 25 February 1994.
2. Speech to 1987 Conference of Welsh Conservatives, quoted in Hansard, 9 June 1993, col. 359.
3. Treasury press release, 23 February 1994.
4. *The Best Future for Britain – The Conservative Manifesto 1992* (Conservative Central Office, London 1992) p. 6.
5. Hansard, 25 November 1993, col. 604.
6. Hansard, 15 July 1993, col. 1109.
7. *Guardian*, 17 July 1993.
8. Hansard, 30 November 1993, cols. 919, 921 and 922.
9. Ibid., col. 938.
10. Philip Stephens, *Financial Times*, 2 December 1993.
11. Will Hutton, *Guardian*, 1 December 1993.
12. *Guardian*, 1 December 1993.
13. *Consultation on the Medical Assessment for Incapacity Benefit* (Department of Social Security, December 1993).
14. Hansard, 30 November 1993, col. 925.
15. Ibid., col. 941.
16. *The Best Future for Britain*, p. 7.
17. "Tax Truths", *Sunday Times*, 7 November 1993.
18. Stephen Dorrell, written answer, Hansard, 26 October 1993, col. 568.
19. Stephen Dorrell, written answer, Hansard, 30 November 1993 cols. 389–90.
20. *Daily Telegraph*, 2 December 1993.
21. *Today*, 3 March 1994.
22. *Daily Telegraph*, 4 March 1994.
23. Interview, Kenneth Clarke.
24. Hansard, 4 November 1993, col. 501.
25. Hansard, 30 November 1993, col. 931.
26. *Financial Times*, 1 December 1993.
27. Hansard, 30 November 1993, col. 932.
28. Hansard, 25 November 1993, col. 610.
29. House of Commons Treasury and Civil Service Committee Session 1993–94, *Second Report, The November 1993 Budget* (HMSO, London 1994) pp. 87–8.

30. *Daily Telegraph*, 8 June 1993.
31. *Daily Telegraph*, 2 August 1993.
32. Interview, Kenneth Clarke.
33. Stephen Dorrell, written answer, Hansard, 30 November 1993, cols. 389–90; *Observer*, 4 December 1993.
34. *Financial Statement and Budget Report 1994–95* (HM Treasury, November 1993) p. 23.
35. *Financial Times*, 2 December 1993.

15. THE UNREAD TREATY AND THE "DREADFUL HOLE"

1. *Desert Island Discs*, BBC Radio 4, 20 February 1994.
2. *Nottingham Evening Post*, 12 March 1986.
3. Beatrix Campbell, *The Iron Ladies – Why do Women Vote Tory?* (Virago, London 1987) p. 153.
4. *The Times*, 29 May 1993.
5. *Daily Mail*, 8 December 1993.
6. *Guardian*, 16 December 1993.
7. For example, Bruce Anderson ("Hezza shares are riding high, but sell soon", *Independent* 8 April 1994) unfavourably compares Tessa Keswick, who "has many qualities [but] is not an economist", with the "outstanding political advisers" employed by previous Chancellors.
8. "Britain's Richest 500: 1994 edition", *Sunday Times*, 10 April 1994.
9. Hansard, 25 November 1993, col. 607.
10. *Sun*, 7 October 1992.
11. *Guardian*, 9 October 1992.
12. *Guardian*, 26 October 1992.
13. Hansard, 22 July 1971, col. 1778.
14. *Guardian*, 9 October 1992.
15. Interview, Kenneth Clarke.
16. Hansard, 1 February 1993, col. 43.
17. Hansard, 27 January 1993, col. 1109.
18. Hansard, 1 February 1993, col. 36.
19. *The House Magazine*, 11 January 1993.
20. Hansard, 1 February 1993, cols. 33–34.
21. Channel Four News, 24 September 1992.
22. Hansard, 15 July 1993, col. 1109.
23. Interview, *The World at One*, BBC Radio 4, 20 September 1993.
24. *The Times*, 8 October 1993.

25. *Guardian*, 9 November 1993.
26. Channel Four News, 15 November 1993.
27. *Daily Mirror*, 7 March 1994.
28. *Guardian*, 11 March 1994.
29. *Daily Telegraph*, 22 February 1994; *Guardian*, 22 February 1994.
30. *Question Time*, BBC 1, 13 January 1994.
31. *Daily Mail*, 1 March 1994.
32. *Independent*, 8 March 1994.
33. *Today*, BBC Radio 4, 8 March 1994.
34. *Sunday Express*, 13 March 1994.
35. Interview, Kenneth Clarke.
36. *The Times*, 13 January 1994.
37. *Sun*, 14 January 1994.
38. Hansard, 23 February 1977, col. 1447.
39. Hansard, 9 June 1993, col. 367.
40. "Walden Interview", London Weekend Television, 3 October 1993.
41. Hansard, 9 June 1993, col. 373.
42. Hansard, 25 November 1993, col. 605.
43. Speech to businessmen, Maidstone, Conservative Central Office press release, 25 February 1993.
44. *Sunday Telegraph*, 24 April 1994.
45. Interview on GMTV, 1 May 1994.
46. *Daily Telegraph*, 2 May 1994.
47. *Guardian*, 4 May 1994.
48. Hansard, 23 February 1977, col. 1445.
49. *The Times*, 8 April 1994.

INDEX

Printed in the United States
by Baker & Taylor Publisher Services